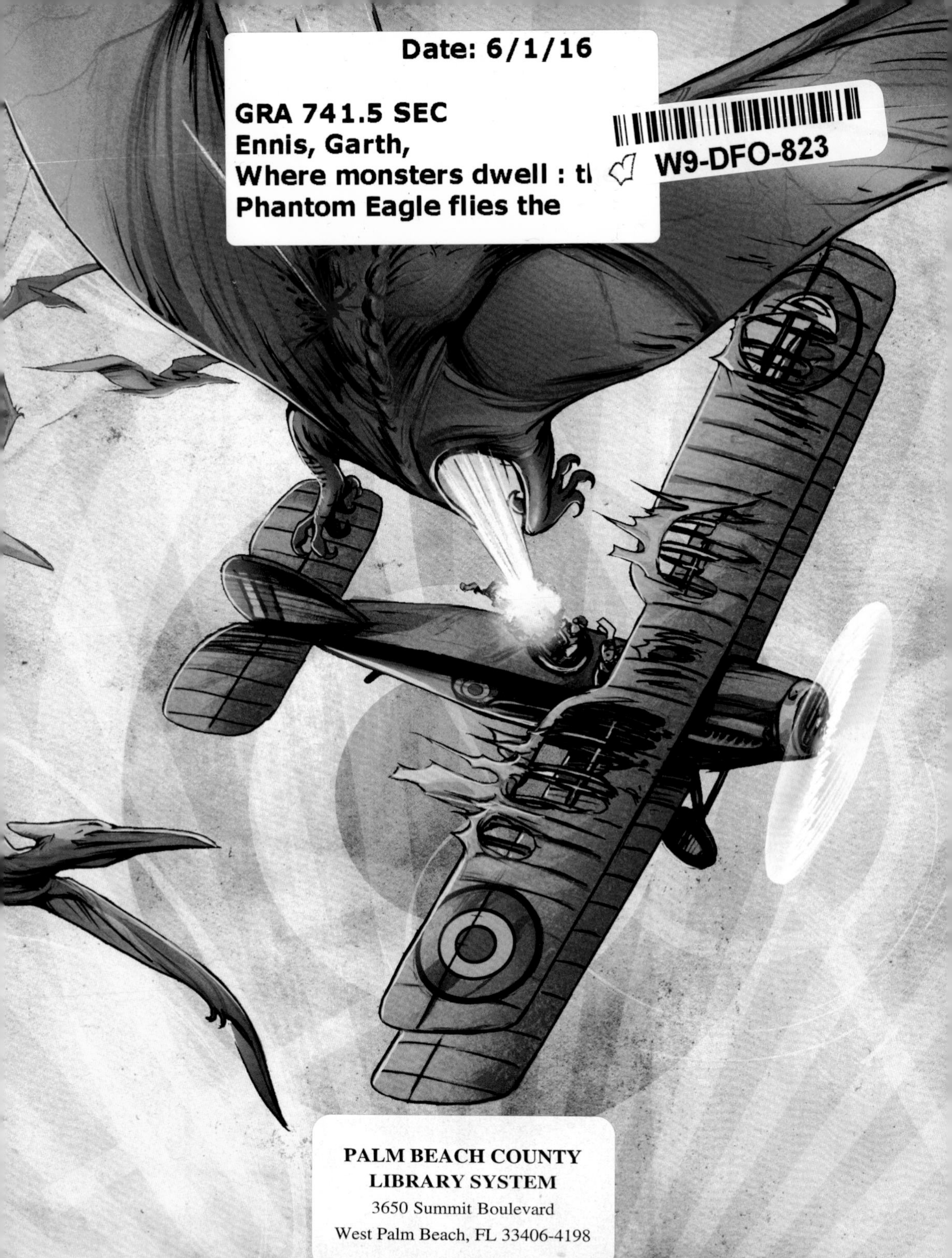

WHERE MONSTERS DWELL

The Phantom Eagle Flies the Savage Skies

[redacted]

THE MULTIVERSE WAS DESTROYED!

•

THE HEROES OF EARTH-616 AND EARTH-1610 WERE POWERLESS TO SAVE IT!

•

NOW, ALL THAT REMAINS...IS BATTLEWORLD!

•

A MASSIVE, PATCHWORK PLANET COMPOSED OF THE FRAGMENTS OF WORLDS THAT NO LONGER EXIST, MAINTAINED BY THE IRON WILL OF ITS GOD AND MASTER, VICTOR VON DOOM!

•

EACH REGION IS A DOMAIN UNTO ITSELF!

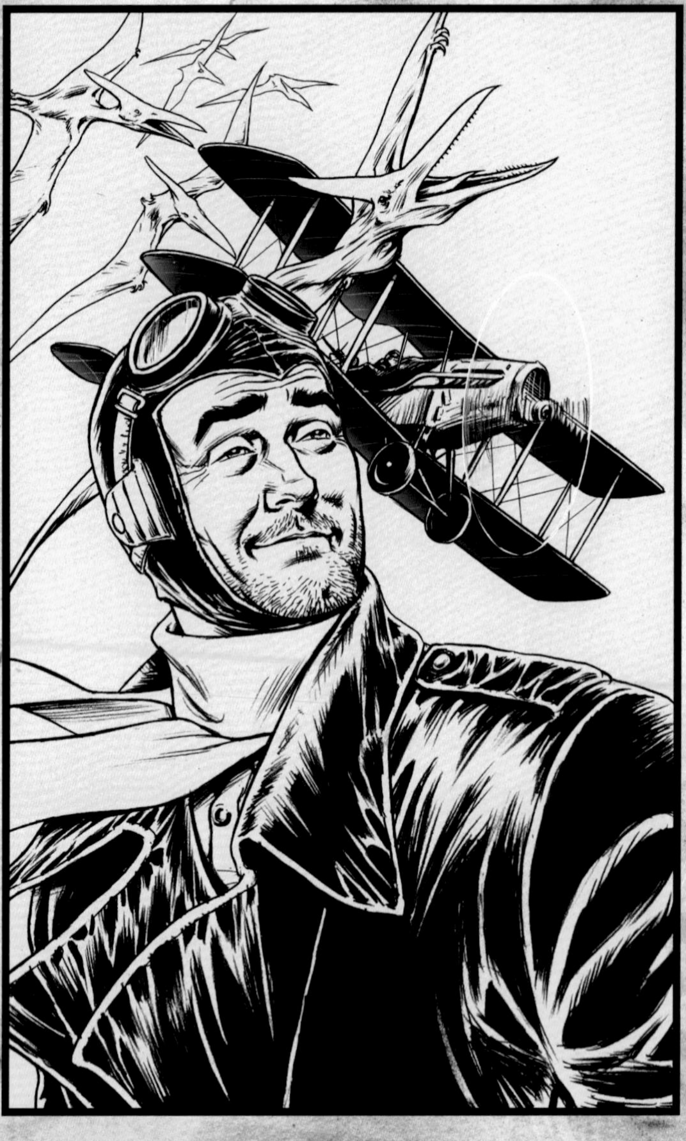

WHERE MONSTERS DWELL

The Phantom Eagle Flies the Savage Skies

WRITER
GARTH ENNIS

ARTIST
RUSS BRAUN

COLOR ARTIST
DONO SANCHEZ ALMARA

LETTERER
ROB STEEN

COVER ART
FRANK CHO & JASON KEITH

ASSISTANT EDITOR
KATHLEEN WISNESKI

ASSOCIATE EDITOR
JAKE THOMAS

EDITOR
NICK LOWE

COLLECTION EDITOR: **JENNIFER GRÜNWALD** • ASSISTANT EDITOR: **SARAH BRUNSTAD**
ASSOCIATE MANAGING EDITOR: **ALEX STARBUCK** • EDITOR, SPECIAL PROJECTS: **MARK D. BEAZLEY**
SENIOR EDITOR, SPECIAL PROJECTS: **JEFF YOUNGQUIST** • SVP PRINT, SALES & MARKETING: **DAVID GABRIEL**

EDITOR IN CHIEF: **AXEL ALONSO** • CHIEF CREATIVE OFFICER: **JOE QUESADA**
PUBLISHER: **DAN BUCKLEY** • EXECUTIVE PRODUCER: **ALAN FINE**

WHERE MONSTERS DWELL: THE PHANTOM EAGLE FLIES THE SAVAGE SKIES. Contains material originally published in magazine form as WHERE MONSTERS DWELL #1-5. First printing 2015. ISBN# 978-0-7851-9892-5. Published by MARVEL WORLDWIDE, INC., a subsidiary of MARVEL ENTERTAINMENT, LLC. OFFICE OF PUBLICATION: 135 West 50th Street, New York, NY 10020.

Printed in Canada. ALAN FINE, President, Marvel Entertainment; DAN BUCKLEY, President, TV, Publishing and Brand Management; JOE QUESADA, Chief Creative Officer; TOM BREVOORT, SVP of Publishing; DAVID BOGART, SVP of Operations & Procurement, Publishing; C.B. CEBULSKI, VP of International Development & Brand Management; DAVID GABRIEL, SVP Print, Sales & Marketing; JIM O'KEEFE, VP of Operations & Logistics; DAN CARR, Executive Director of Publishing Technology; SUSAN CRESPI, Editorial Operations Manager; ALEX MORALES, Publishing Operations Manager; STAN LEE, Chairman Emeritus. For information regarding advertising in Marvel Comics or on Marvel.com, please contact Jonathan Rheingold, VP of Custom Solutions & Ad Sales, at jrheingold@marvel.com. For Marvel subscription inquiries, please call 800-217-9158. **Manufactured between 10/30/2015 and 12/7/2015 by SOLISCO PRINTERS, SCOTT, QC, CANADA.**

10 9 8 7 6 5 4 3 2 1

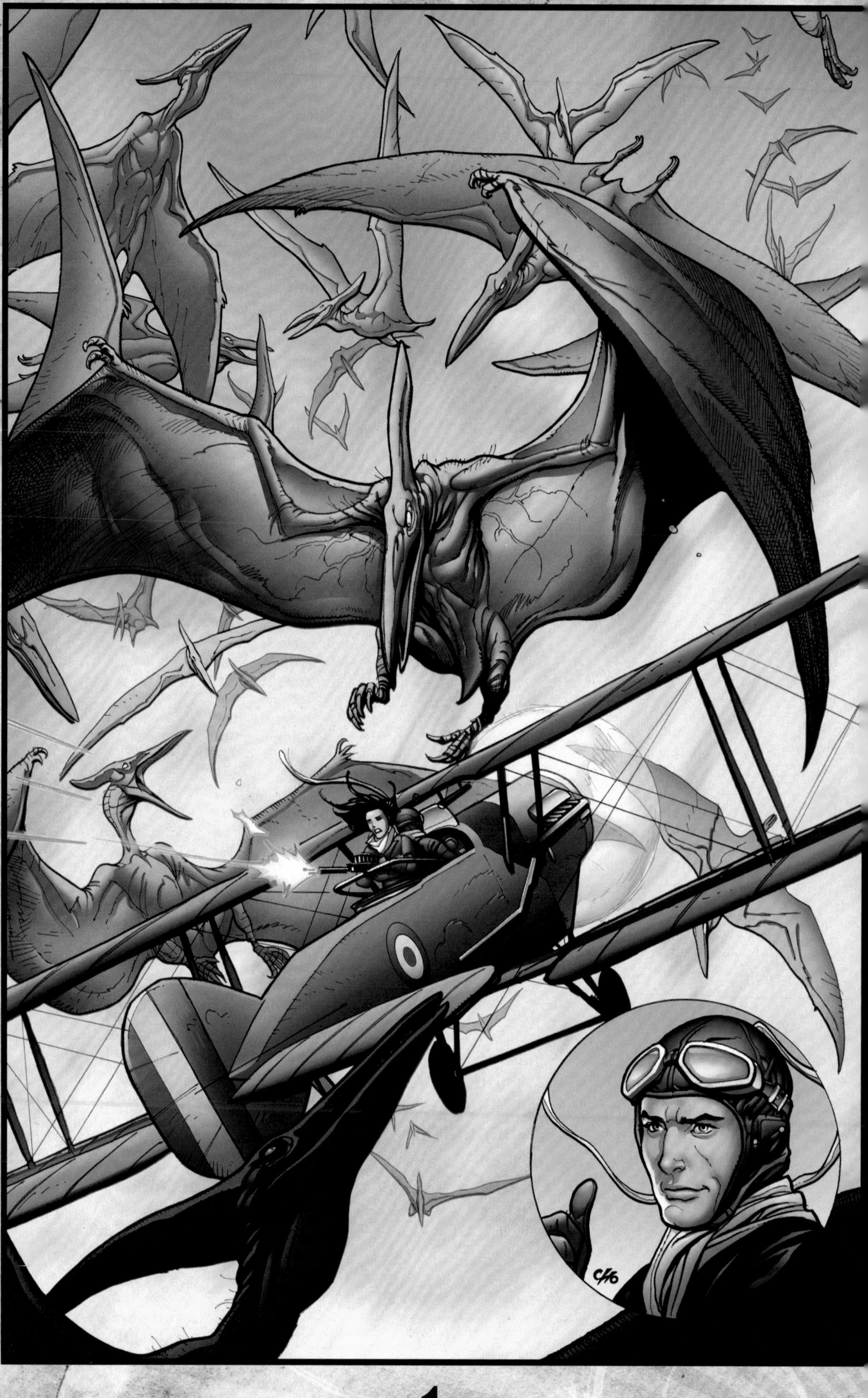

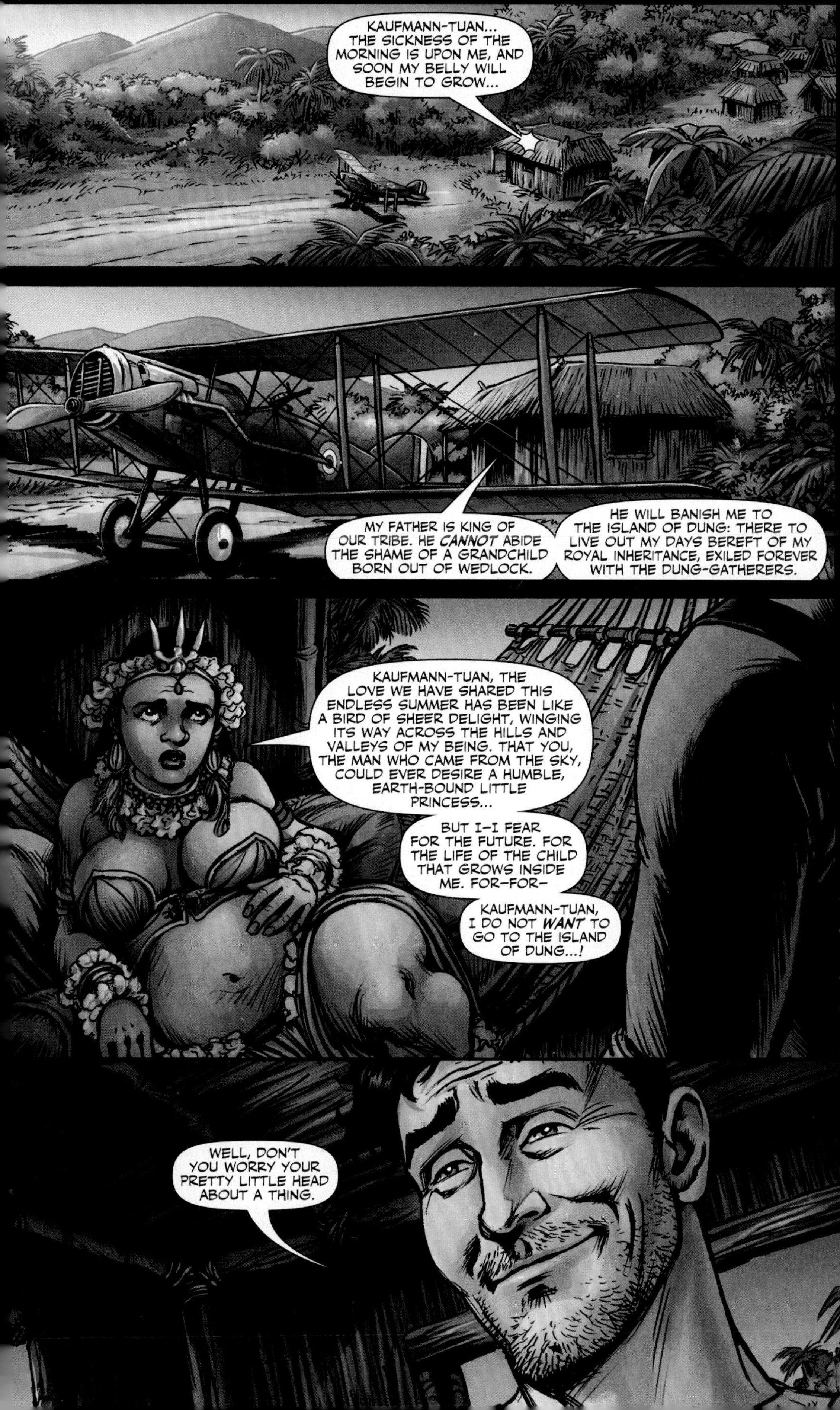
KAUFMANN-TUAN... THE SICKNESS OF THE MORNING IS UPON ME, AND SOON MY BELLY WILL BEGIN TO GROW...
MY FATHER IS KING OF OUR TRIBE. HE *CANNOT* ABIDE THE SHAME OF A GRANDCHILD BORN OUT OF WEDLOCK.
HE WILL BANISH ME TO THE ISLAND OF DUNG: THERE TO LIVE OUT MY DAYS BEREFT OF MY ROYAL INHERITANCE, EXILED FOREVER WITH THE DUNG-GATHERERS.
KAUFMANN-TUAN, THE LOVE WE HAVE SHARED THIS ENDLESS SUMMER HAS BEEN LIKE A BIRD OF SHEER DELIGHT, WINGING ITS WAY ACROSS THE HILLS AND VALLEYS OF MY BEING. THAT YOU, THE MAN WHO CAME FROM THE SKY, COULD EVER DESIRE A HUMBLE, EARTH-BOUND LITTLE PRINCESS...
BUT I--I FEAR FOR THE FUTURE. FOR THE LIFE OF THE CHILD THAT GROWS INSIDE ME. FOR--FOR--
KAUFMANN-TUAN, I DO NOT *WANT* TO GO TO THE ISLAND OF DUNG...!
WELL, DON'T YOU WORRY YOUR PRETTY LITTLE HEAD ABOUT A THING.

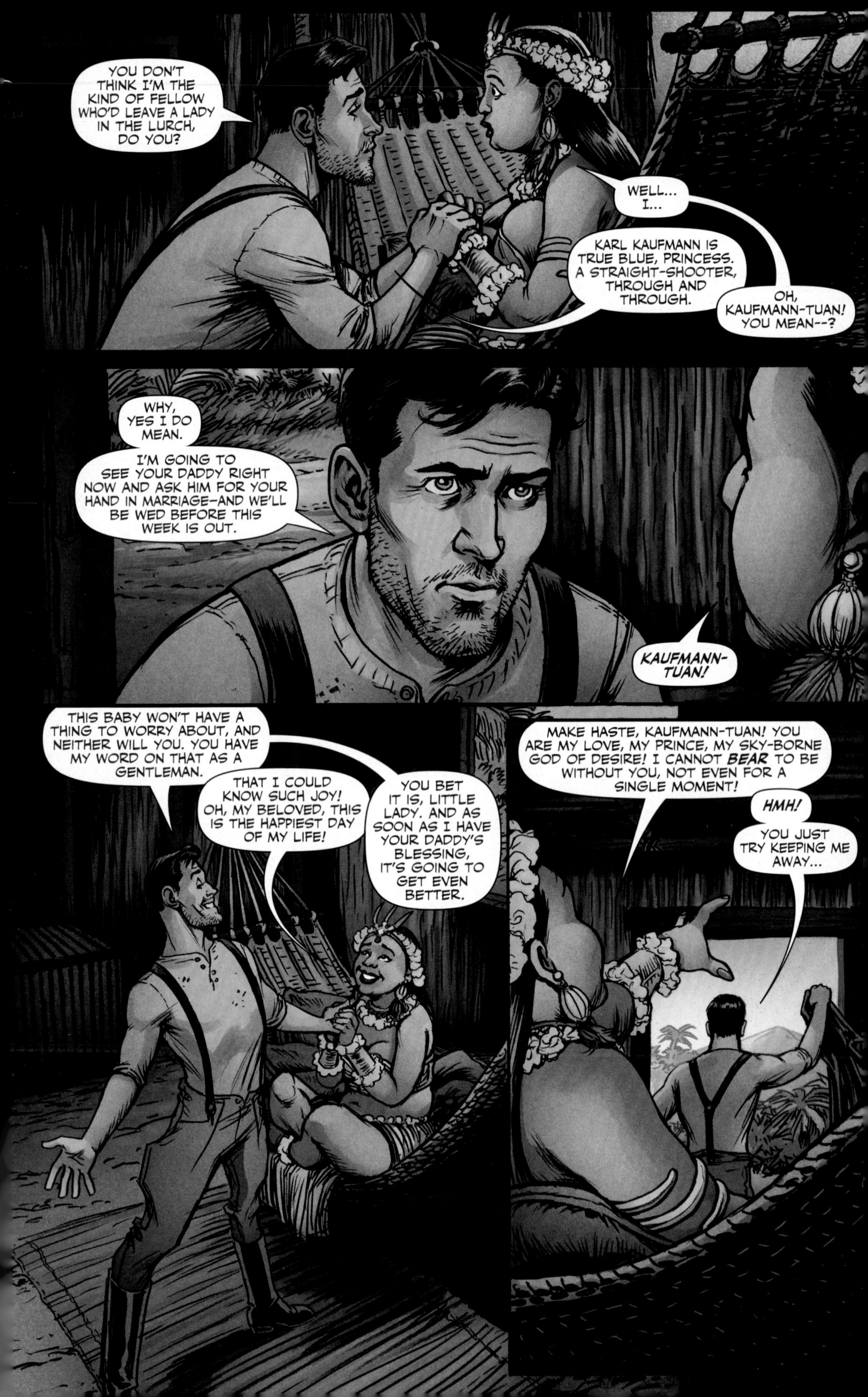
YOU DON'T THINK I'M THE KIND OF FELLOW WHO'D LEAVE A LADY IN THE LURCH, DO YOU?
WELL... I...
KARL KAUFMANN IS TRUE BLUE, PRINCESS. A STRAIGHT-SHOOTER, THROUGH AND THROUGH.
OH, KAUFMANN-TUAN! YOU MEAN--?
WHY, YES I DO MEAN.
I'M GOING TO SEE YOUR DADDY RIGHT NOW AND ASK HIM FOR YOUR HAND IN MARRIAGE--AND WE'LL BE WED BEFORE THIS WEEK IS OUT.
KAUFMANN-TUAN!
THIS BABY WON'T HAVE A THING TO WORRY ABOUT, AND NEITHER WILL YOU. YOU HAVE MY WORD ON THAT AS A GENTLEMAN.
THAT I COULD KNOW SUCH JOY! OH, MY BELOVED, THIS IS THE HAPPIEST DAY OF MY LIFE!
YOU BET IT IS, LITTLE LADY. AND AS SOON AS I HAVE YOUR DADDY'S BLESSING, IT'S GOING TO GET EVEN BETTER.
MAKE HASTE, KAUFMANN-TUAN! YOU ARE MY LOVE, MY PRINCE, MY SKY-BORNE GOD OF DESIRE! I CANNOT *BEAR* TO BE WITHOUT YOU, NOT EVEN FOR A SINGLE MOMENT!
HMH!
YOU JUST TRY KEEPING ME AWAY...

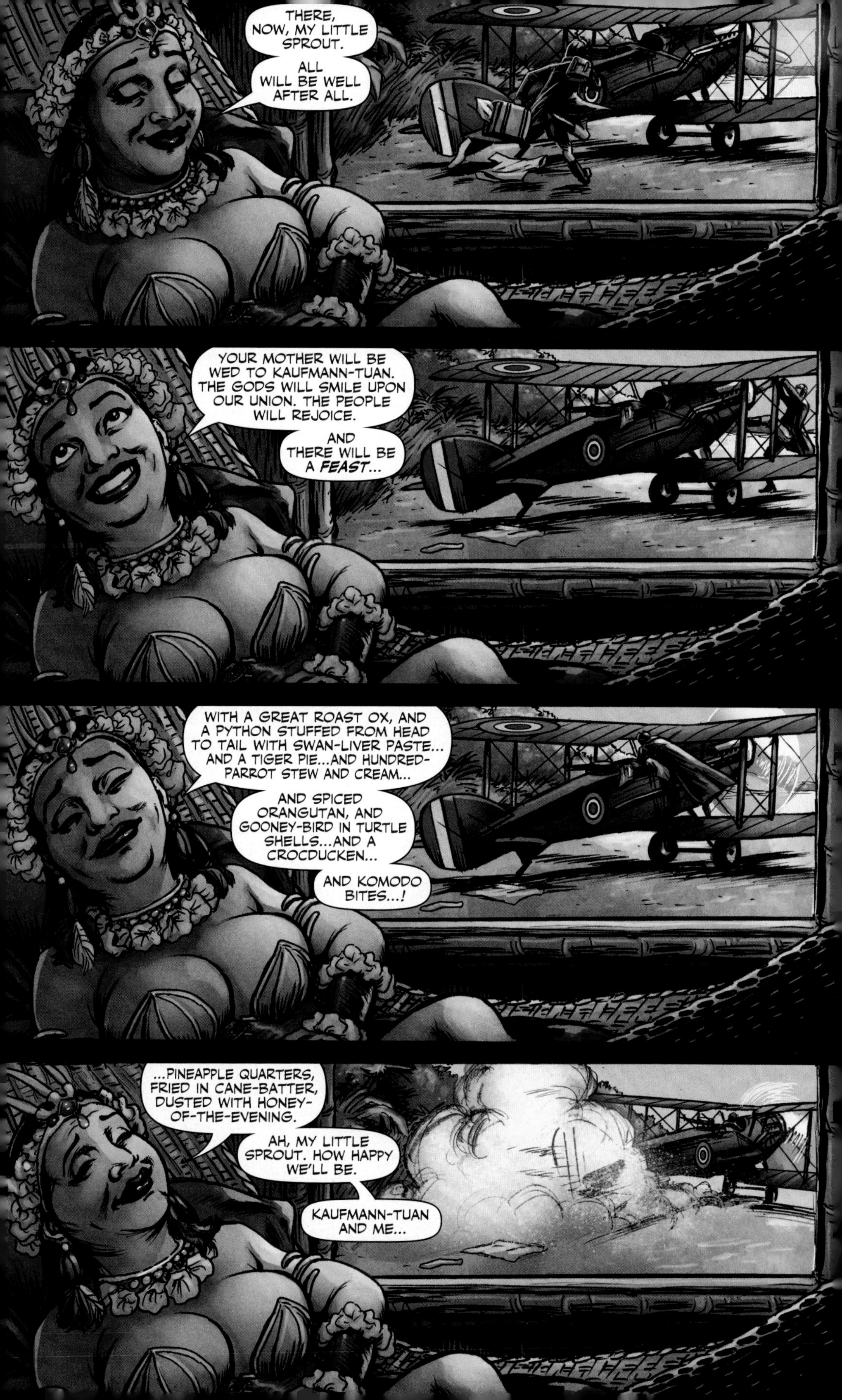
THERE, NOW, MY LITTLE SPROUT.
ALL WILL BE WELL AFTER ALL.
YOUR MOTHER WILL BE WED TO KAUFMANN-TUAN. THE GODS WILL SMILE UPON OUR UNION. THE PEOPLE WILL REJOICE.
AND THERE WILL BE A *FEAST*...
WITH A GREAT ROAST OX, AND A PYTHON STUFFED FROM HEAD TO TAIL WITH SWAN-LIVER PASTE... AND A TIGER PIE...AND HUNDRED-PARROT STEW AND CREAM...
AND SPICED ORANGUTAN, AND GOONEY-BIRD IN TURTLE SHELLS...AND A CROCDUCKEN...
AND KOMODO BITES...!
...PINEAPPLE QUARTERS, FRIED IN CANE-BATTER, DUSTED WITH HONEY-OF-THE-EVENING.
AH, MY LITTLE SPROUT. HOW HAPPY WE'LL BE.
KAUFMANN-TUAN AND ME...

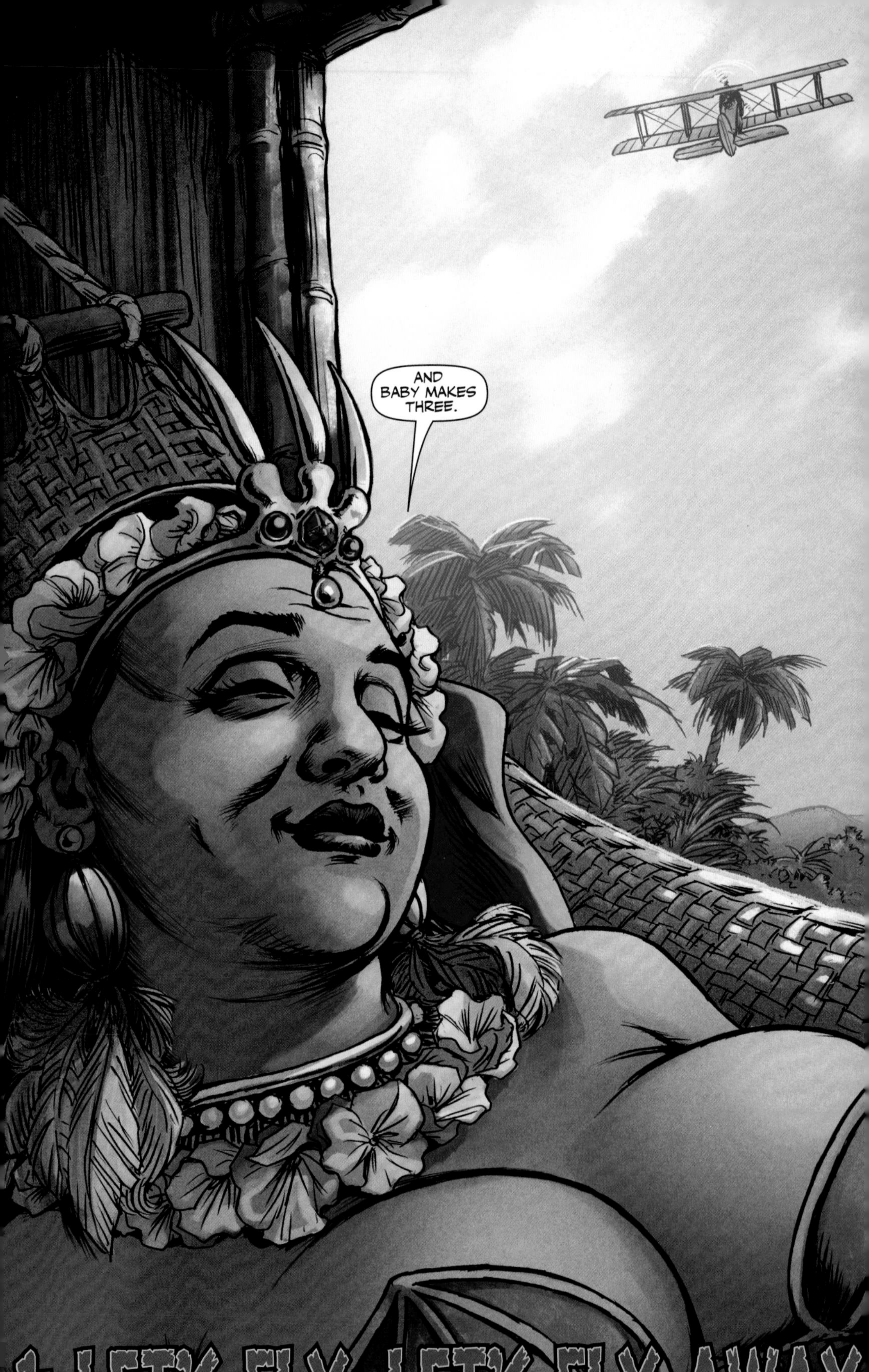
AND BABY MAKES THREE.

1: LET'S FLY, LET'S FLY AWAY

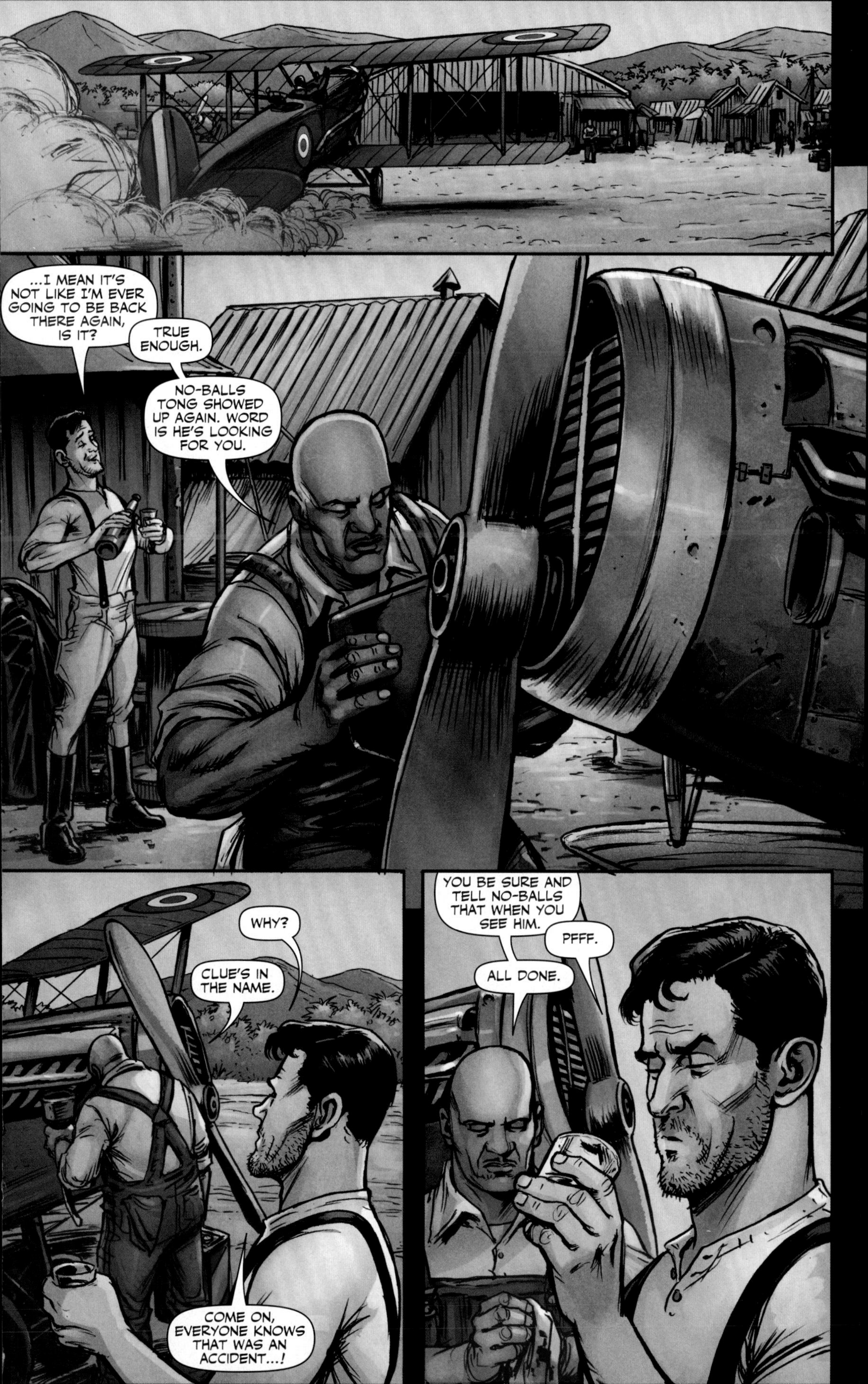
...I MEAN IT'S NOT LIKE I'M EVER GOING TO BE BACK THERE AGAIN, IS IT?
TRUE ENOUGH.
NO-BALLS TONG SHOWED UP AGAIN. WORD IS HE'S LOOKING FOR YOU.
WHY?
CLUE'S IN THE NAME.
COME ON, EVERYONE KNOWS THAT WAS AN ACCIDENT...!
YOU BE SURE AND TELL NO-BALLS THAT WHEN YOU SEE HIM.
PFFF.
ALL DONE.

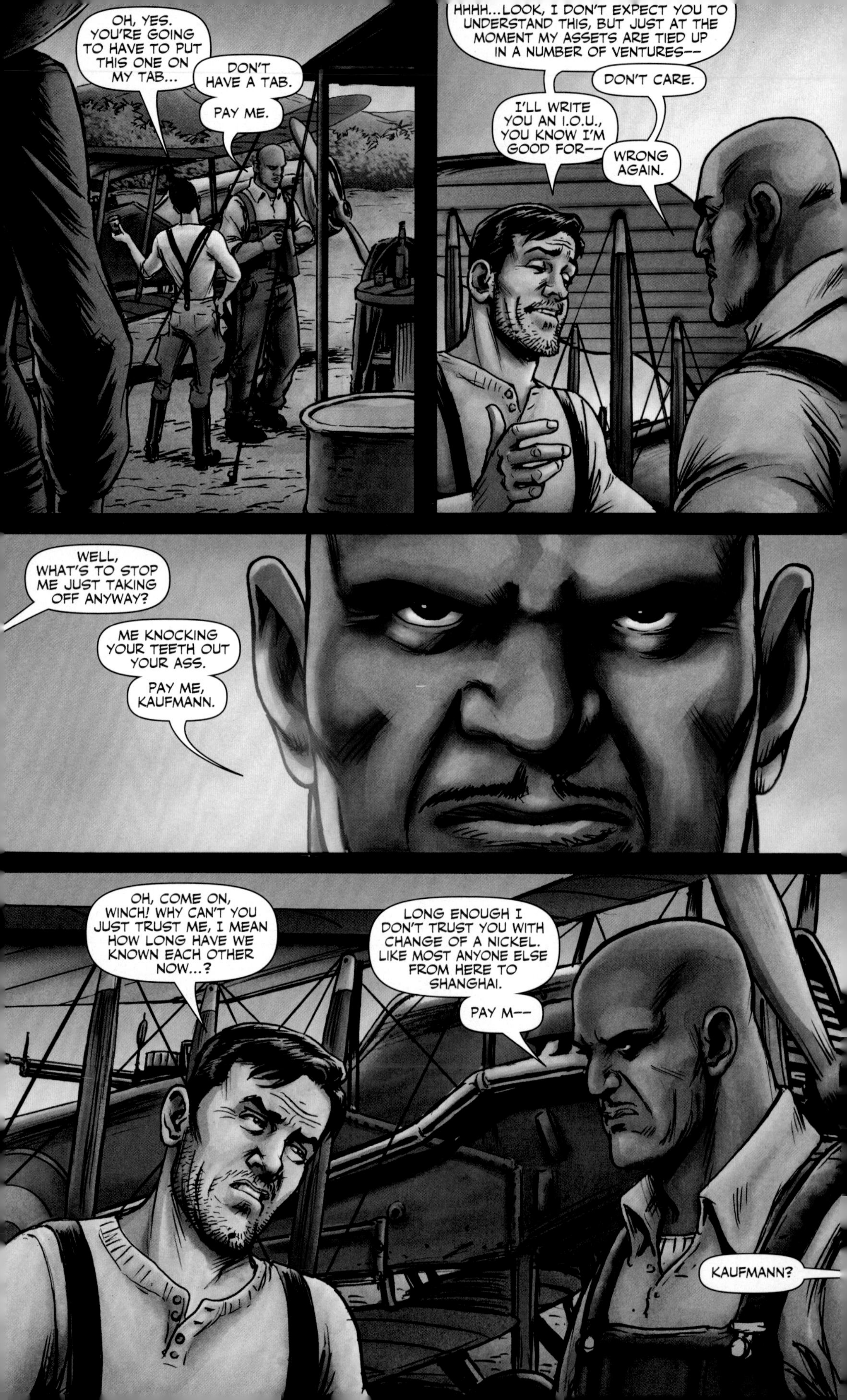
OH, YES. YOU'RE GOING TO HAVE TO PUT THIS ONE ON MY TAB...
DON'T HAVE A TAB.
PAY ME.
HHHH...LOOK, I DON'T EXPECT YOU TO UNDERSTAND THIS, BUT JUST AT THE MOMENT MY ASSETS ARE TIED UP IN A NUMBER OF VENTURES--
DON'T CARE.
I'LL WRITE YOU AN I.O.U., YOU KNOW I'M GOOD FOR--
WRONG AGAIN.
WELL, WHAT'S TO STOP ME JUST TAKING OFF ANYWAY?
ME KNOCKING YOUR TEETH OUT YOUR ASS.
PAY ME, KAUFMANN.
OH, COME ON, WINCH! WHY CAN'T YOU JUST TRUST ME, I MEAN HOW LONG HAVE WE KNOWN EACH OTHER NOW...?
LONG ENOUGH I DON'T TRUST YOU WITH CHANGE OF A NICKEL. LIKE MOST ANYONE ELSE FROM HERE TO SHANGHAI.
PAY M--
KAUFMANN?

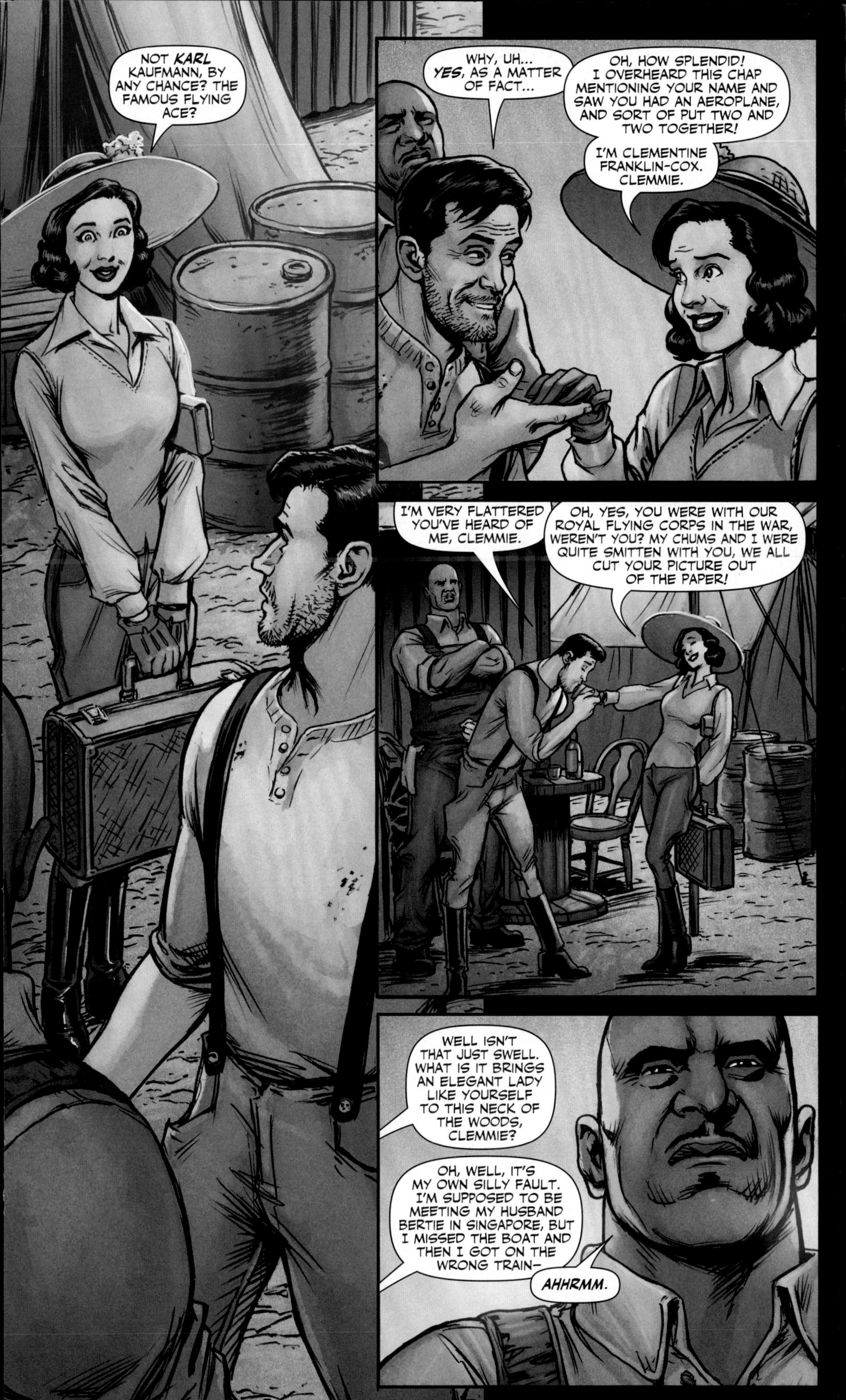
NOT KARL KAUFMANN, BY ANY CHANCE? THE FAMOUS FLYING ACE?
WHY, UH... YES, AS A MATTER OF FACT...
OH, HOW SPLENDID! I OVERHEARD THIS CHAP MENTIONING YOUR NAME AND SAW YOU HAD AN AEROPLANE, AND SORT OF PUT TWO AND TWO TOGETHER!
I'M CLEMENTINE FRANKLIN-COX. CLEMMIE.
I'M VERY FLATTERED YOU'VE HEARD OF ME, CLEMMIE.
OH, YES, YOU WERE WITH OUR ROYAL FLYING CORPS IN THE WAR, WEREN'T YOU? MY CHUMS AND I WERE QUITE SMITTEN WITH YOU, WE ALL CUT YOUR PICTURE OUT OF THE PAPER!
WELL ISN'T THAT JUST SWELL. WHAT IS IT BRINGS AN ELEGANT LADY LIKE YOURSELF TO THIS NECK OF THE WOODS, CLEMMIE?
OH, WELL, IT'S MY OWN SILLY FAULT. I'M SUPPOSED TO BE MEETING MY HUSBAND BERTIE IN SINGAPORE, BUT I MISSED THE BOAT AND THEN I GOT ON THE WRONG TRAIN—
AHHRMM.

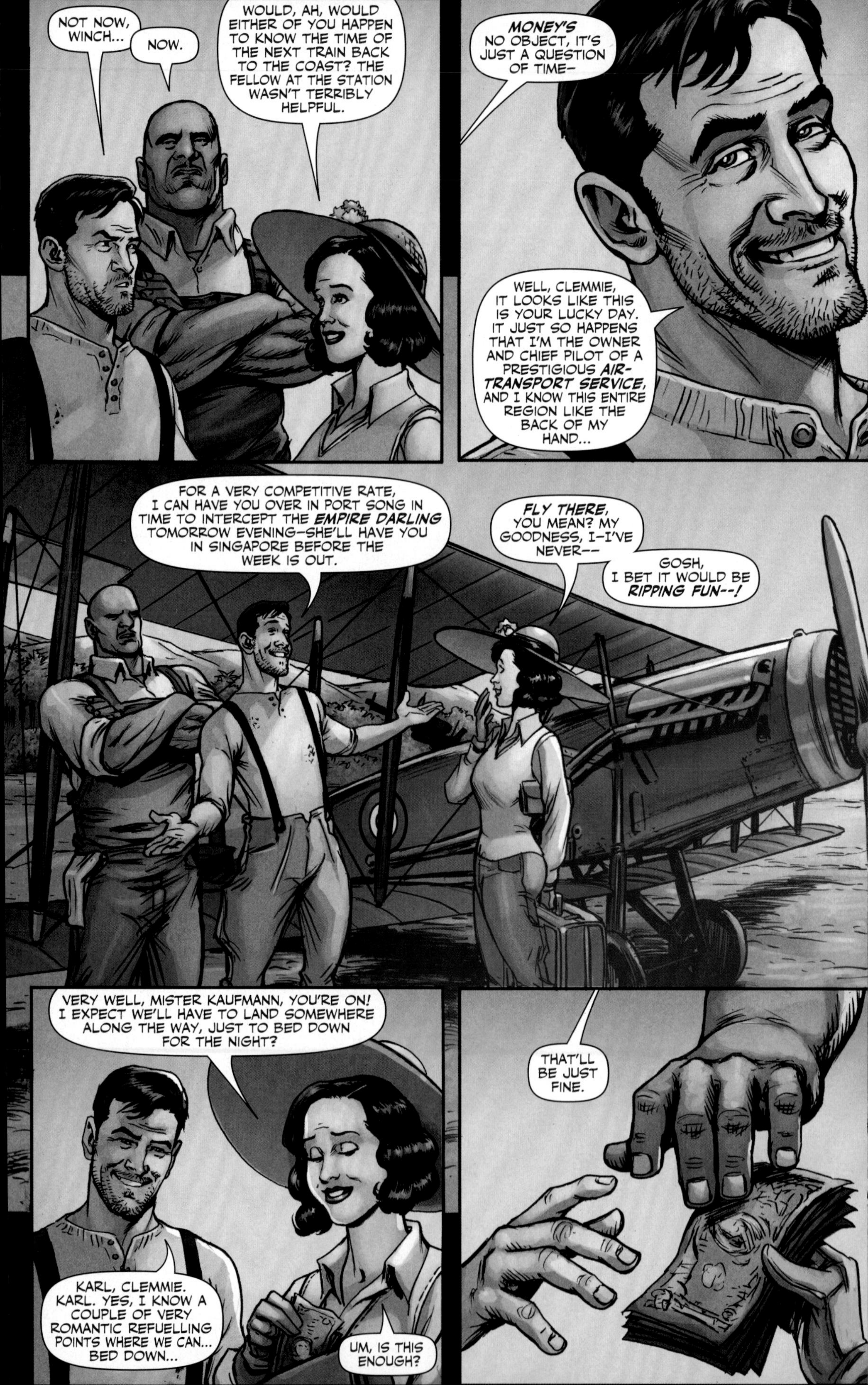
NOT NOW, WINCH...
NOW.
WOULD, AH, WOULD EITHER OF YOU HAPPEN TO KNOW THE TIME OF THE NEXT TRAIN BACK TO THE COAST? THE FELLOW AT THE STATION WASN'T TERRIBLY HELPFUL.
MONEY'S NO OBJECT, IT'S JUST A QUESTION OF TIME–
WELL, CLEMMIE, IT LOOKS LIKE THIS IS YOUR LUCKY DAY. IT JUST SO HAPPENS THAT I'M THE OWNER AND CHIEF PILOT OF A PRESTIGIOUS AIR-TRANSPORT SERVICE, AND I KNOW THIS ENTIRE REGION LIKE THE BACK OF MY HAND...
FOR A VERY COMPETITIVE RATE, I CAN HAVE YOU OVER IN PORT SONG IN TIME TO INTERCEPT THE EMPIRE DARLING TOMORROW EVENING–SHE'LL HAVE YOU IN SINGAPORE BEFORE THE WEEK IS OUT.
FLY THERE, YOU MEAN? MY GOODNESS, I–I'VE NEVER--
GOSH, I BET IT WOULD BE RIPPING FUN--!
VERY WELL, MISTER KAUFMANN, YOU'RE ON! I EXPECT WE'LL HAVE TO LAND SOMEWHERE ALONG THE WAY, JUST TO BED DOWN FOR THE NIGHT?
KARL, CLEMMIE. KARL. YES, I KNOW A COUPLE OF VERY ROMANTIC REFUELLING POINTS WHERE WE CAN... BED DOWN...
UM, IS THIS ENOUGH?
THAT'LL BE JUST FINE.

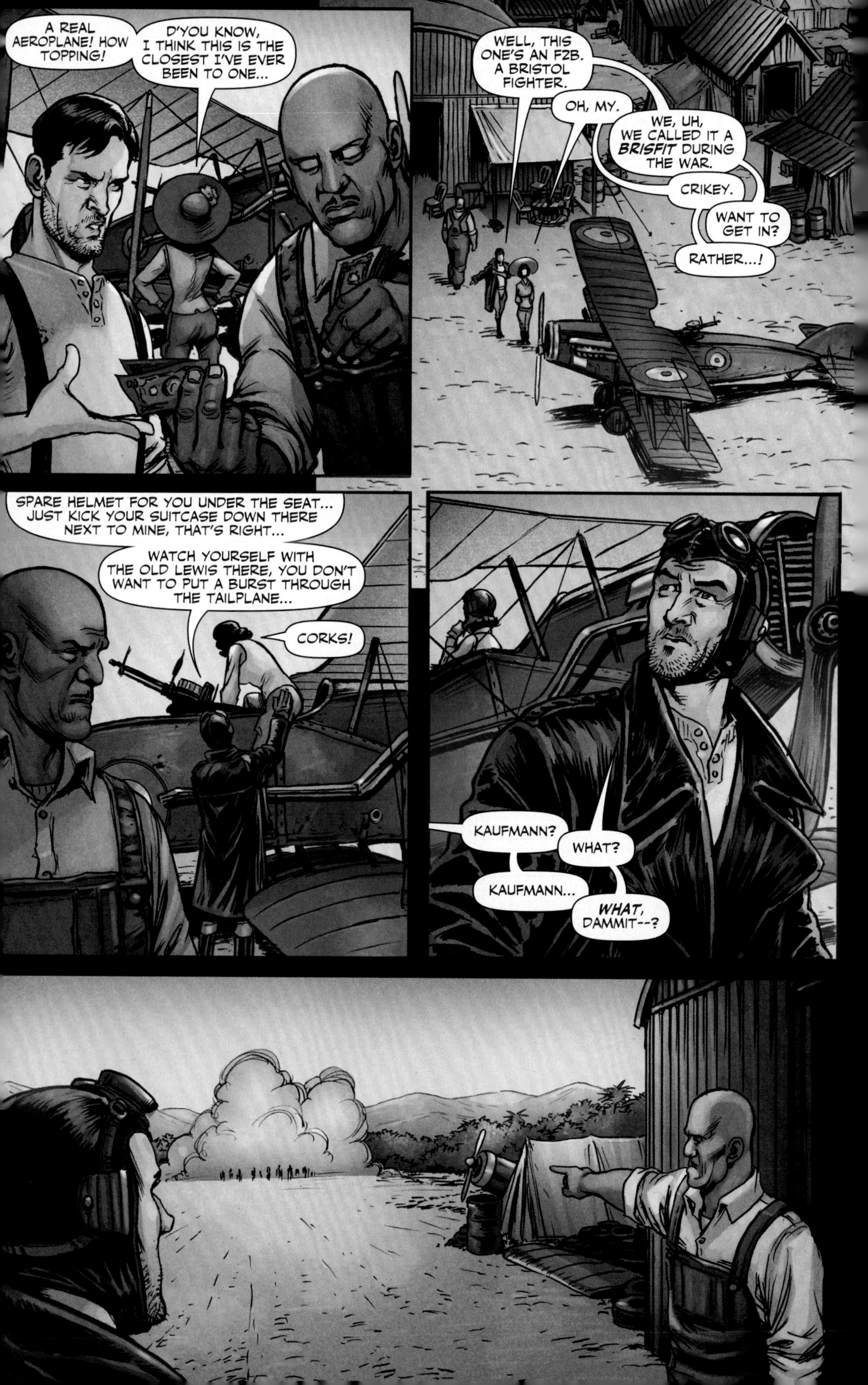
A REAL AEROPLANE! HOW TOPPING!
D'YOU KNOW, I THINK THIS IS THE CLOSEST I'VE EVER BEEN TO ONE...
WELL, THIS ONE'S AN F2B. A BRISTOL FIGHTER.
OH, MY.
WE, UH, WE CALLED IT A *BRISFIT* DURING THE WAR.
CRIKEY.
WANT TO GET IN?
RATHER...!
SPARE HELMET FOR YOU UNDER THE SEAT... JUST KICK YOUR SUITCASE DOWN THERE NEXT TO MINE, THAT'S RIGHT...
WATCH YOURSELF WITH THE OLD LEWIS THERE, YOU DON'T WANT TO PUT A BURST THROUGH THE TAILPLANE...
CORKS!
KAUFMANN?
WHAT?
KAUFMANN...
WHAT, DAMMIT--?

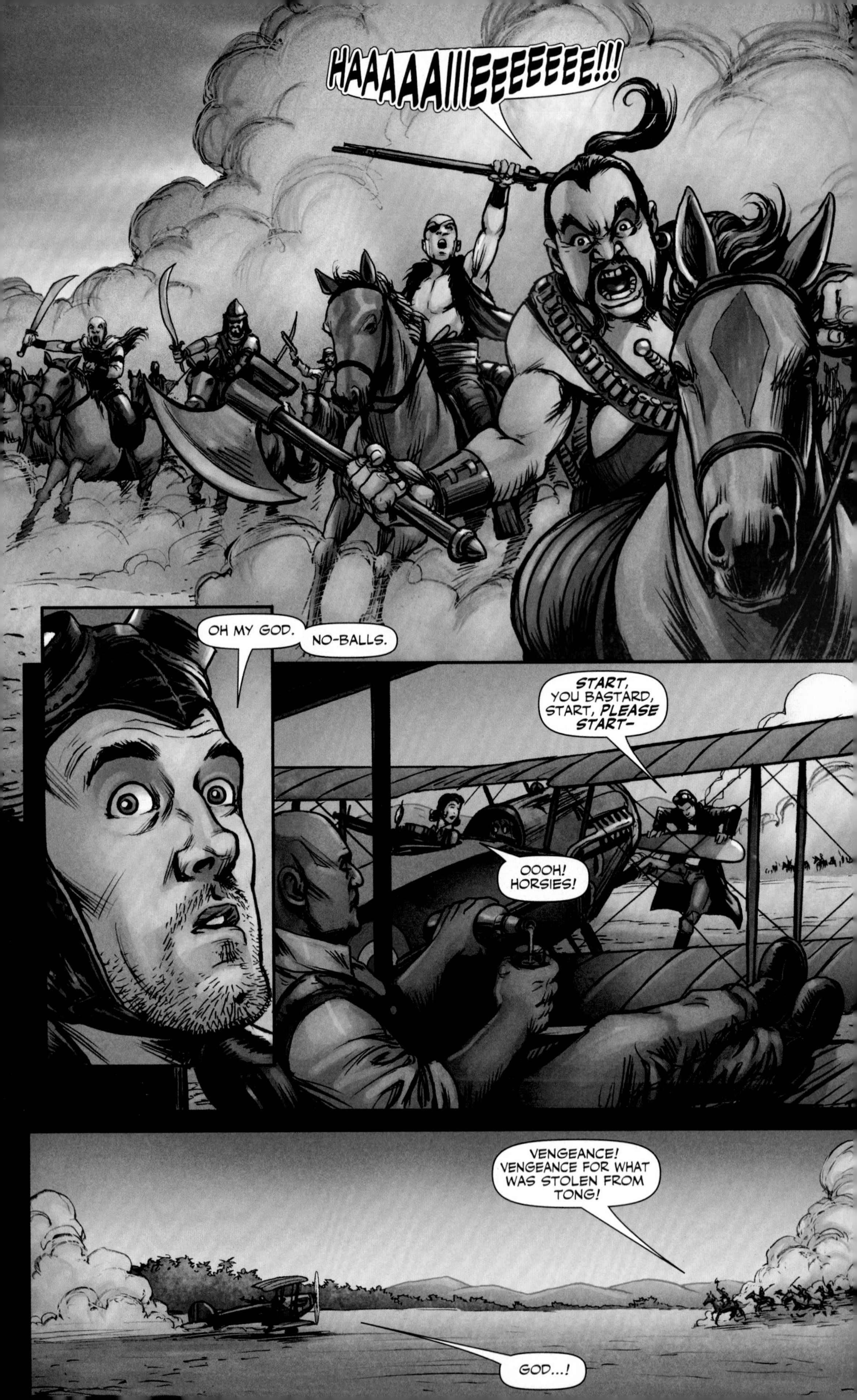
HAAAAAIIIIEEEEEEE!!!
OH MY GOD.
NO-BALLS.
START, YOU BASTARD, START, PLEASE START-
OOOH! HORSIES!
VENGEANCE! VENGEANCE FOR WHAT WAS STOLEN FROM TONG!
GOD...!

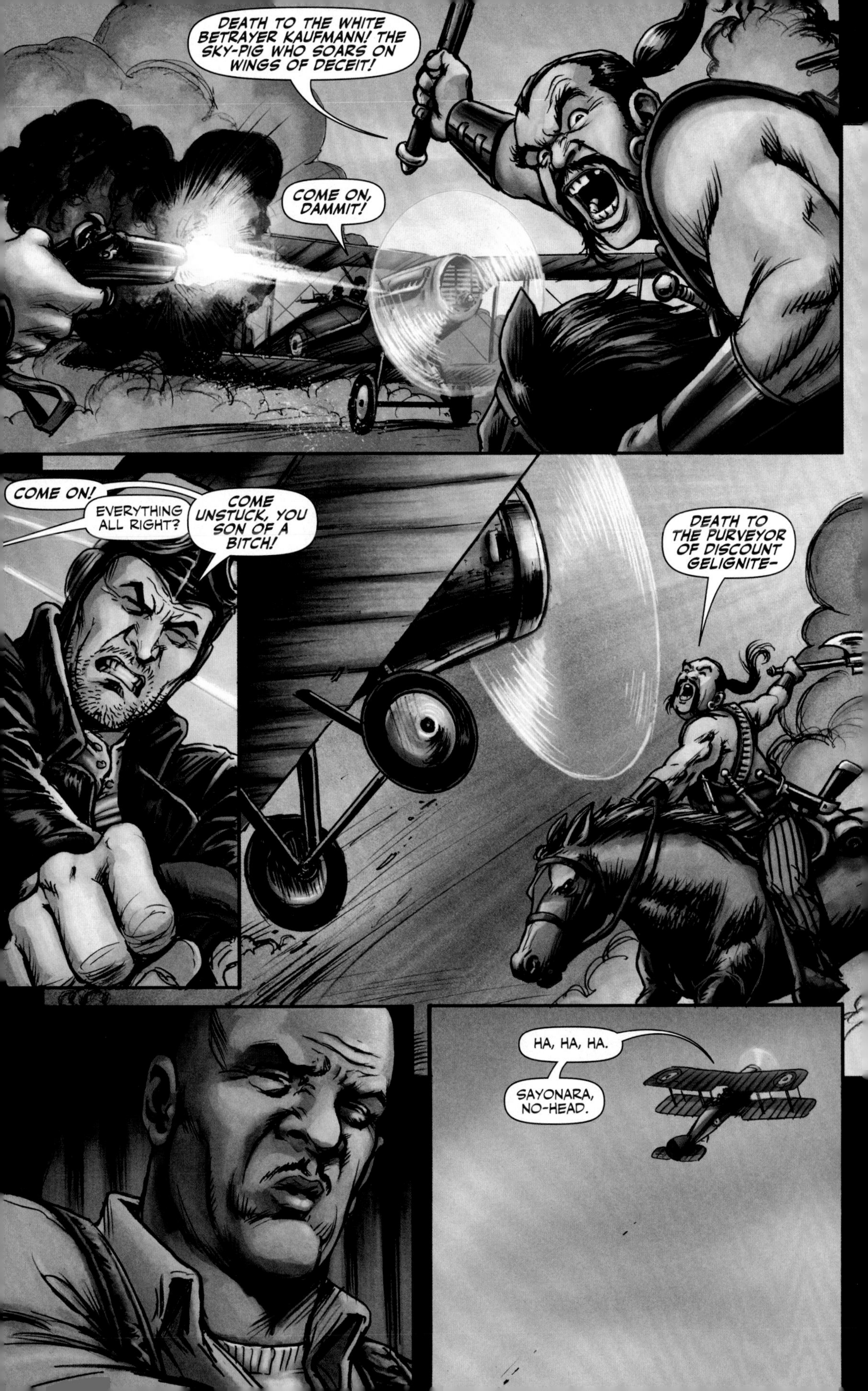
DEATH TO THE WHITE BETRAYER KAUFMANN! THE SKY-PIG WHO SOARS ON WINGS OF DECEIT!
COME ON, DAMMIT!
COME ON!
EVERYTHING ALL RIGHT?
COME UNSTUCK, YOU SON OF A BITCH!
DEATH TO THE PURVEYOR OF DISCOUNT GELIGNITE-
HA, HA, HA.
SAYONARA, NO-HEAD.

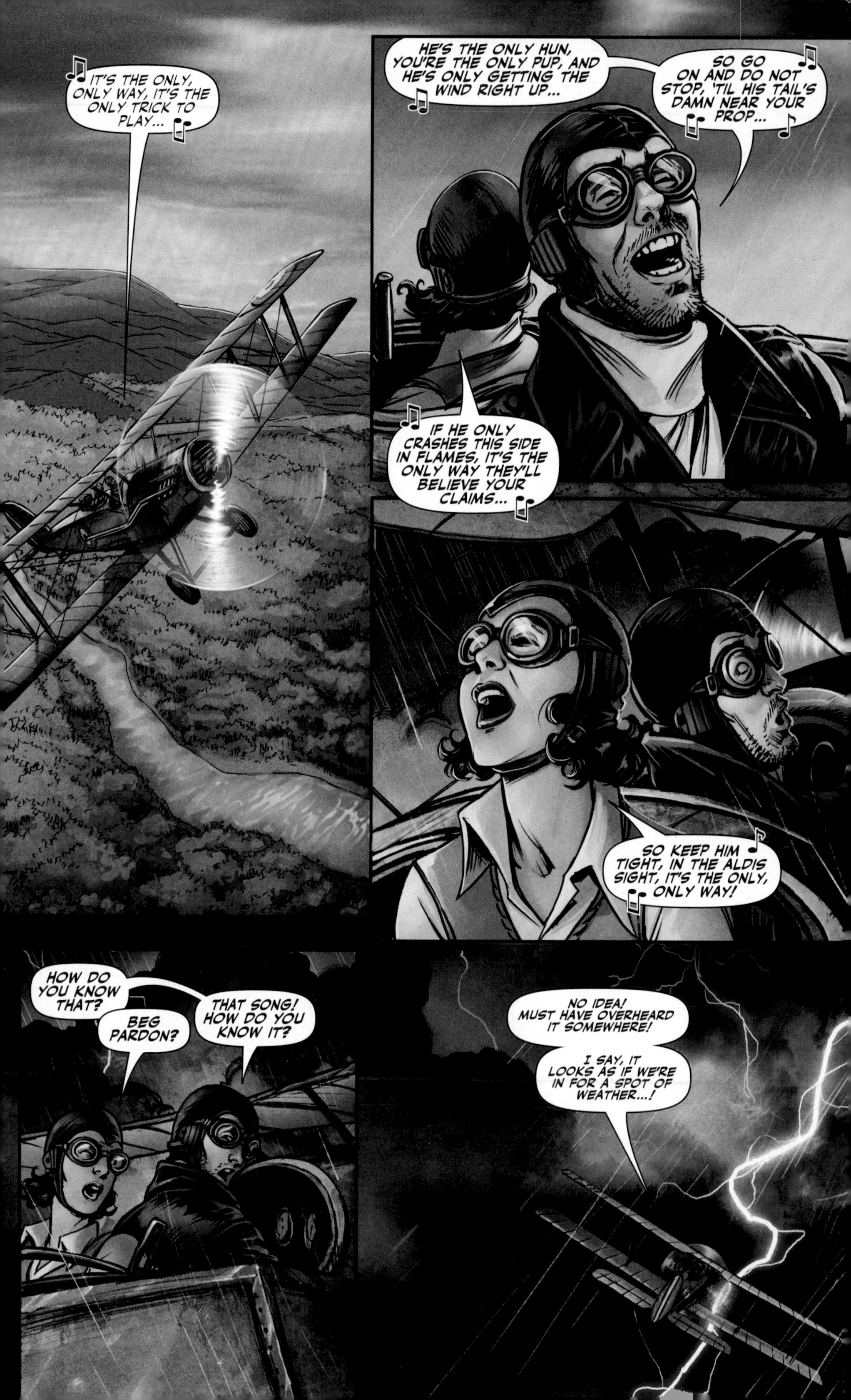
IT'S THE ONLY, ONLY WAY, IT'S THE ONLY TRICK TO PLAY...
HE'S THE ONLY HUN, YOU'RE THE ONLY PUP, AND HE'S ONLY GETTING THE WIND RIGHT UP...
SO GO ON AND DO NOT STOP, 'TIL HIS TAIL'S DAMN NEAR YOUR PROP...
IF HE ONLY CRASHES THIS SIDE IN FLAMES, IT'S THE ONLY WAY THEY'LL BELIEVE YOUR CLAIMS...
SO KEEP HIM TIGHT, IN THE ALDIS SIGHT, IT'S THE ONLY, ONLY WAY!
HOW DO YOU KNOW THAT?
BEG PARDON?
THAT SONG! HOW DO YOU KNOW IT?
NO IDEA! MUST HAVE OVERHEARD IT SOMEWHERE!
I SAY, IT LOOKS AS IF WE'RE IN FOR A SPOT OF WEATHER...!

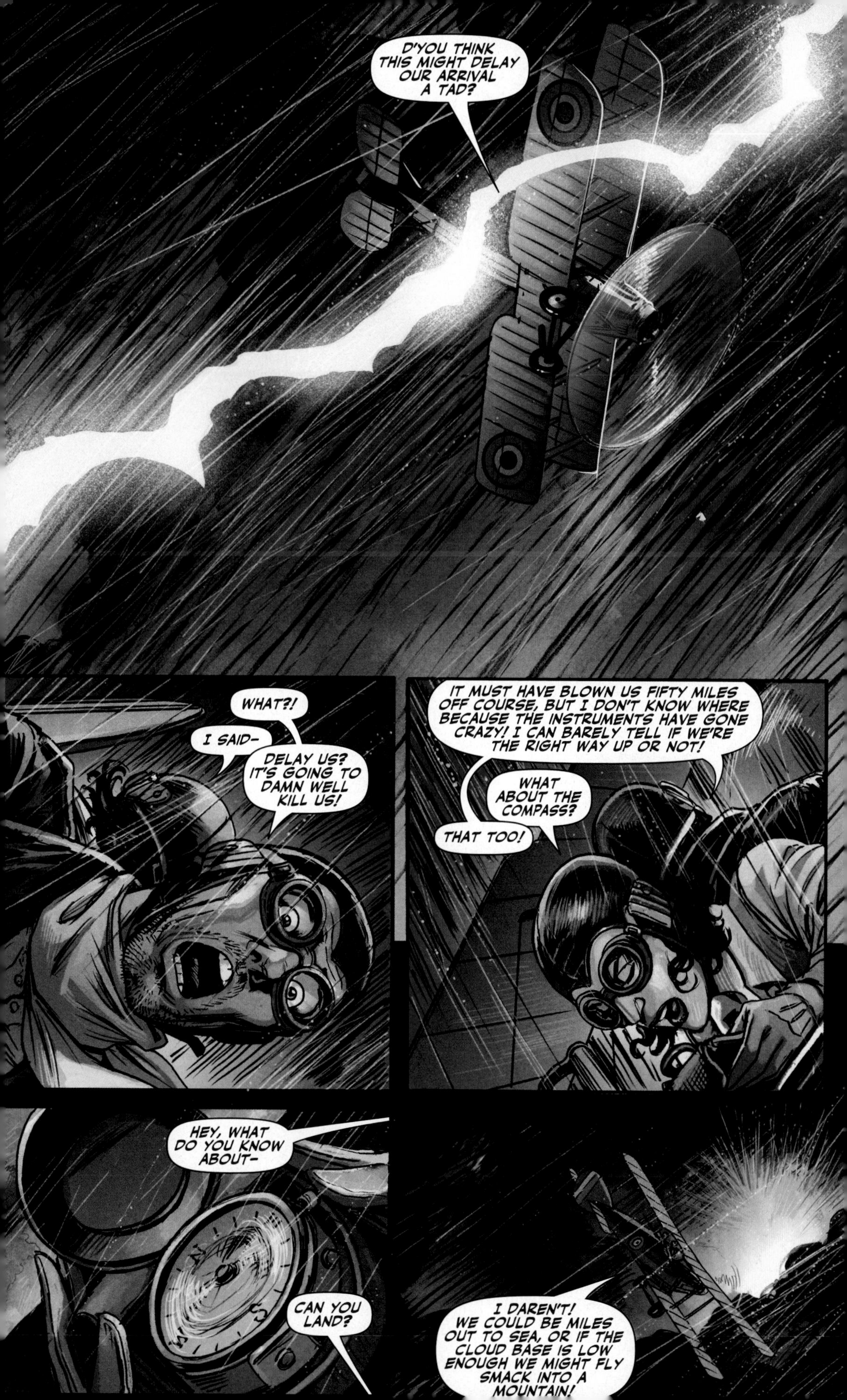
D'YOU THINK THIS MIGHT DELAY OUR ARRIVAL A TAD?
WHAT?!
I SAID-
DELAY US? IT'S GOING TO DAMN WELL KILL US!
IT MUST HAVE BLOWN US FIFTY MILES OFF COURSE, BUT I DON'T KNOW WHERE BECAUSE THE INSTRUMENTS HAVE GONE CRAZY! I CAN BARELY TELL IF WE'RE THE RIGHT WAY UP OR NOT!
WHAT ABOUT THE COMPASS?
THAT TOO!
HEY, WHAT DO YOU KNOW ABOUT-
CAN YOU LAND?
I DAREN'T! WE COULD BE MILES OUT TO SEA, OR IF THE CLOUD BASE IS LOW ENOUGH WE MIGHT FLY SMACK INTO A MOUNTAIN!

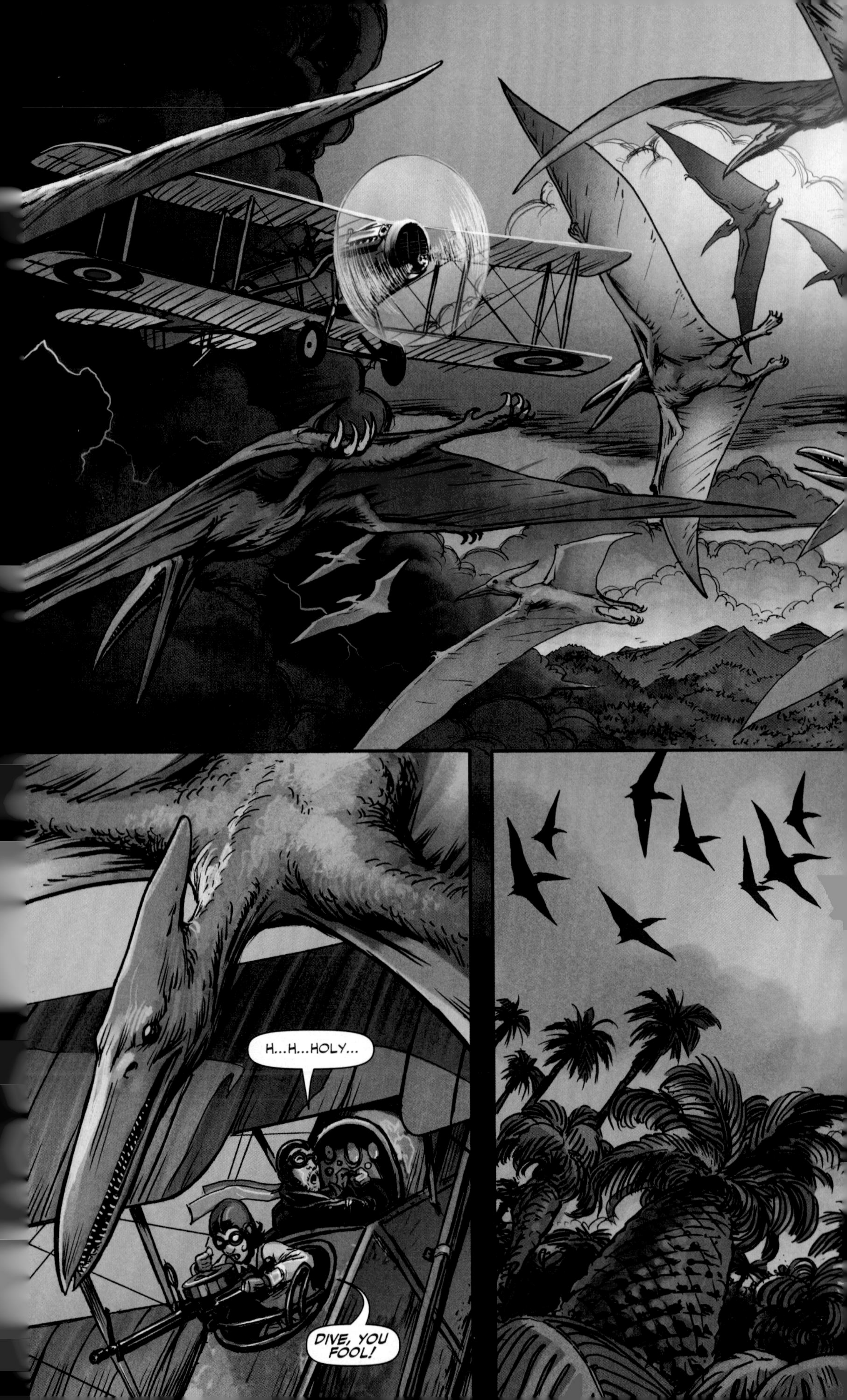
H...H...HOLY...
DIVE, YOU FOOL!

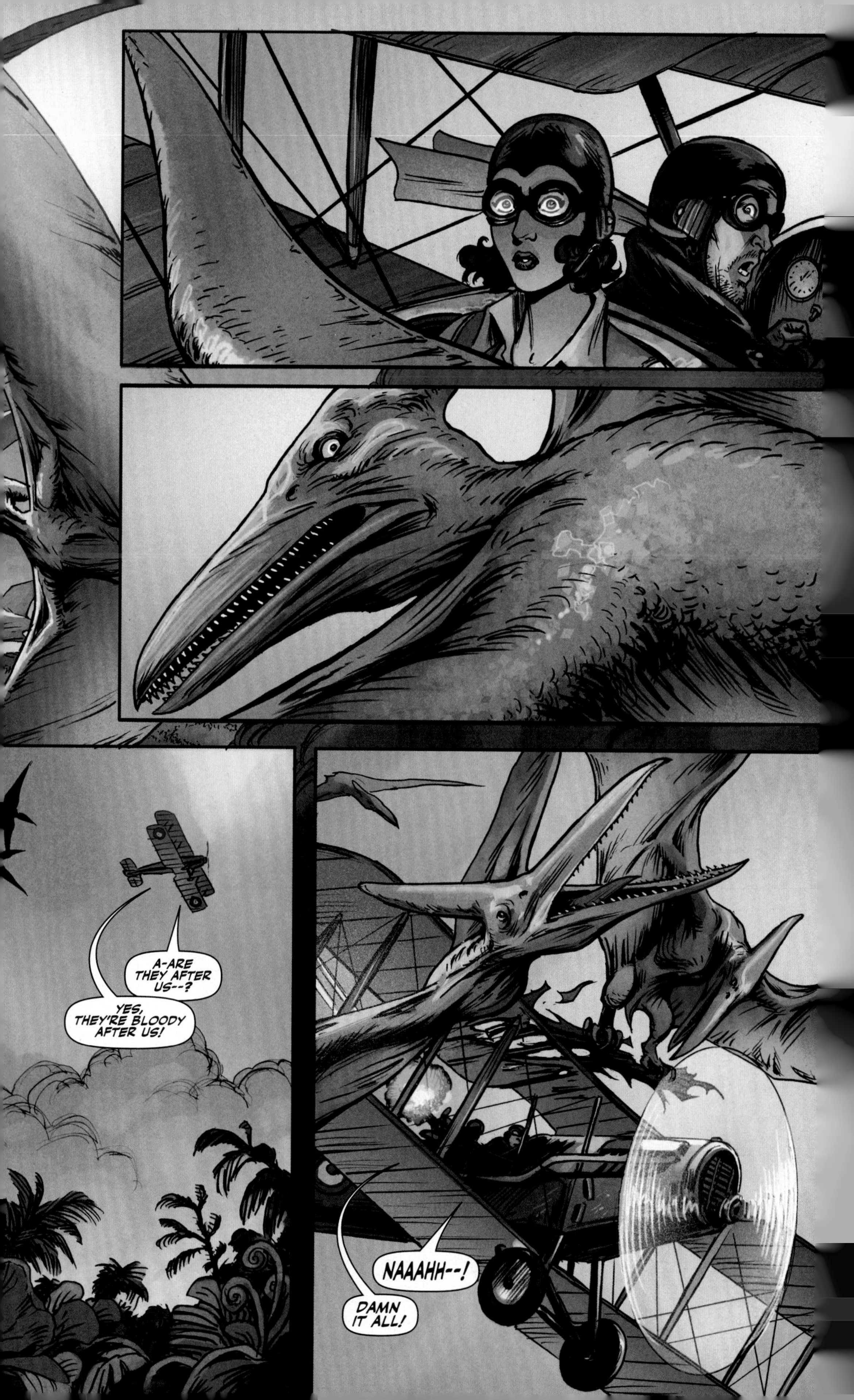
A-ARE THEY AFTER US--?
YES, THEY'RE BLOODY AFTER US!
NAAAHH--!
DAMN IT ALL!

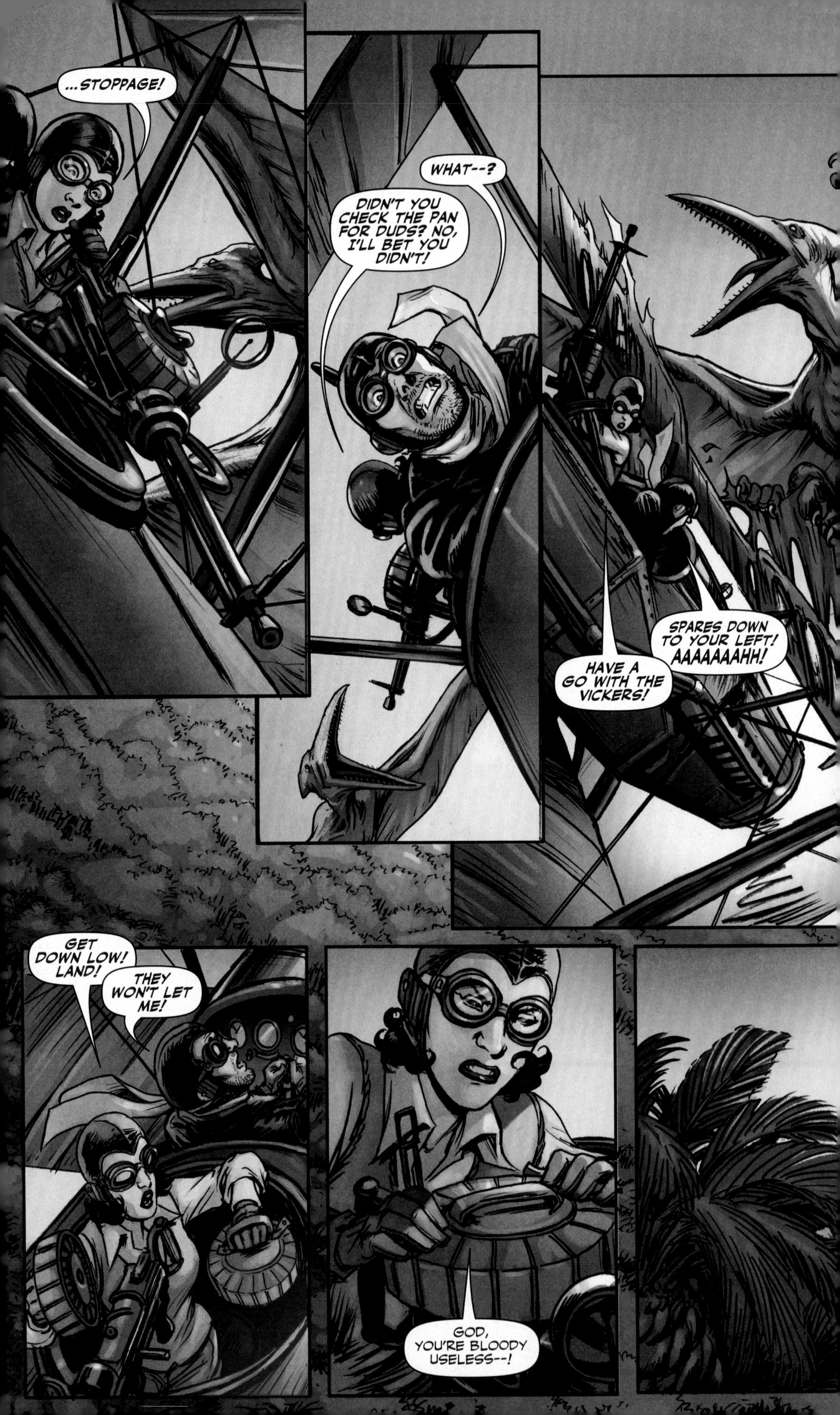

...STOPPAGE!
WHAT--?
DIDN'T YOU CHECK THE PAN FOR DUDS? NO, I'LL BET YOU DIDN'T!
SPARES DOWN TO YOUR LEFT! AAAAAAAAHH!
HAVE A GO WITH THE VICKERS!
GET DOWN LOW! LAND!
THEY WON'T LET ME!
GOD, YOU'RE BLOODY USELESS--!

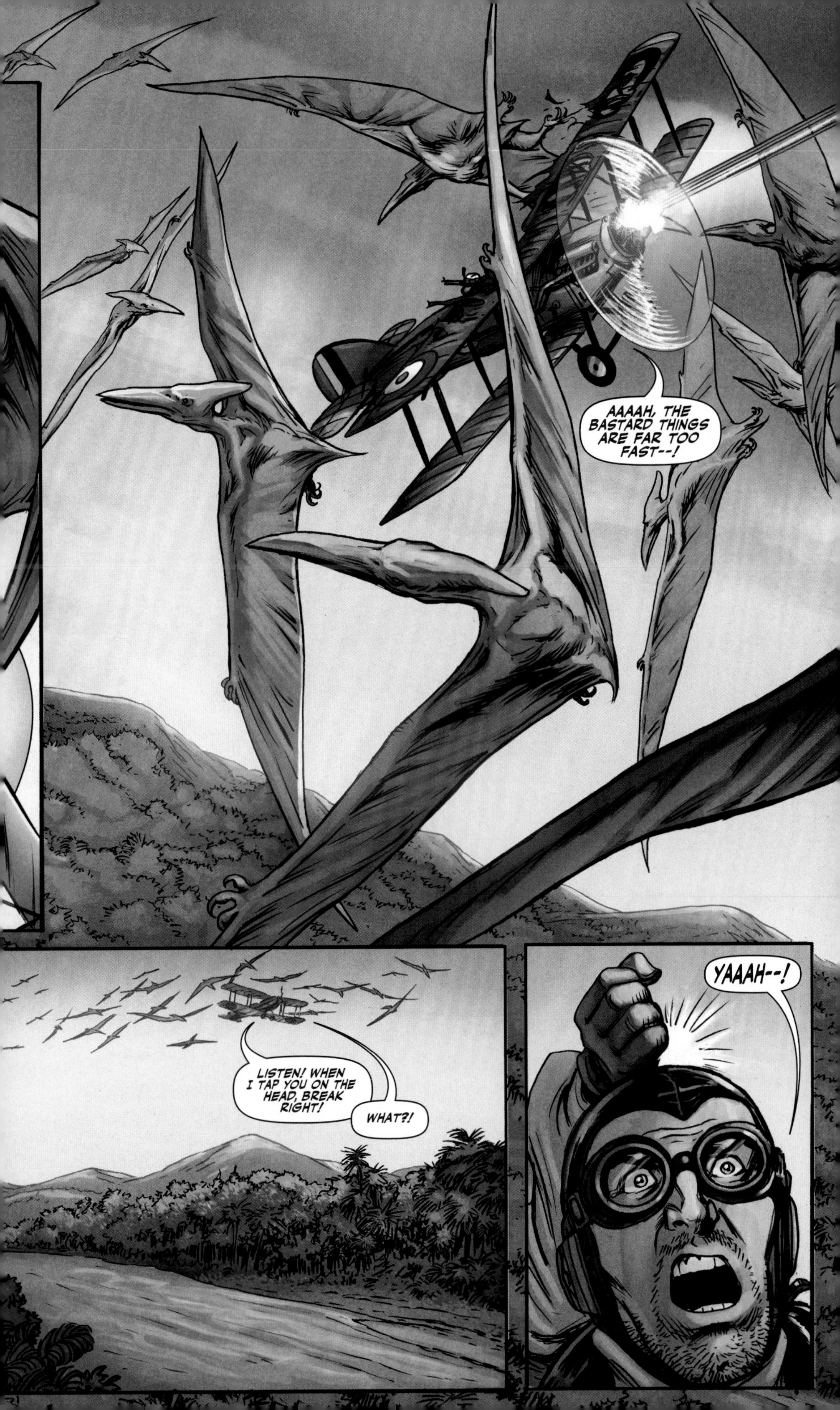
AAAAH, THE BASTARD THINGS ARE FAR TOO FAST--!
LISTEN! WHEN I TAP YOU ON THE HEAD, BREAK RIGHT!
WHAT?!
YAAAH--!

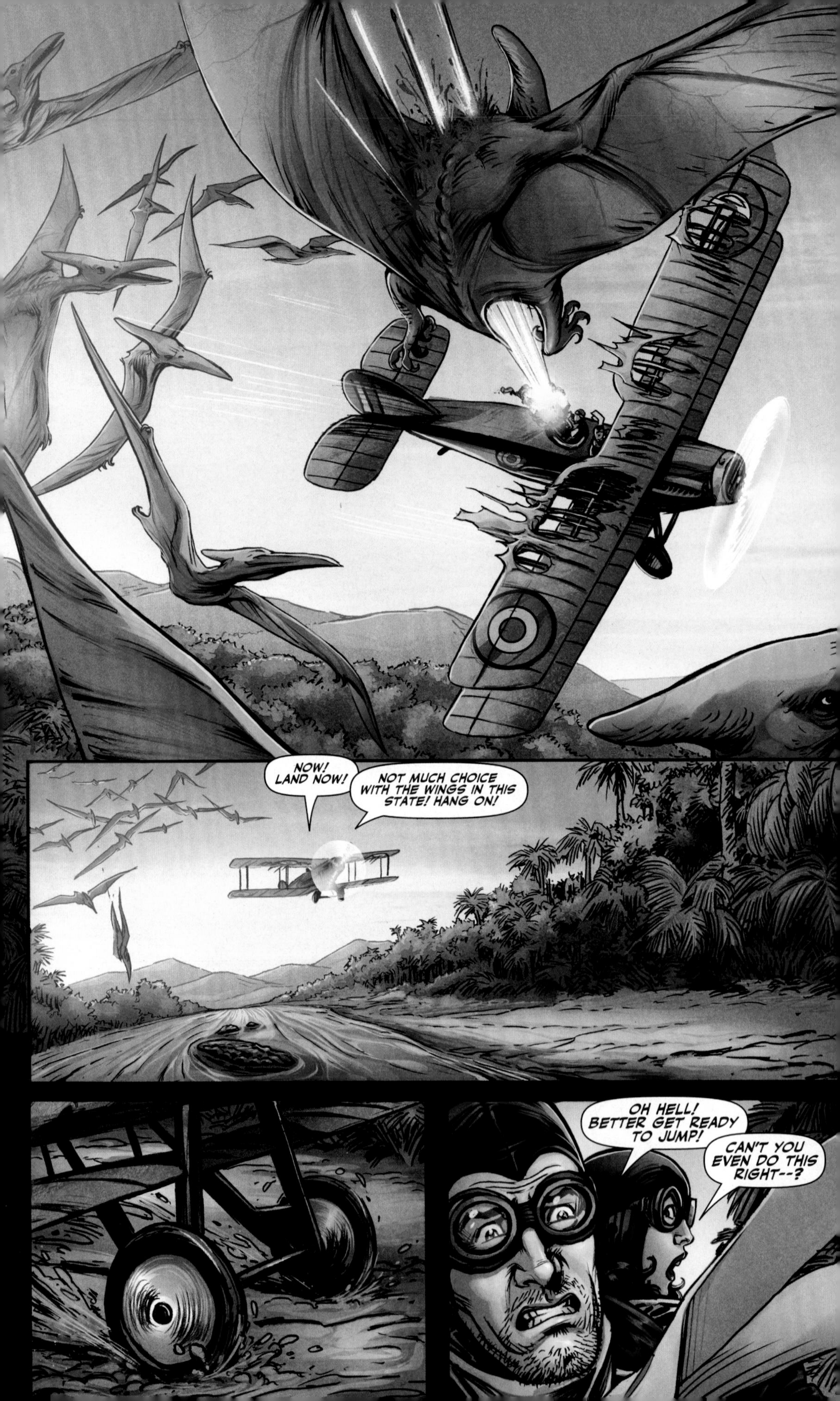
NOW! LAND NOW!
NOT MUCH CHOICE WITH THE WINGS IN THIS STATE! HANG ON!
OH HELL! BETTER GET READY TO JUMP!
CAN'T YOU EVEN DO THIS RIGHT--?

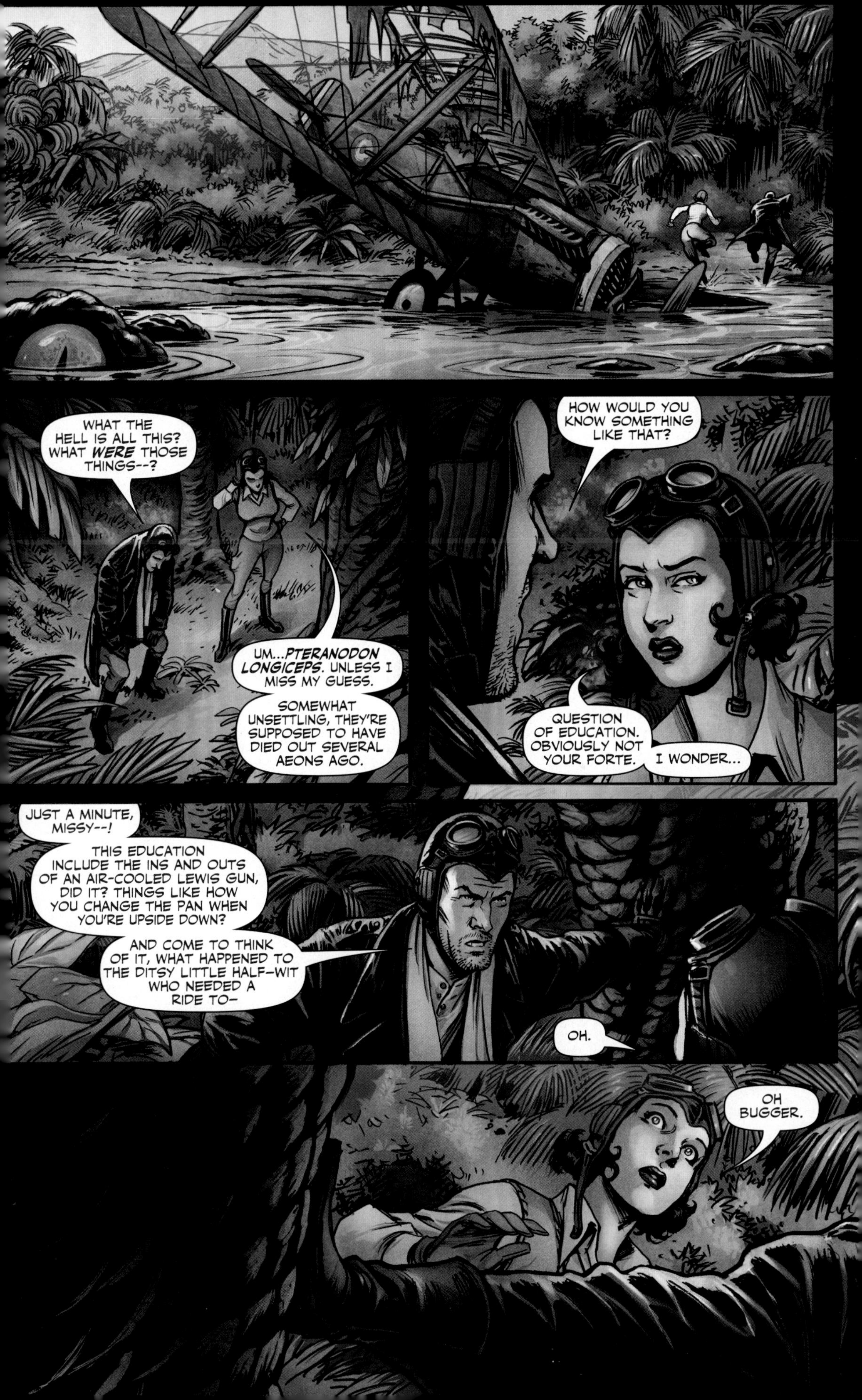
WHAT THE HELL IS ALL THIS? WHAT *WERE* THOSE THINGS--?
UM...*PTERANODON LONGICEPS*. UNLESS I MISS MY GUESS.
SOMEWHAT UNSETTLING, THEY'RE SUPPOSED TO HAVE DIED OUT SEVERAL AEONS AGO.
HOW WOULD YOU KNOW SOMETHING LIKE THAT?
QUESTION OF EDUCATION. OBVIOUSLY NOT YOUR FORTE.
I WONDER...
JUST A MINUTE, MISSY--!
THIS EDUCATION INCLUDE THE INS AND OUTS OF AN AIR-COOLED LEWIS GUN, DID IT? THINGS LIKE HOW YOU CHANGE THE PAN WHEN YOU'RE UPSIDE DOWN?
AND COME TO THINK OF IT, WHAT HAPPENED TO THE DITSY LITTLE HALF-WIT WHO NEEDED A RIDE TO-
OH.
OH BUGGER.

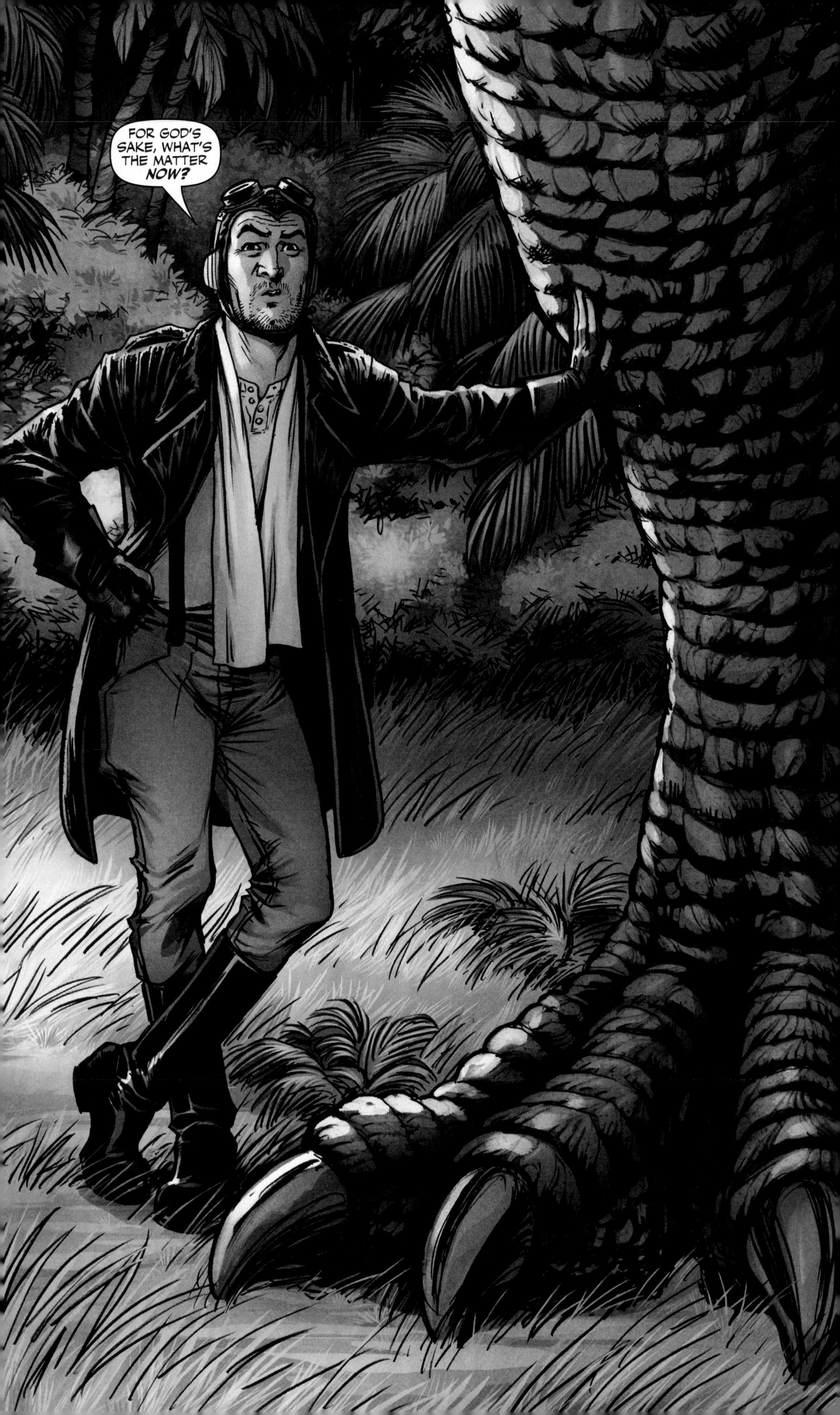
FOR GOD'S SAKE, WHAT'S THE MATTER *NOW?*

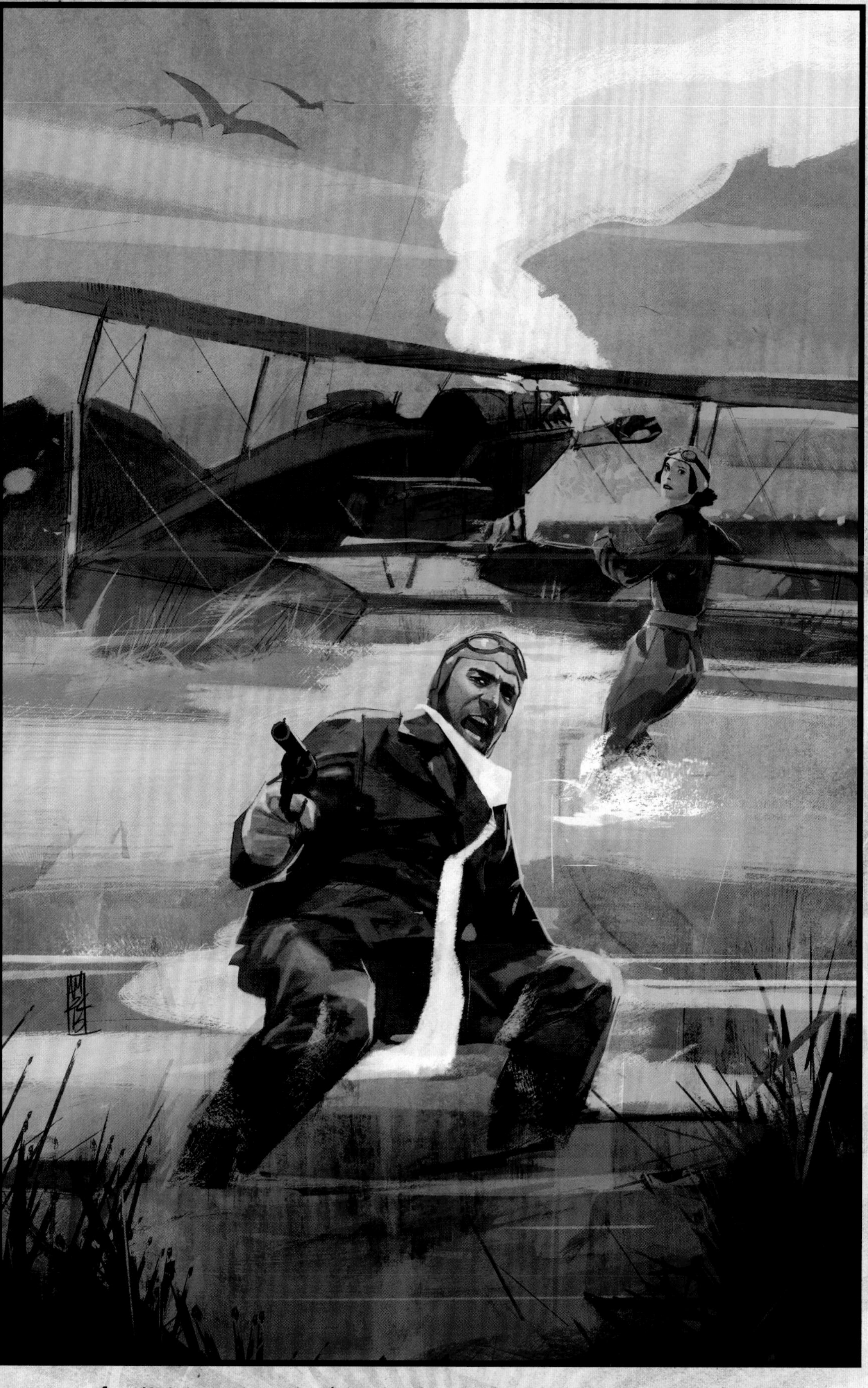

#1 VARIANT COVER BY ALEX MALEEV

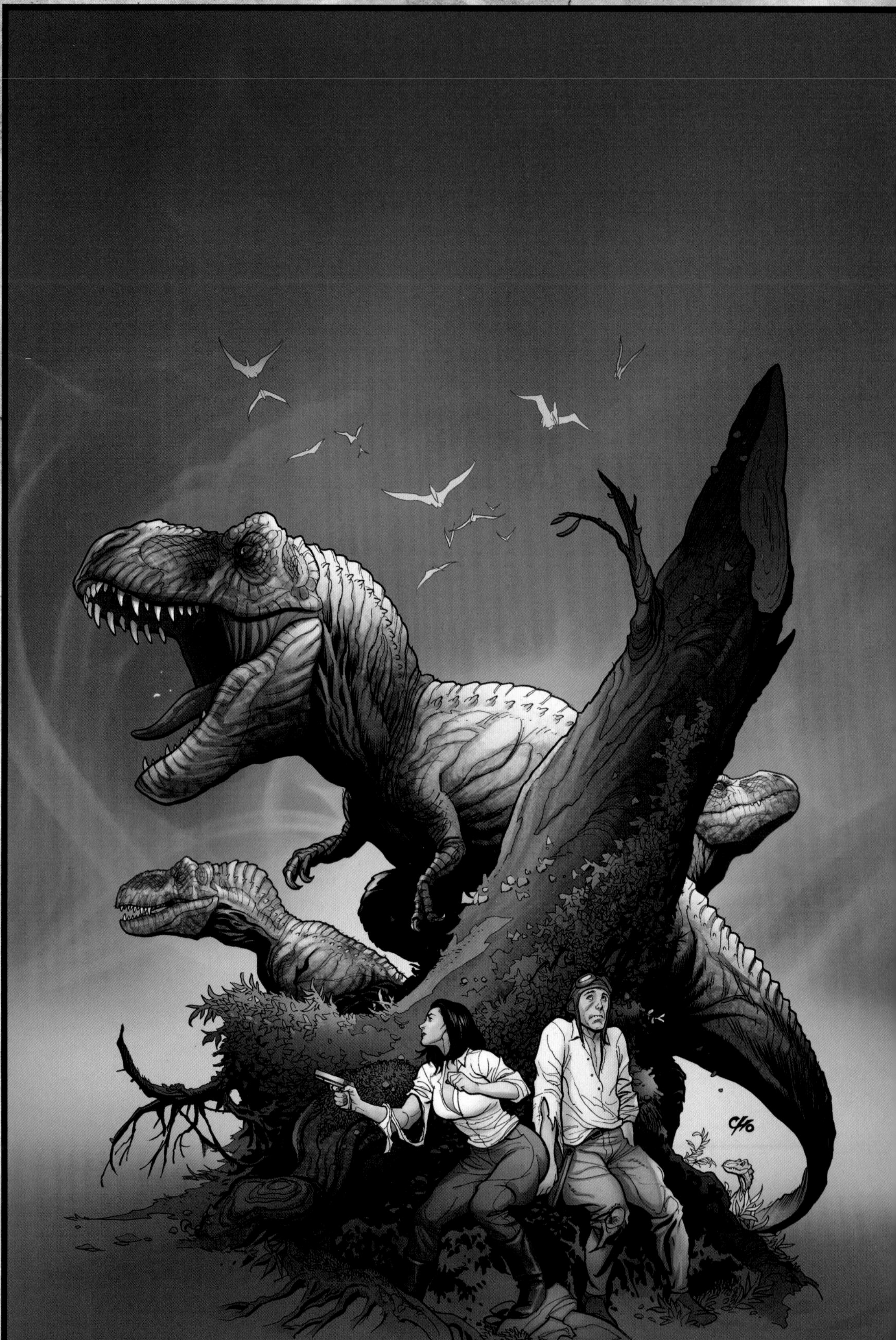

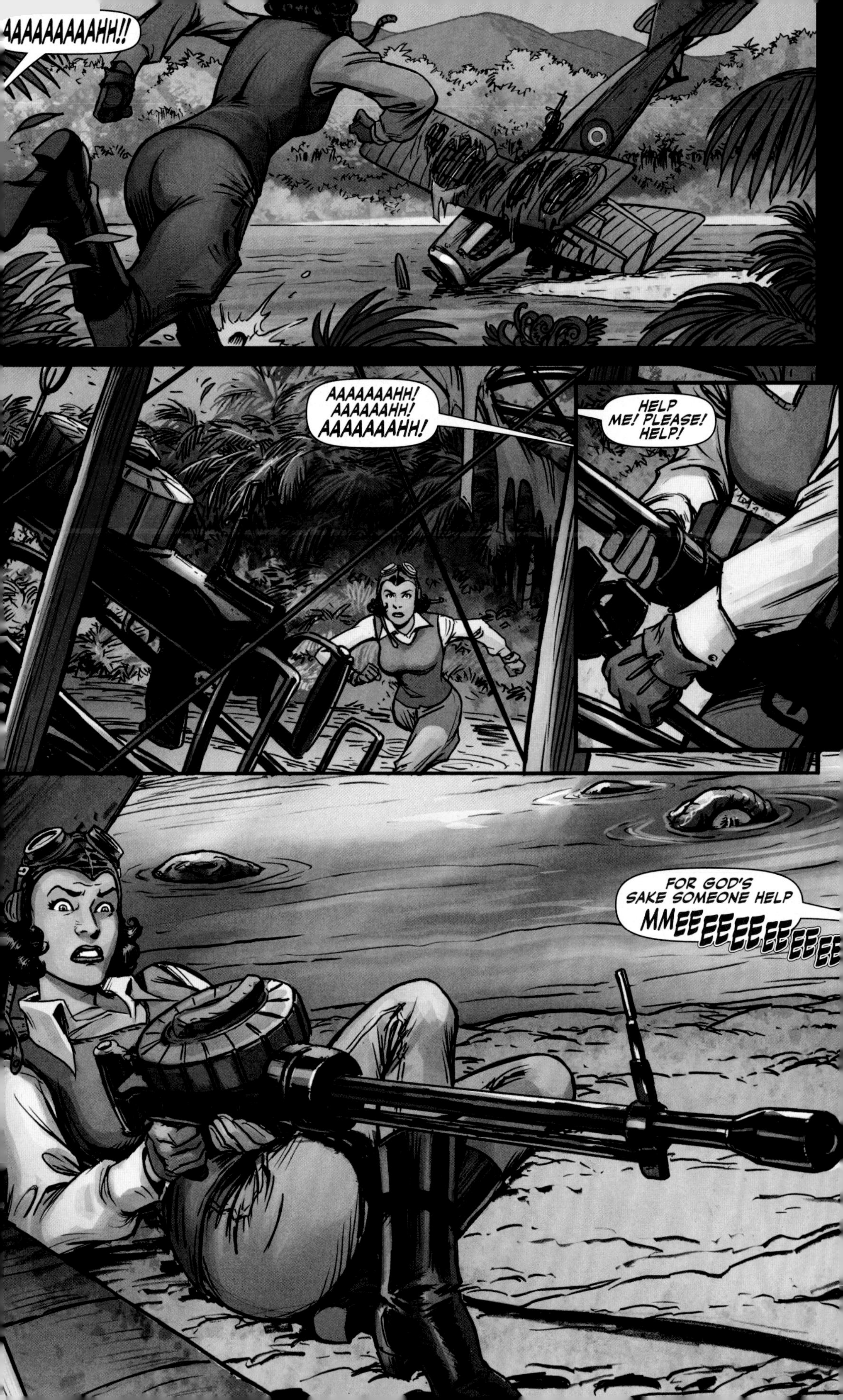
AAAAAAAAAAHH!!
AAAAAAAHH! AAAAAAAHH! AAAAAAAAHH!
HELP ME! PLEASE! HELP!
FOR GOD'S SAKE SOMEONE HELP MMEEEEEEEEEEEE

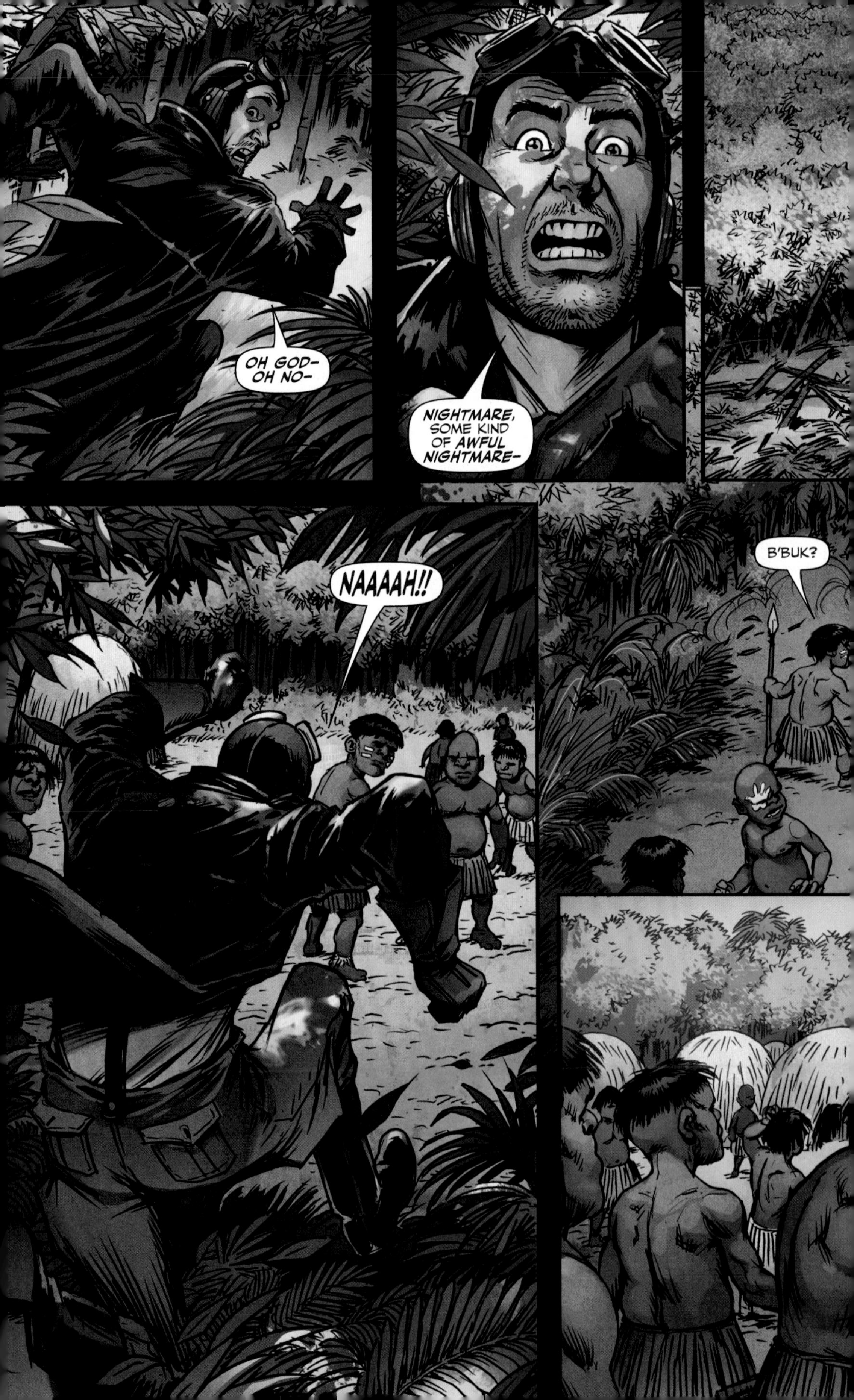
OH GOD-
OH NO-
NIGHTMARE, SOME KIND OF AWFUL NIGHTMARE-
NAAAAH!!
B'BUK?

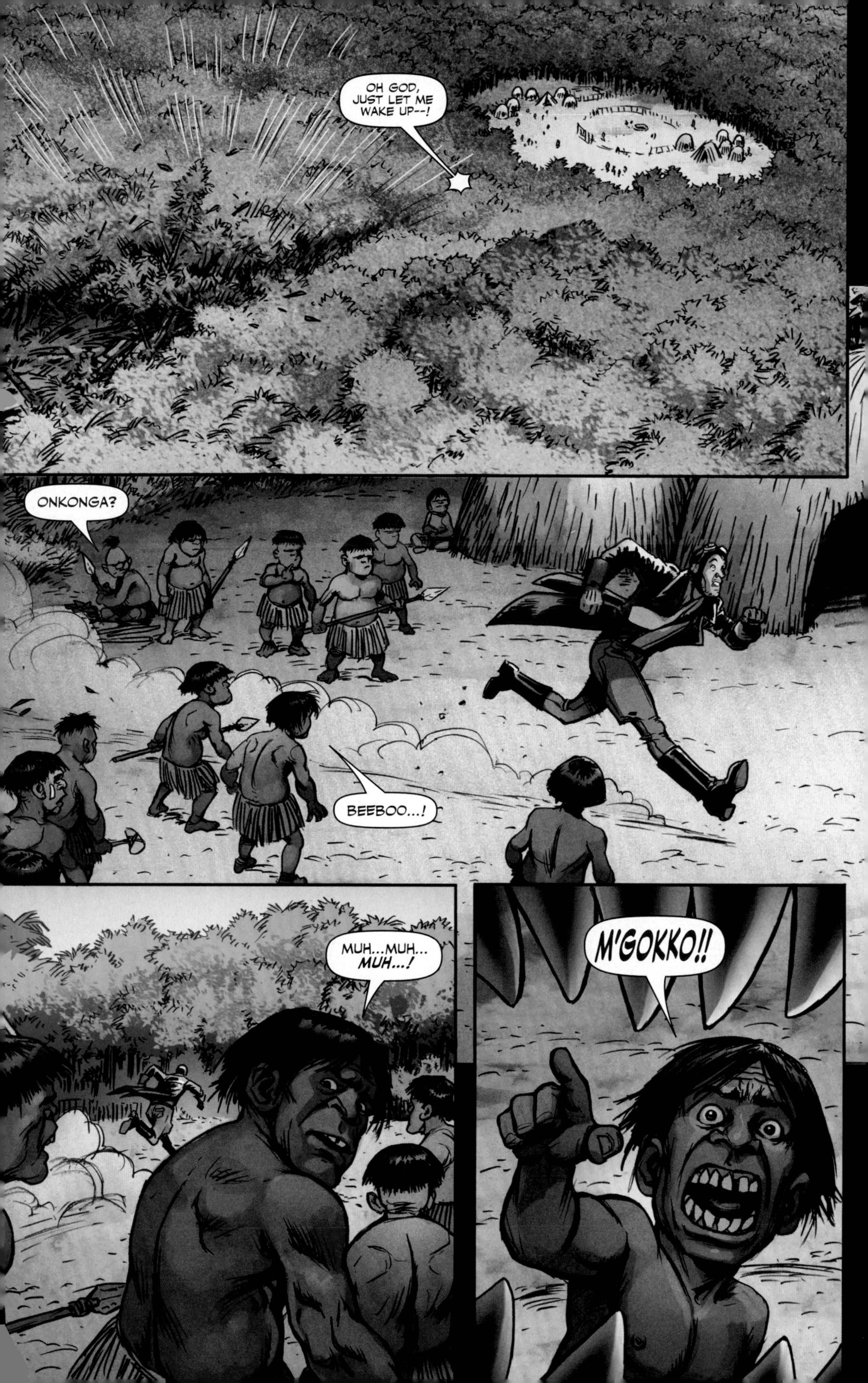
OH GOD, JUST LET ME WAKE UP--!
ONKONGA?
BEEBOO...!
MUH...MUH... *MUH...!*
M'GOKKO!!

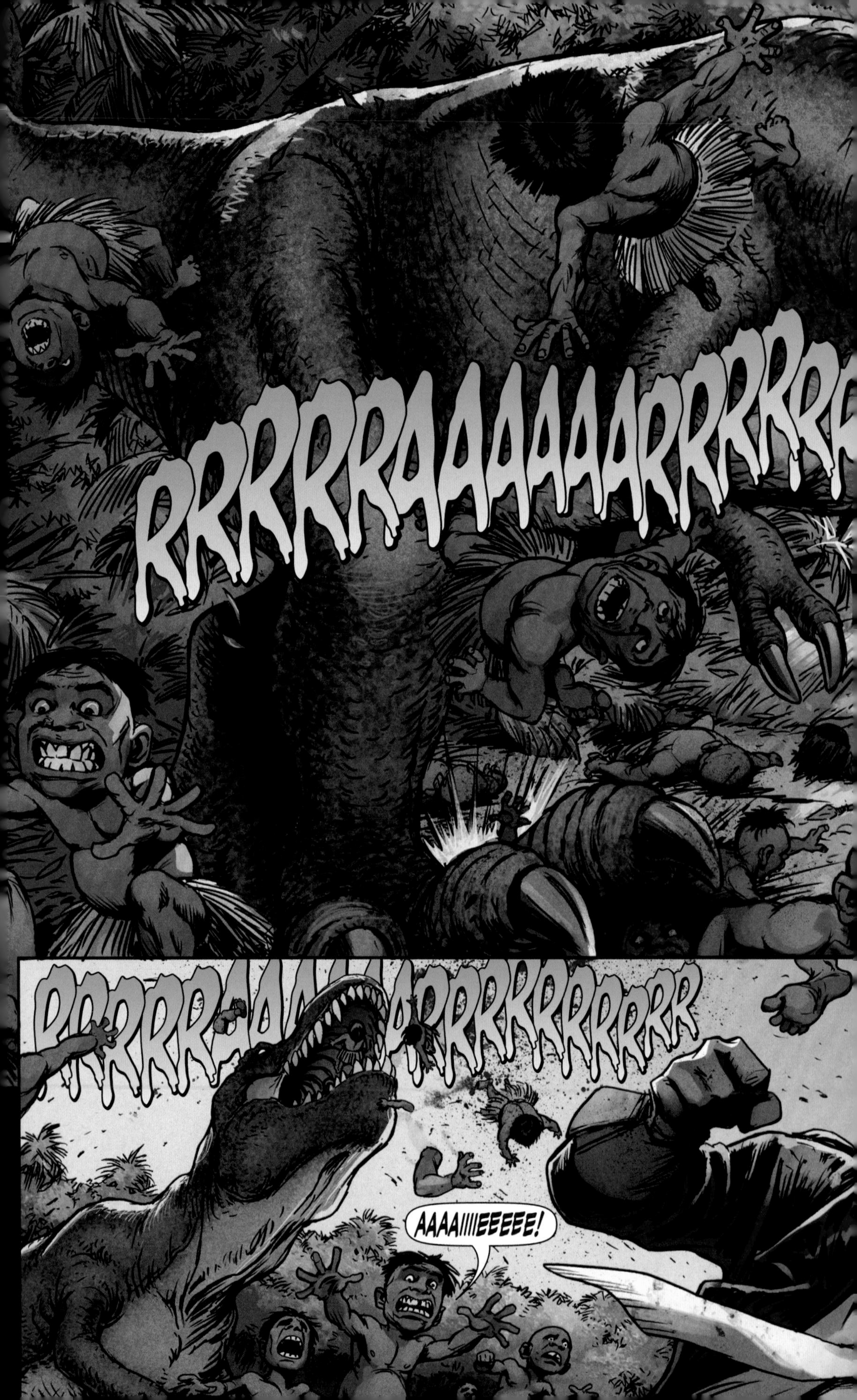
RRRRAAAAAAARRRRR
AAAAIIIIEEEEE!

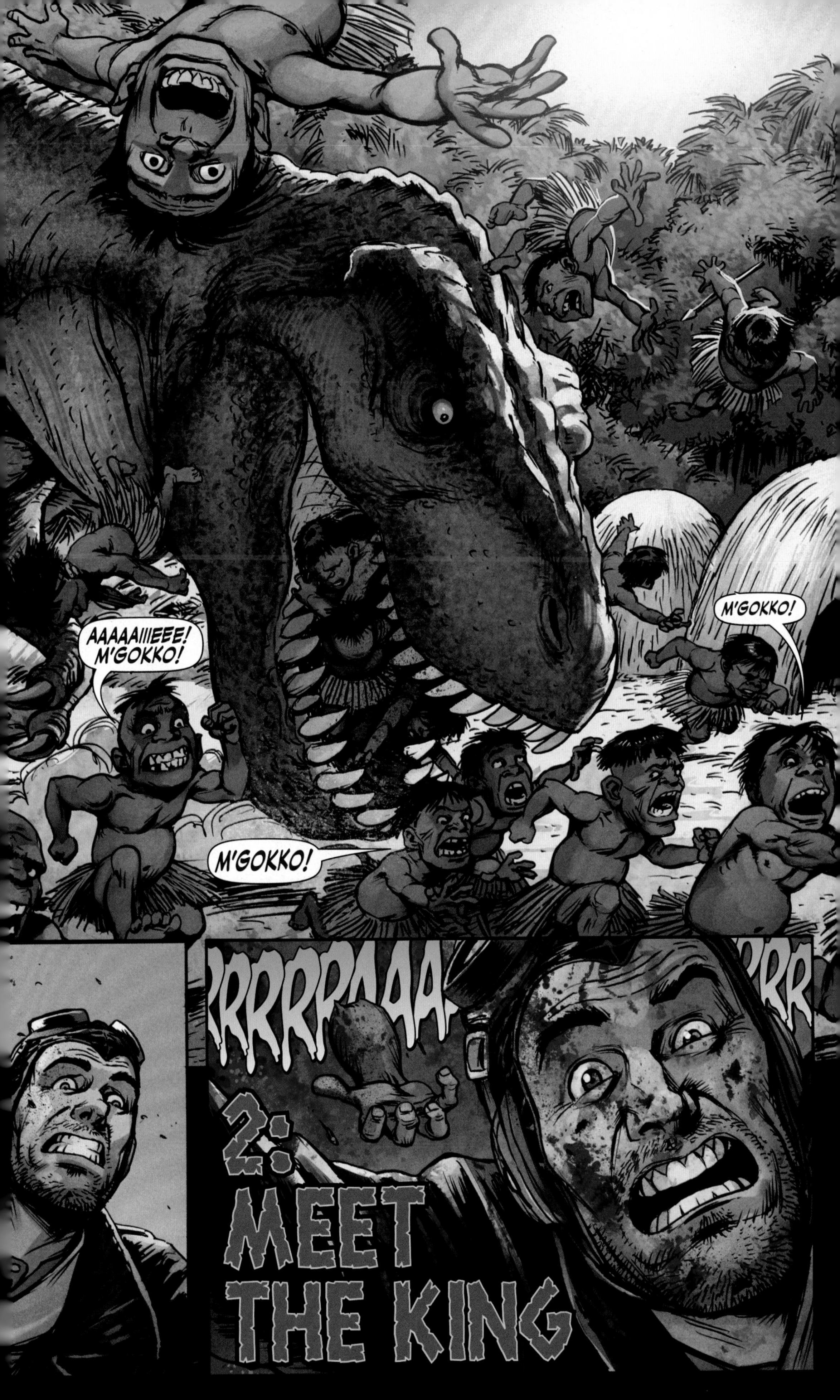

AAAAAIIIEEE! M'GOKKO!
M'GOKKO!
M'GOKKO!
RRRRRAAA
RRR
2: MEET THE KING

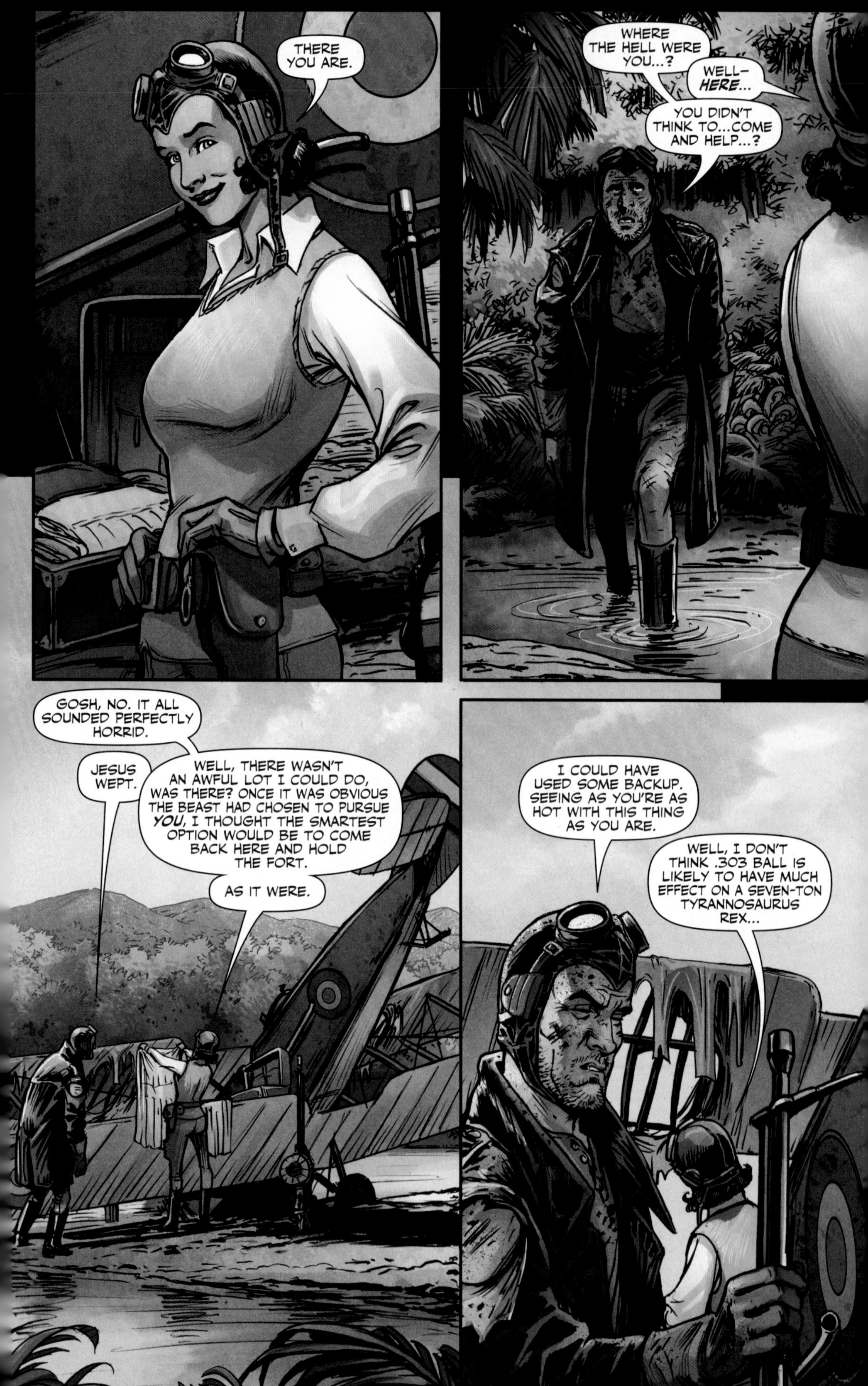
THERE YOU ARE.
WHERE THE HELL WERE YOU...?
WELL– HERE...
YOU DIDN'T THINK TO...COME AND HELP...?
GOSH, NO. IT ALL SOUNDED PERFECTLY HORRID.
JESUS WEPT.
WELL, THERE WASN'T AN AWFUL LOT I COULD DO, WAS THERE? ONCE IT WAS OBVIOUS THE BEAST HAD CHOSEN TO PURSUE YOU, I THOUGHT THE SMARTEST OPTION WOULD BE TO COME BACK HERE AND HOLD THE FORT.
AS IT WERE.
I COULD HAVE USED SOME BACKUP. SEEING AS YOU'RE AS HOT WITH THIS THING AS YOU ARE.
WELL, I DON'T THINK .303 BALL IS LIKELY TO HAVE MUCH EFFECT ON A SEVEN-TON TYRANNOSAURUS REX...

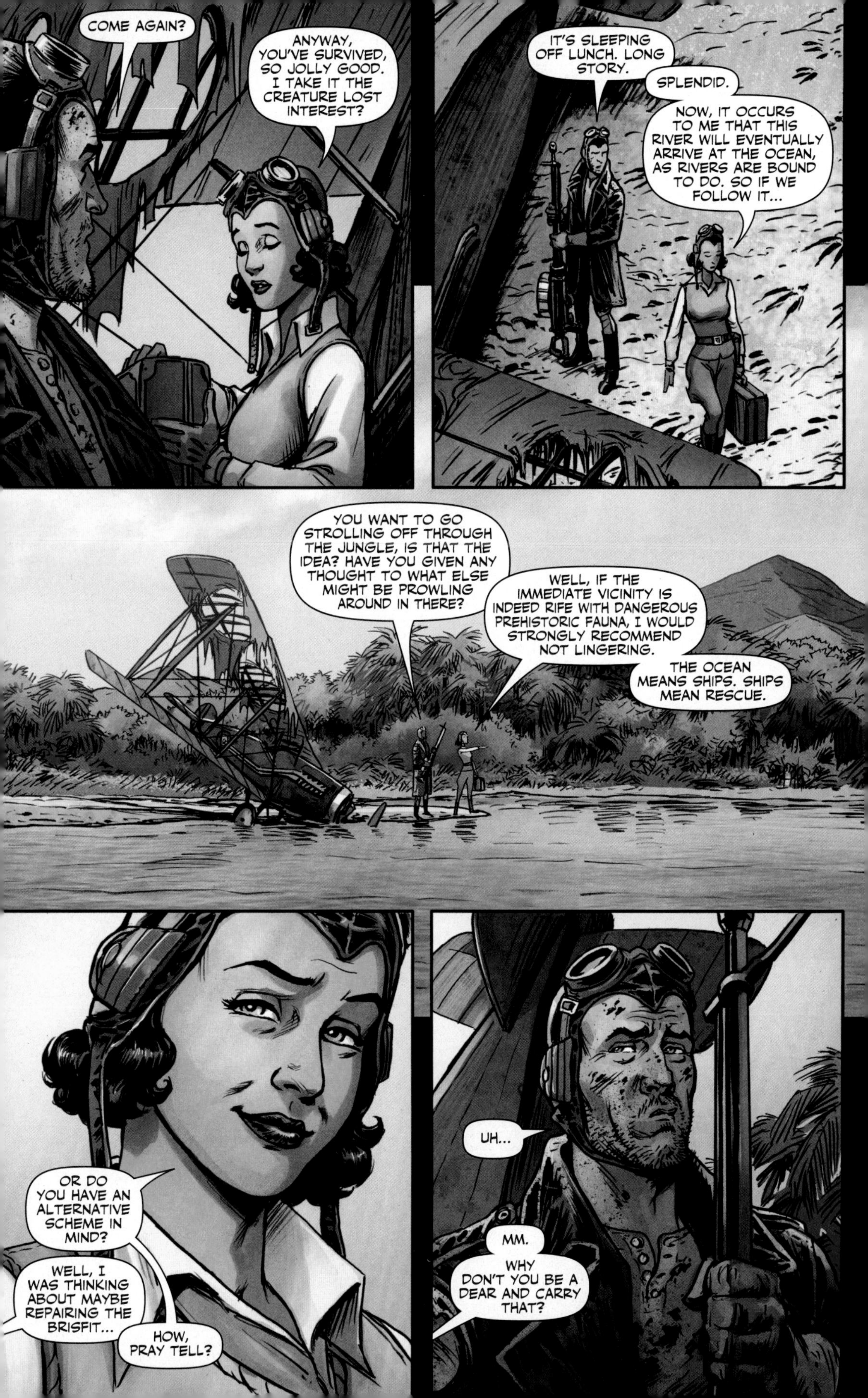
COME AGAIN?
ANYWAY, YOU'VE SURVIVED, SO JOLLY GOOD. I TAKE IT THE CREATURE LOST INTEREST?
IT'S SLEEPING OFF LUNCH. LONG STORY.
SPLENDID.
NOW, IT OCCURS TO ME THAT THIS RIVER WILL EVENTUALLY ARRIVE AT THE OCEAN, AS RIVERS ARE BOUND TO DO. SO IF WE FOLLOW IT...
YOU WANT TO GO STROLLING OFF THROUGH THE JUNGLE, IS THAT THE IDEA? HAVE YOU GIVEN ANY THOUGHT TO WHAT ELSE MIGHT BE PROWLING AROUND IN THERE?
WELL, IF THE IMMEDIATE VICINITY IS INDEED RIFE WITH DANGEROUS PREHISTORIC FAUNA, I WOULD STRONGLY RECOMMEND NOT LINGERING.
THE OCEAN MEANS SHIPS. SHIPS MEAN RESCUE.
OR DO YOU HAVE AN ALTERNATIVE SCHEME IN MIND?
WELL, I WAS THINKING ABOUT MAYBE REPAIRING THE BRISFIT...
HOW, PRAY TELL?
UH...
MM.
WHY DON'T YOU BE A DEAR AND CARRY THAT?

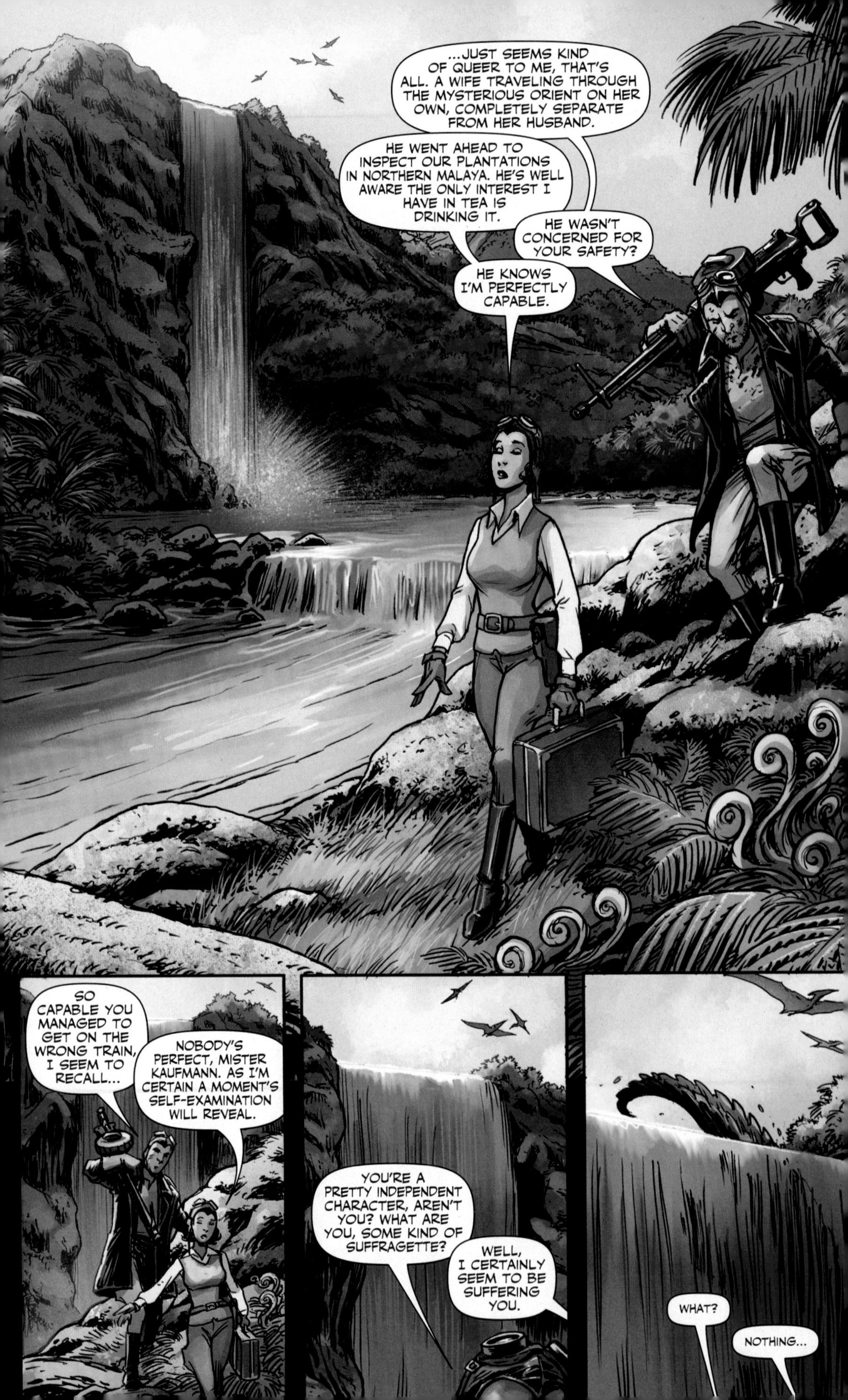
...JUST SEEMS KIND OF QUEER TO ME, THAT'S ALL. A WIFE TRAVELING THROUGH THE MYSTERIOUS ORIENT ON HER OWN, COMPLETELY SEPARATE FROM HER HUSBAND.
HE WENT AHEAD TO INSPECT OUR PLANTATIONS IN NORTHERN MALAYA. HE'S WELL AWARE THE ONLY INTEREST I HAVE IN TEA IS DRINKING IT.
HE WASN'T CONCERNED FOR YOUR SAFETY?
HE KNOWS I'M PERFECTLY CAPABLE.
SO CAPABLE YOU MANAGED TO GET ON THE WRONG TRAIN, I SEEM TO RECALL...
NOBODY'S PERFECT, MISTER KAUFMANN. AS I'M CERTAIN A MOMENT'S SELF-EXAMINATION WILL REVEAL.
YOU'RE A PRETTY INDEPENDENT CHARACTER, AREN'T YOU? WHAT ARE YOU, SOME KIND OF SUFFRAGETTE?
WELL, I CERTAINLY SEEM TO BE SUFFERING YOU.
WHAT?
NOTHING...

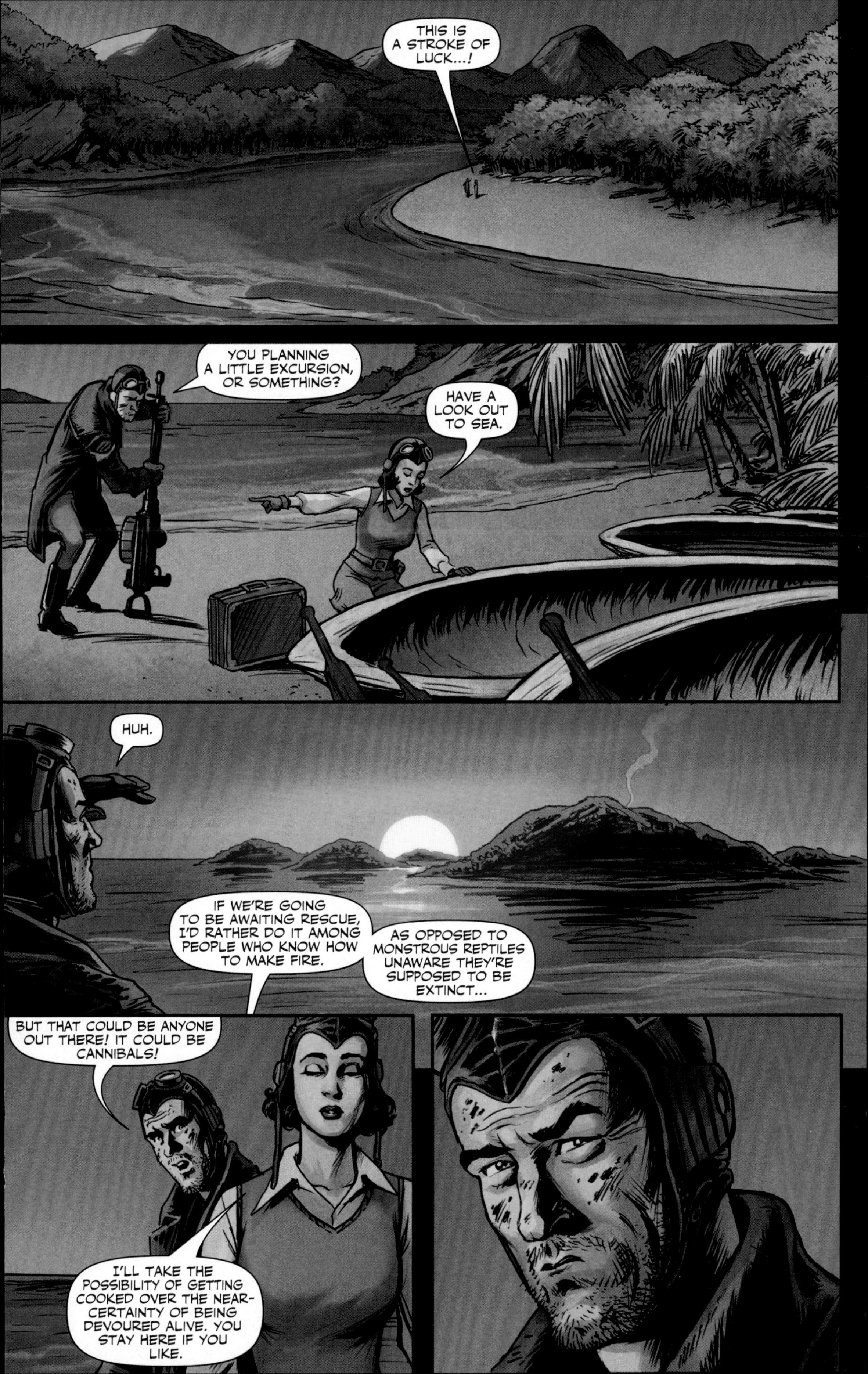
THIS IS A STROKE OF LUCK...!
YOU PLANNING A LITTLE EXCURSION, OR SOMETHING?
HAVE A LOOK OUT TO SEA.
HUH.
IF WE'RE GOING TO BE AWAITING RESCUE, I'D RATHER DO IT AMONG PEOPLE WHO KNOW HOW TO MAKE FIRE.
AS OPPOSED TO MONSTROUS REPTILES UNAWARE THEY'RE SUPPOSED TO BE EXTINCT...
BUT THAT COULD BE ANYONE OUT THERE! IT COULD BE CANNIBALS!
I'LL TAKE THE POSSIBILITY OF GETTING COOKED OVER THE NEAR-CERTAINTY OF BEING DEVOURED ALIVE. YOU STAY HERE IF YOU LIKE.

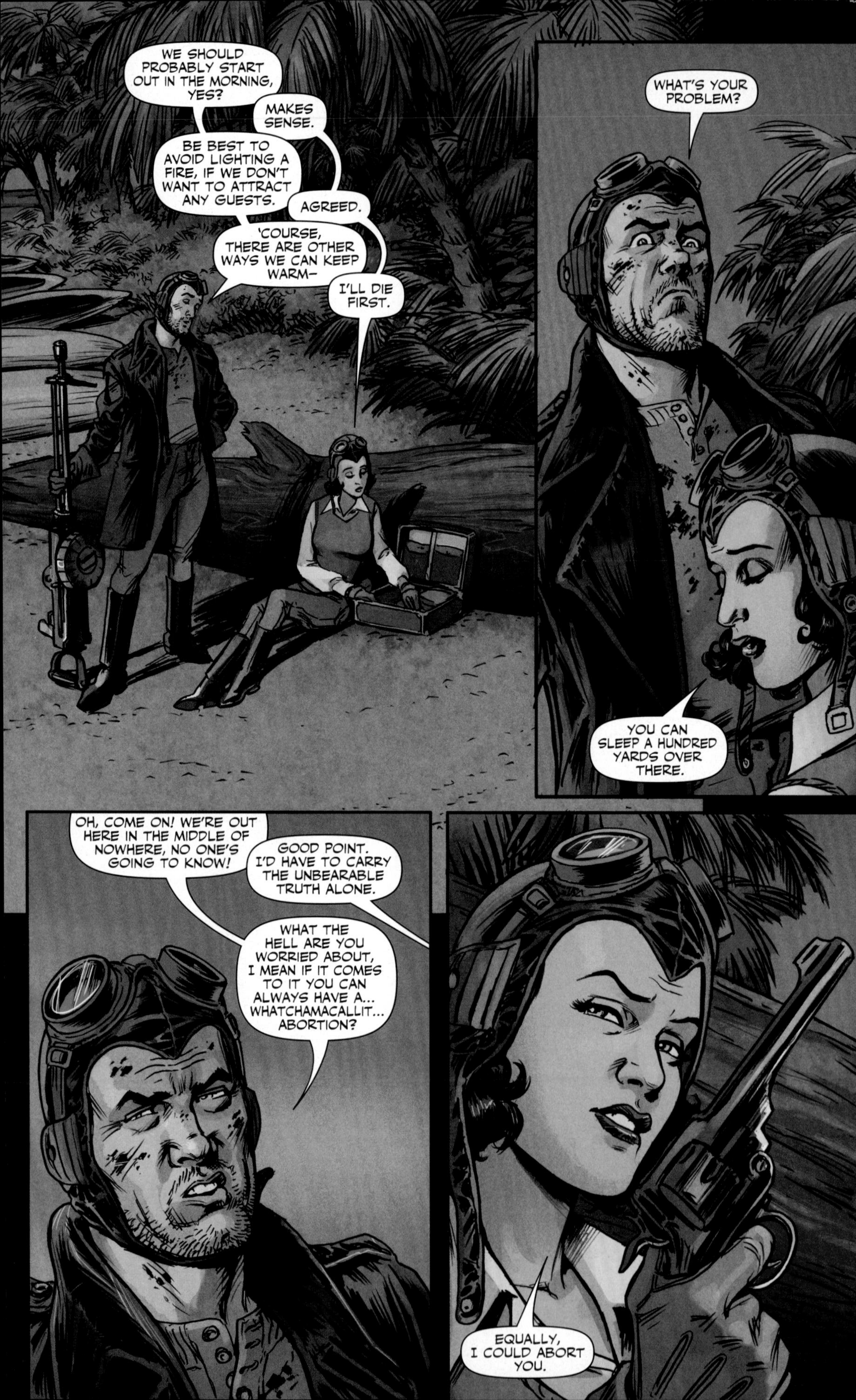
WE SHOULD PROBABLY START OUT IN THE MORNING, YES?
MAKES SENSE.
BE BEST TO AVOID LIGHTING A FIRE, IF WE DON'T WANT TO ATTRACT ANY GUESTS.
AGREED.
'COURSE, THERE ARE OTHER WAYS WE CAN KEEP WARM–
I'LL DIE FIRST.
WHAT'S YOUR PROBLEM?
YOU CAN SLEEP A HUNDRED YARDS OVER THERE.
OH, COME ON! WE'RE OUT HERE IN THE MIDDLE OF NOWHERE, NO ONE'S GOING TO KNOW!
GOOD POINT. I'D HAVE TO CARRY THE UNBEARABLE TRUTH ALONE.
WHAT THE HELL ARE YOU WORRIED ABOUT, I MEAN IF IT COMES TO IT YOU CAN ALWAYS HAVE A... WHATCHAMACALLIT... ABORTION?
EQUALLY, I COULD ABORT YOU.

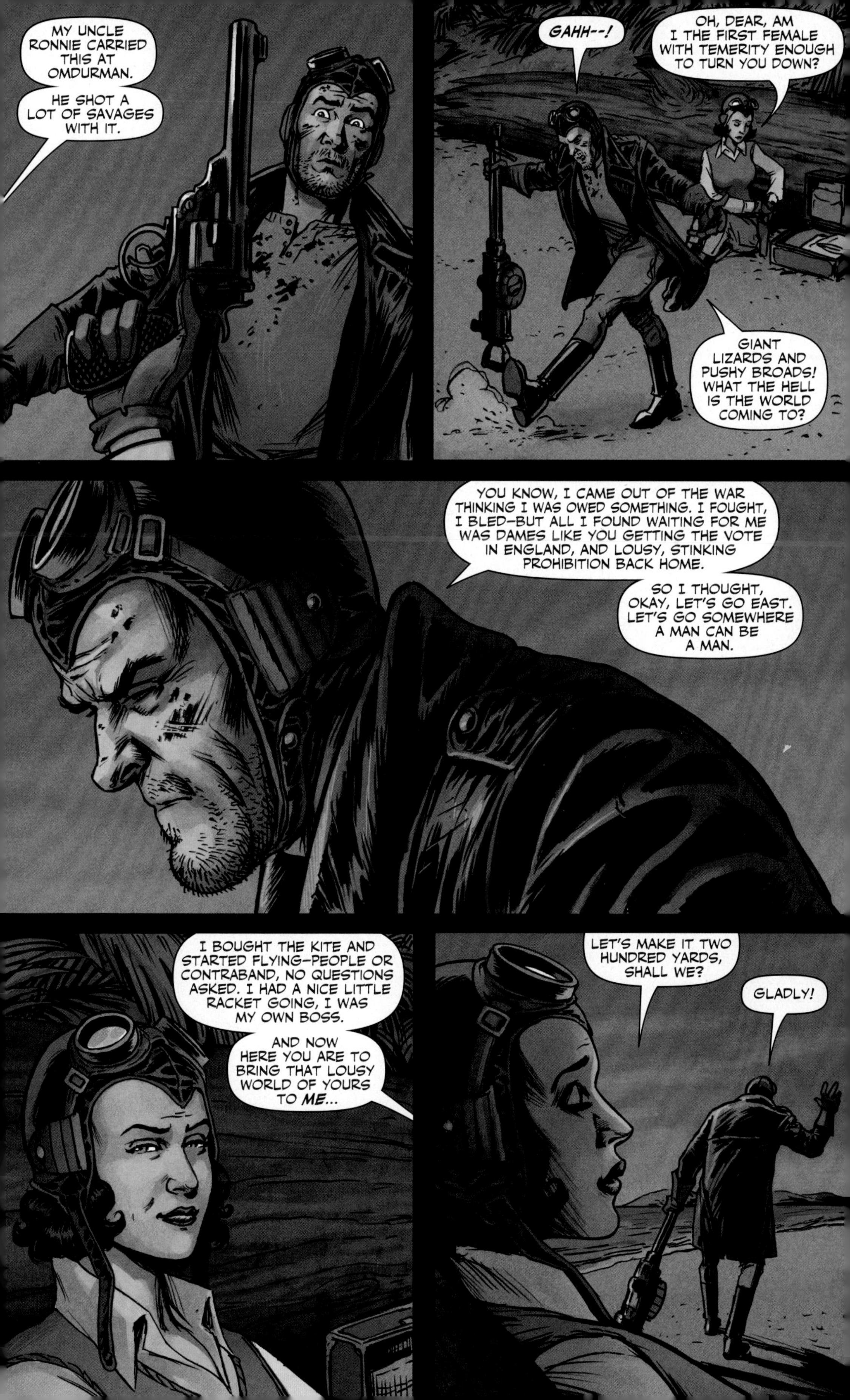
MY UNCLE RONNIE CARRIED THIS AT OMDURMAN.
HE SHOT A LOT OF SAVAGES WITH IT.
GAHH--!
OH, DEAR, AM I THE FIRST FEMALE WITH TEMERITY ENOUGH TO TURN YOU DOWN?
GIANT LIZARDS AND PUSHY BROADS! WHAT THE HELL IS THE WORLD COMING TO?
YOU KNOW, I CAME OUT OF THE WAR THINKING I WAS OWED SOMETHING. I FOUGHT, I BLED—BUT ALL I FOUND WAITING FOR ME WAS DAMES LIKE YOU GETTING THE VOTE IN ENGLAND, AND LOUSY, STINKING PROHIBITION BACK HOME.
SO I THOUGHT, OKAY, LET'S GO EAST. LET'S GO SOMEWHERE A MAN CAN BE A MAN.
I BOUGHT THE KITE AND STARTED FLYING—PEOPLE OR CONTRABAND, NO QUESTIONS ASKED. I HAD A NICE LITTLE RACKET GOING, I WAS MY OWN BOSS.
AND NOW HERE YOU ARE TO BRING THAT LOUSY WORLD OF YOURS TO ***ME***...
LET'S MAKE IT TWO HUNDRED YARDS, SHALL WE?
GLADLY!

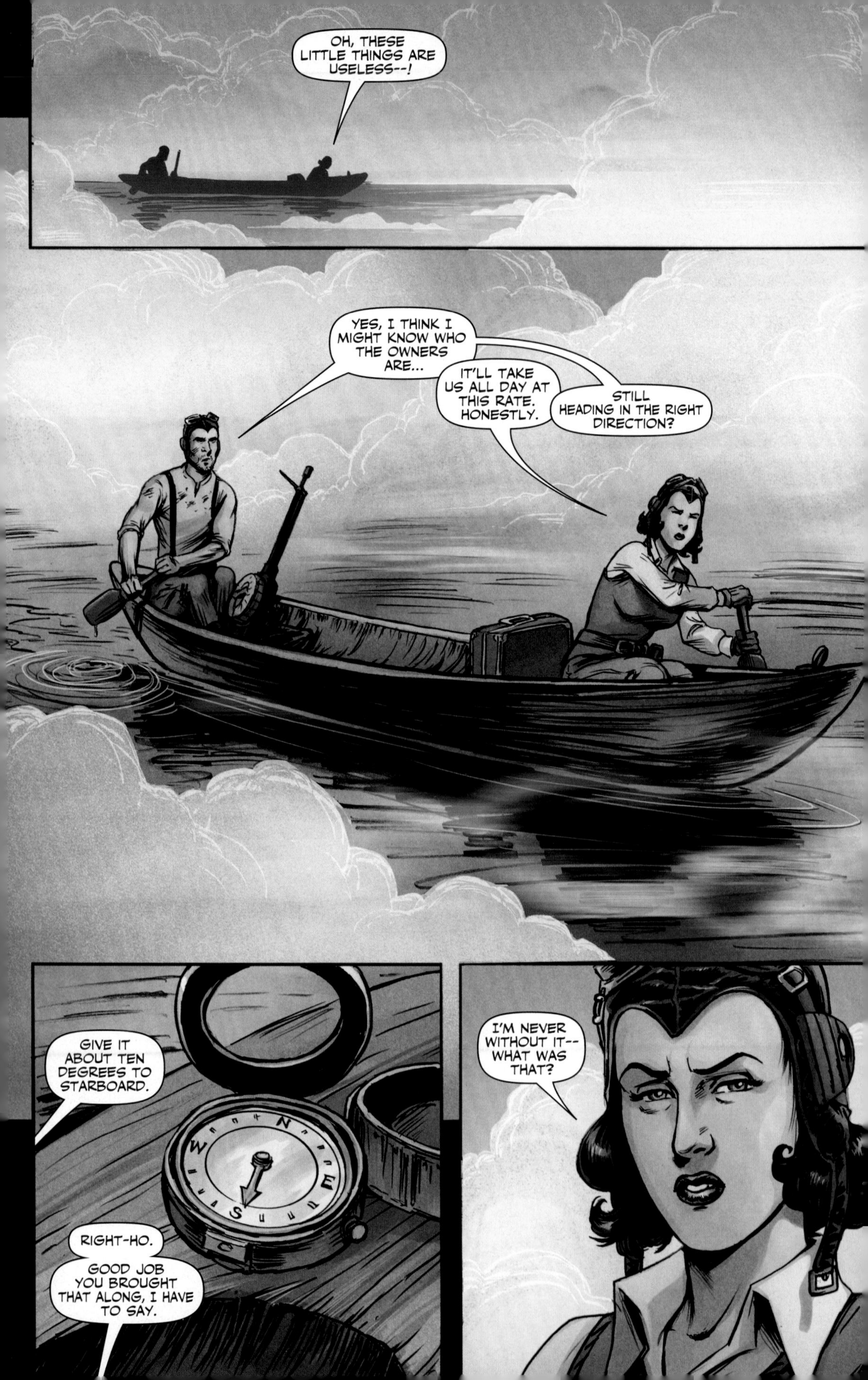
OH, THESE LITTLE THINGS ARE USELESS--!
YES, I THINK I MIGHT KNOW WHO THE OWNERS ARE...
STILL HEADING IN THE RIGHT DIRECTION?
IT'LL TAKE US ALL DAY AT THIS RATE. HONESTLY.
GIVE IT ABOUT TEN DEGREES TO STARBOARD.
RIGHT-HO.
GOOD JOB YOU BROUGHT THAT ALONG, I HAVE TO SAY.
N
W
E
S
I'M NEVER WITHOUT IT-- WHAT WAS THAT?

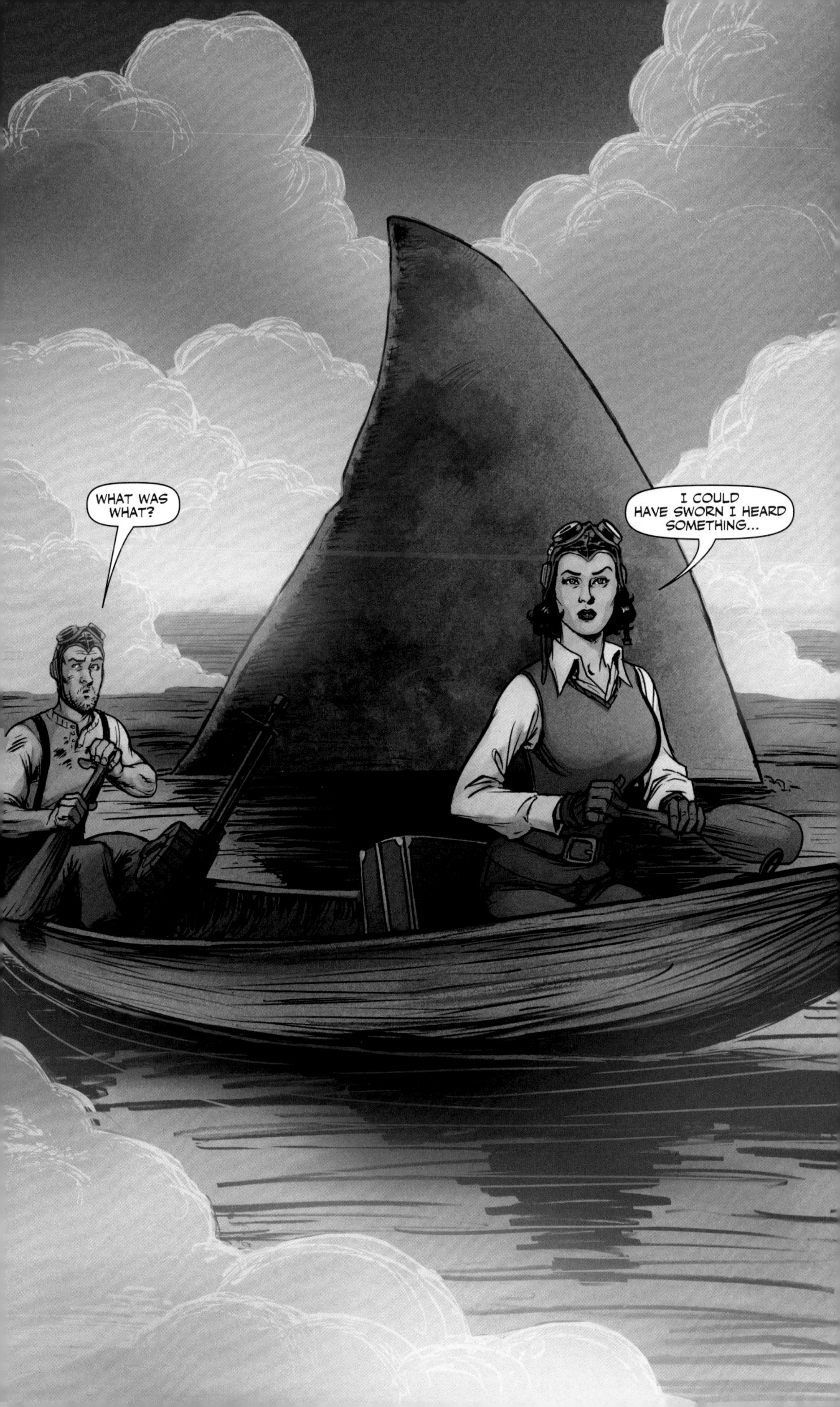
I COULD HAVE SWORN I HEARD SOMETHING...
WHAT WAS WHAT?

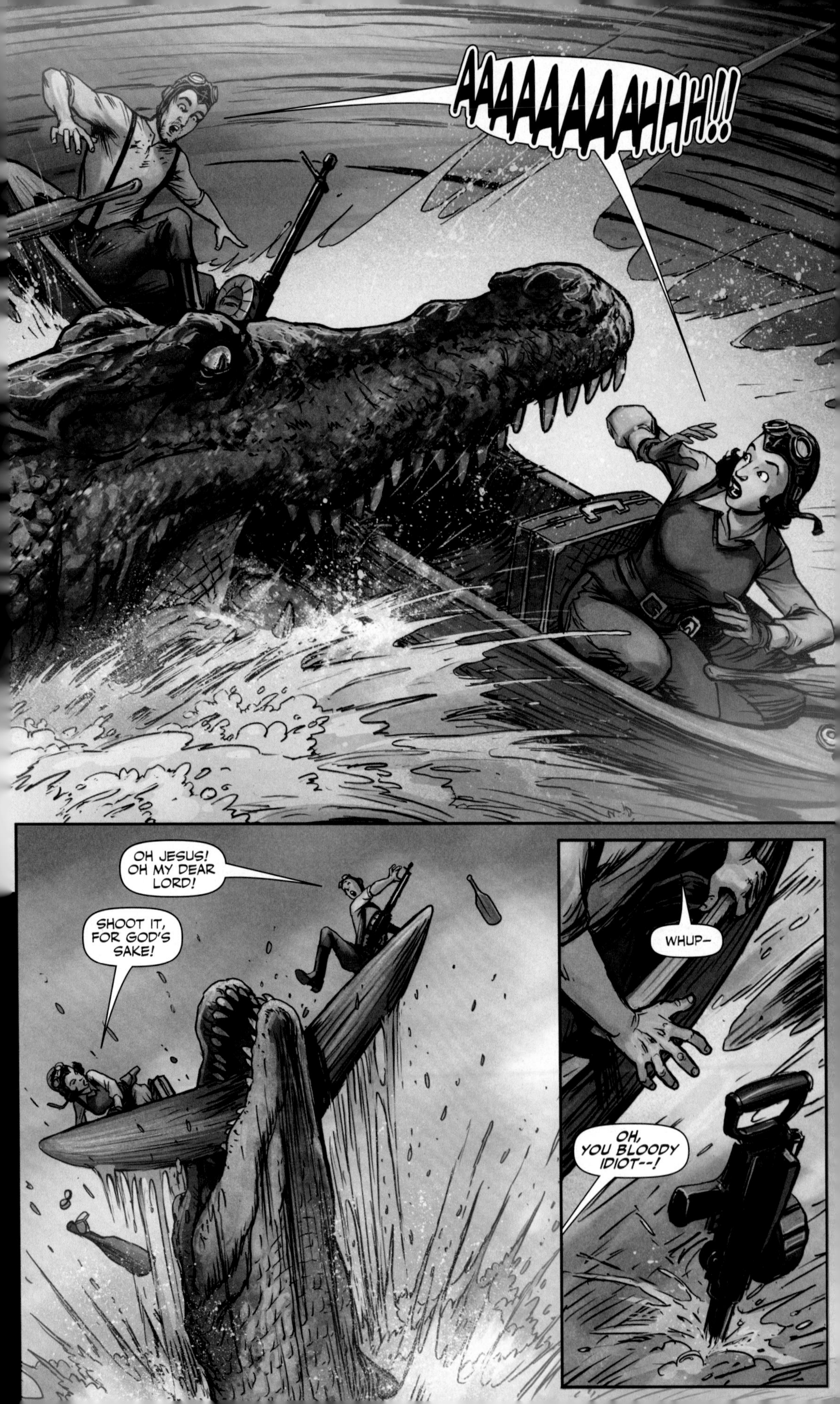
AAAAAAAAAHHH!!
OH JESUS! OH MY DEAR LORD!
SHOOT IT, FOR GOD'S SAKE!
WHUP–
OH, YOU BLOODY IDIOT--!

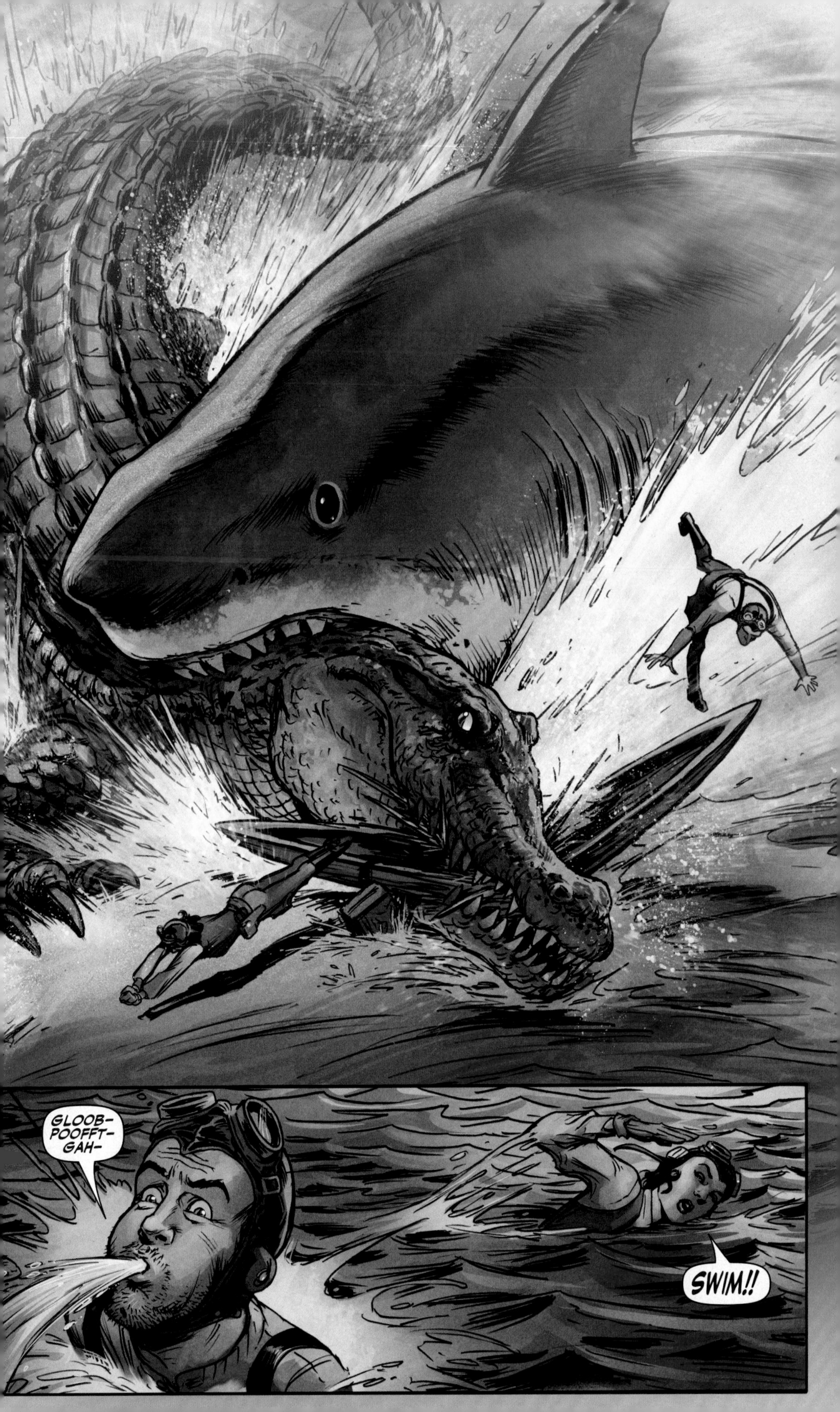
GLOOB-POOFFT-GAH-
SWIM!!

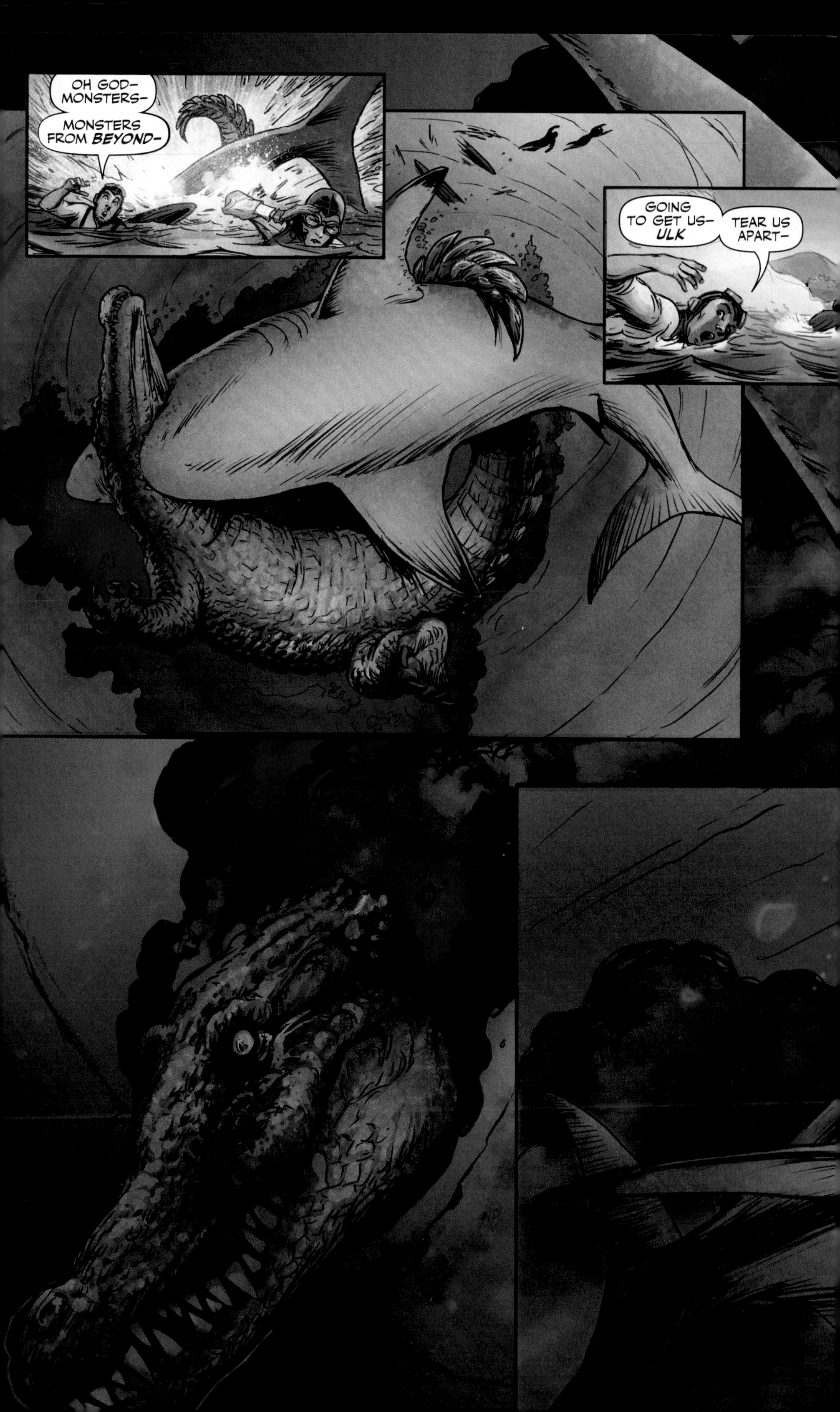
OH GOD-
MONSTERS-
MONSTERS FROM BEYOND-
GOING TO GET US-
ULK
TEAR US APART-

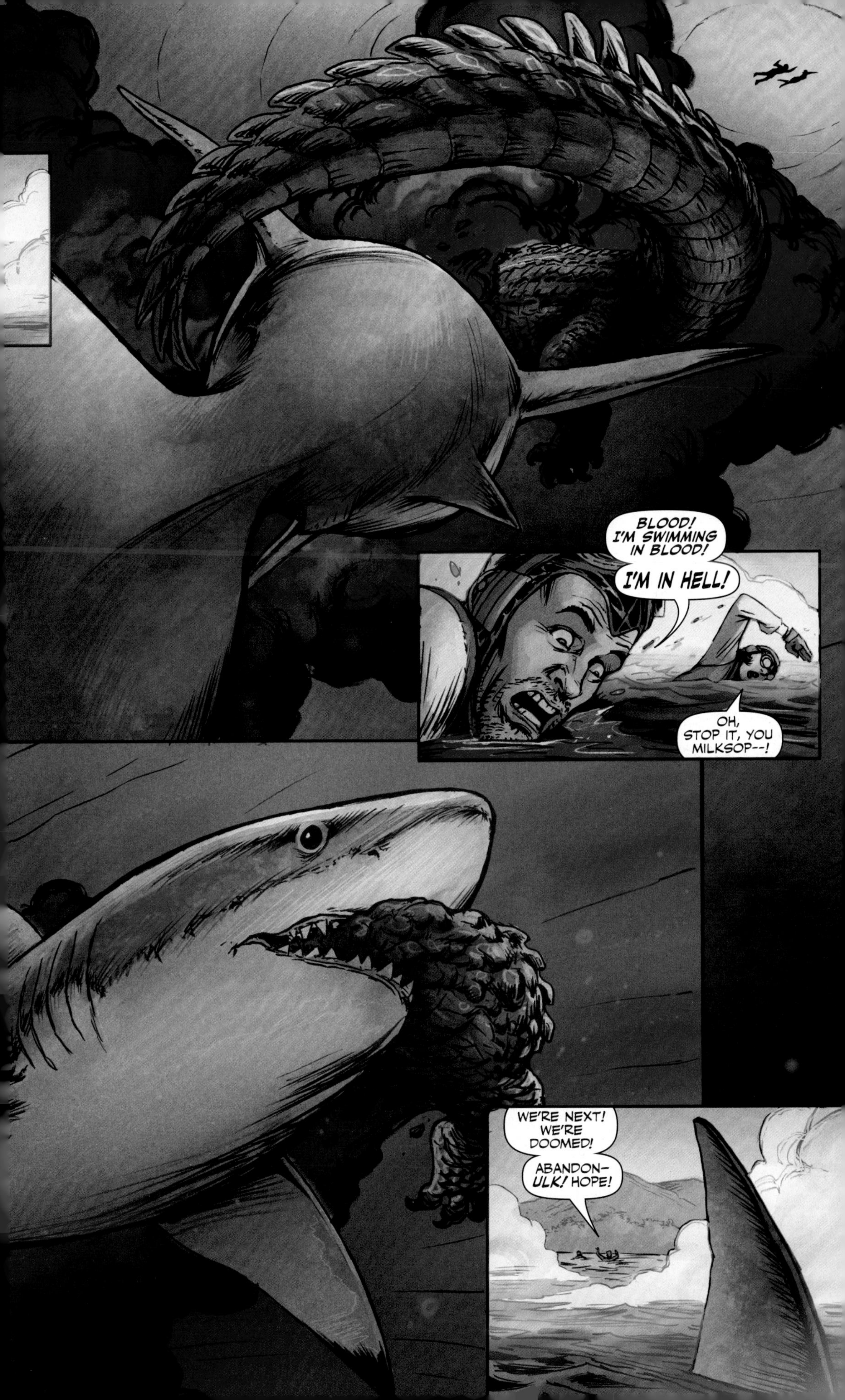
BLOOD! I'M SWIMMING IN BLOOD!
I'M IN HELL!
OH, STOP IT, YOU MILKSOP--!
WE'RE NEXT! WE'RE DOOMED!
ABANDON--ULK! HOPE!

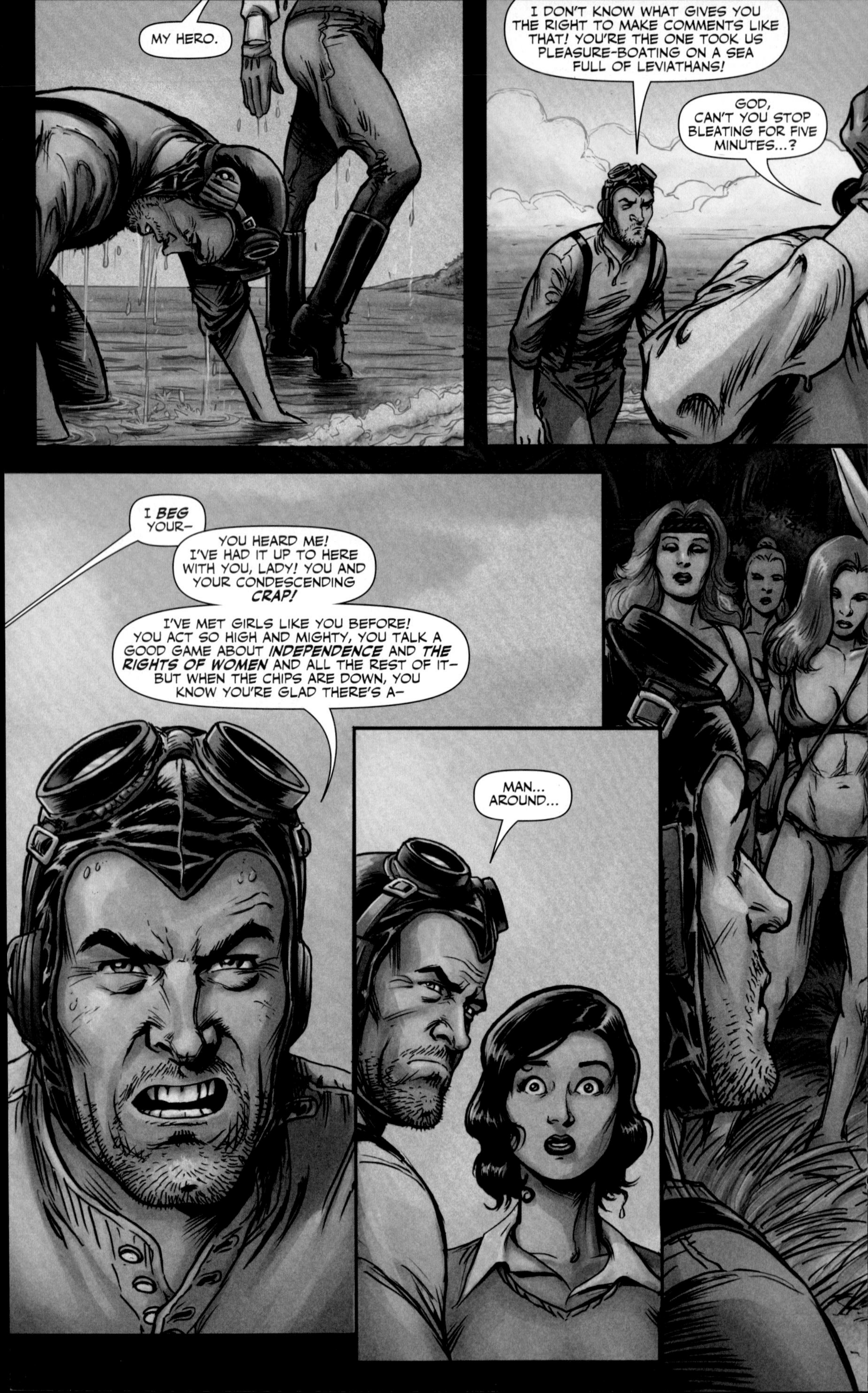
MY HERO.
I DON'T KNOW WHAT GIVES YOU THE RIGHT TO MAKE COMMENTS LIKE THAT! YOU'RE THE ONE TOOK US PLEASURE-BOATING ON A SEA FULL OF LEVIATHANS!
GOD, CAN'T YOU STOP BLEATING FOR FIVE MINUTES...?
I BEG YOUR-
YOU HEARD ME! I'VE HAD IT UP TO HERE WITH YOU, LADY! YOU AND YOUR CONDESCENDING CRAP!
I'VE MET GIRLS LIKE YOU BEFORE! YOU ACT SO HIGH AND MIGHTY, YOU TALK A GOOD GAME ABOUT INDEPENDENCE AND THE RIGHTS OF WOMEN AND ALL THE REST OF IT- BUT WHEN THE CHIPS ARE DOWN, YOU KNOW YOU'RE GLAD THERE'S A-
MAN... AROUND...

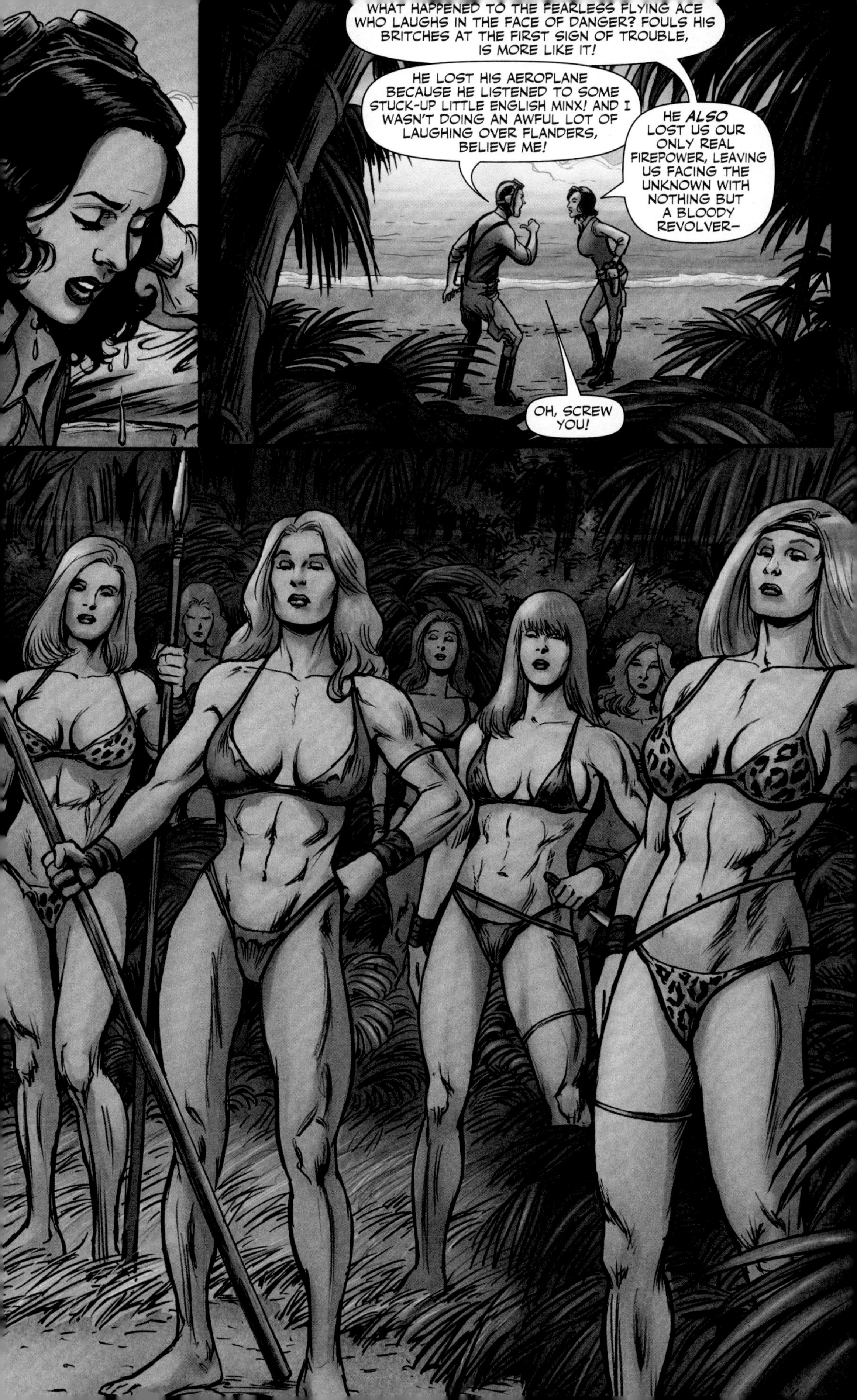
WHAT HAPPENED TO THE FEARLESS FLYING ACE WHO LAUGHS IN THE FACE OF DANGER? FOULS HIS BRITCHES AT THE FIRST SIGN OF TROUBLE, IS MORE LIKE IT!
HE LOST HIS AEROPLANE BECAUSE HE LISTENED TO SOME STUCK-UP LITTLE ENGLISH MINX! AND I WASN'T DOING AN AWFUL LOT OF LAUGHING OVER FLANDERS, BELIEVE ME!
HE ALSO LOST US OUR ONLY REAL FIREPOWER, LEAVING US FACING THE UNKNOWN WITH NOTHING BUT A BLOODY REVOLVER–
OH, SCREW YOU!

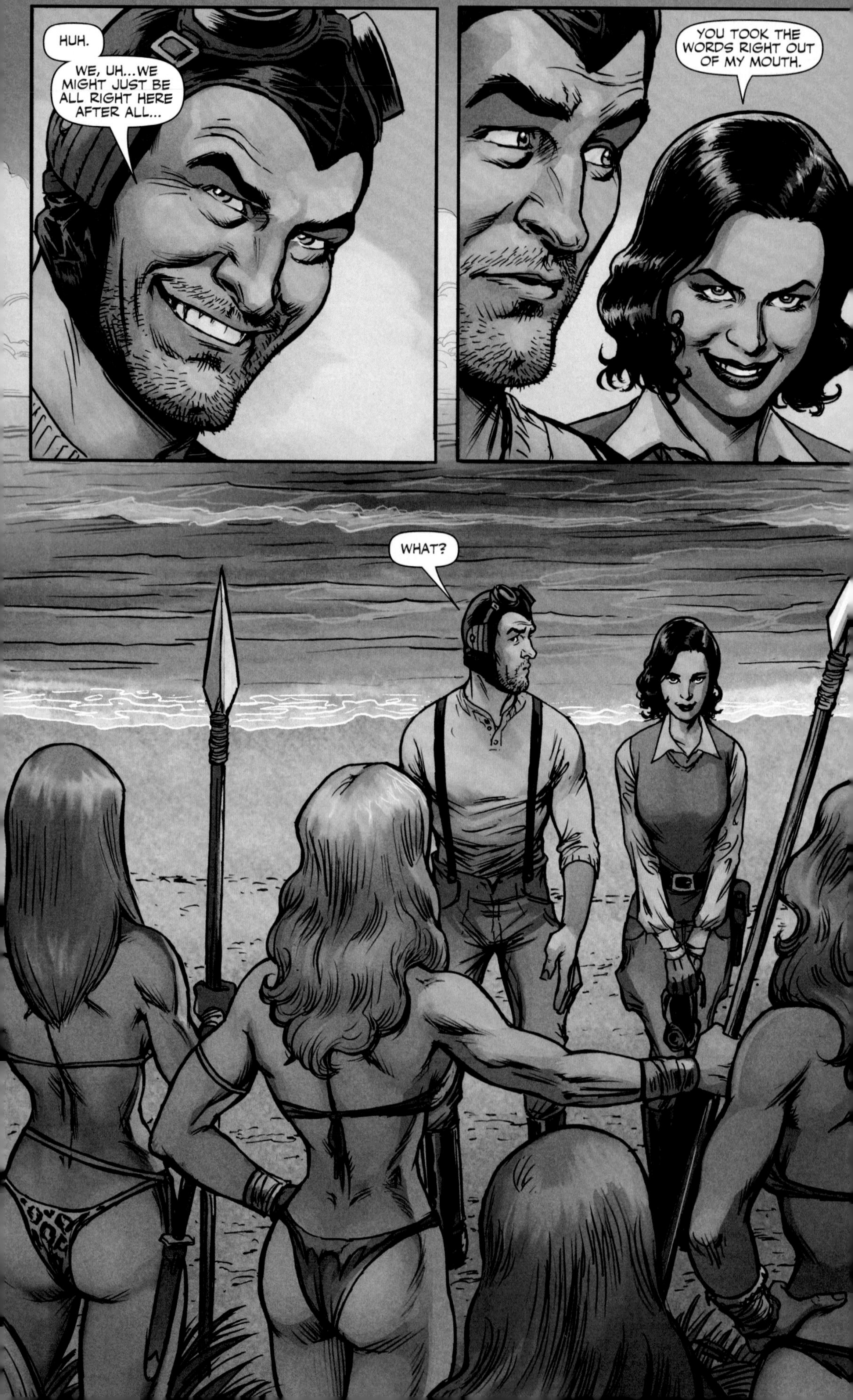
HUH.
WE, UH...WE MIGHT JUST BE ALL RIGHT HERE AFTER ALL...
YOU TOOK THE WORDS RIGHT OUT OF MY MOUTH.
WHAT?

KARL KAUFMANN BY RUSS BRAUN

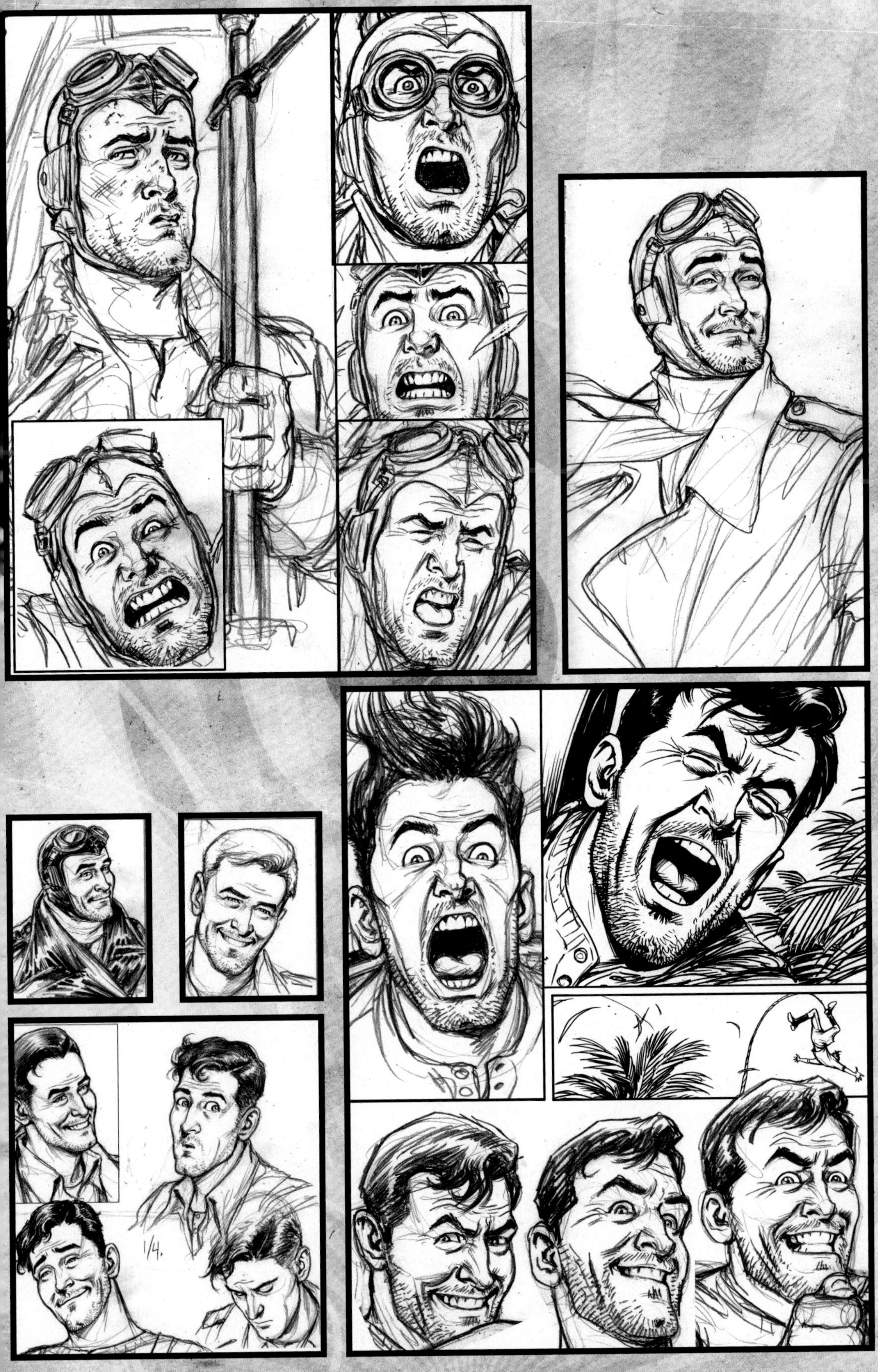
1/4.

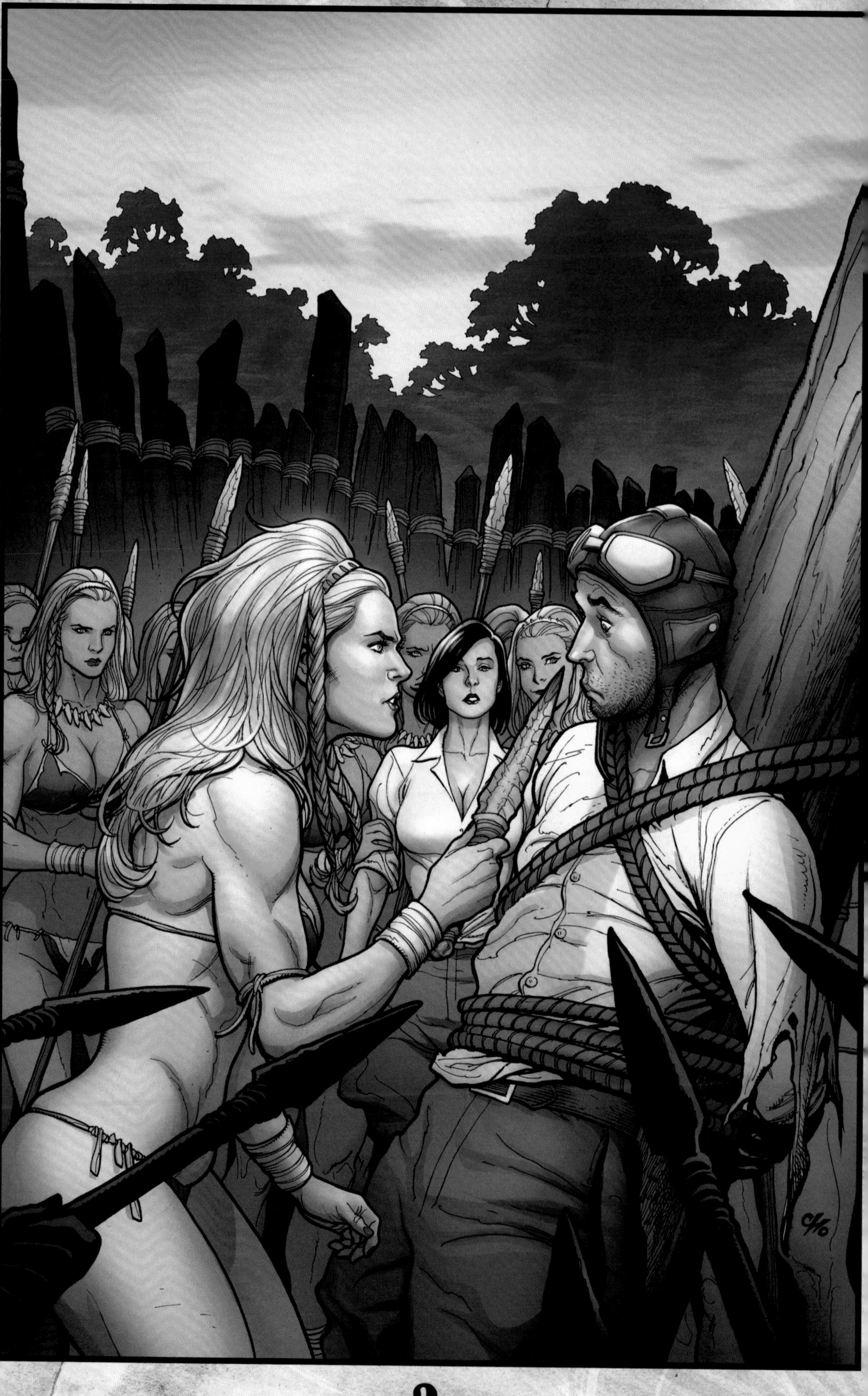

★ 3 ★

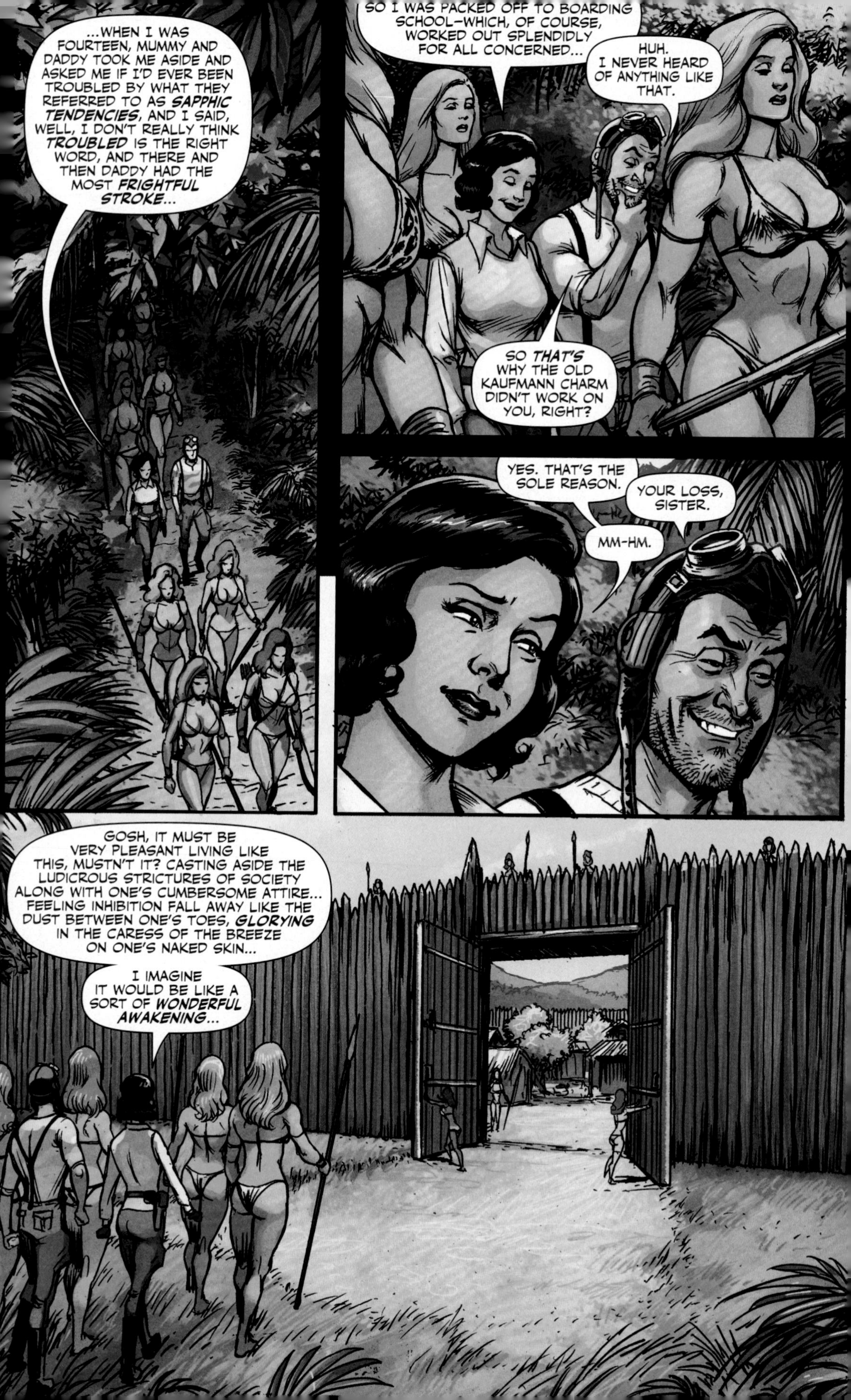
...WHEN I WAS FOURTEEN, MUMMY AND DADDY TOOK ME ASIDE AND ASKED ME IF I'D EVER BEEN TROUBLED BY WHAT THEY REFERRED TO AS *SAPPHIC TENDENCIES*, AND I SAID, WELL, I DON'T REALLY THINK *TROUBLED* IS THE RIGHT WORD, AND THERE AND THEN DADDY HAD THE MOST *FRIGHTFUL STROKE*...
SO I WAS PACKED OFF TO BOARDING SCHOOL—WHICH, OF COURSE, WORKED OUT SPLENDIDLY FOR ALL CONCERNED...
HUH. I NEVER HEARD OF ANYTHING LIKE THAT.
SO *THAT'S* WHY THE OLD KAUFMANN CHARM DIDN'T WORK ON YOU, RIGHT?
YES. THAT'S THE SOLE REASON.
YOUR LOSS, SISTER.
MM-HM.
GOSH, IT MUST BE VERY PLEASANT LIVING LIKE THIS, MUSTN'T IT? CASTING ASIDE THE LUDICROUS STRICTURES OF SOCIETY ALONG WITH ONE'S CUMBERSOME ATTIRE... FEELING INHIBITION FALL AWAY LIKE THE DUST BETWEEN ONE'S TOES, *GLORYING* IN THE CARESS OF THE BREEZE ON ONE'S NAKED SKIN...
I IMAGINE IT WOULD BE LIKE A SORT OF *WONDERFUL AWAKENING*...

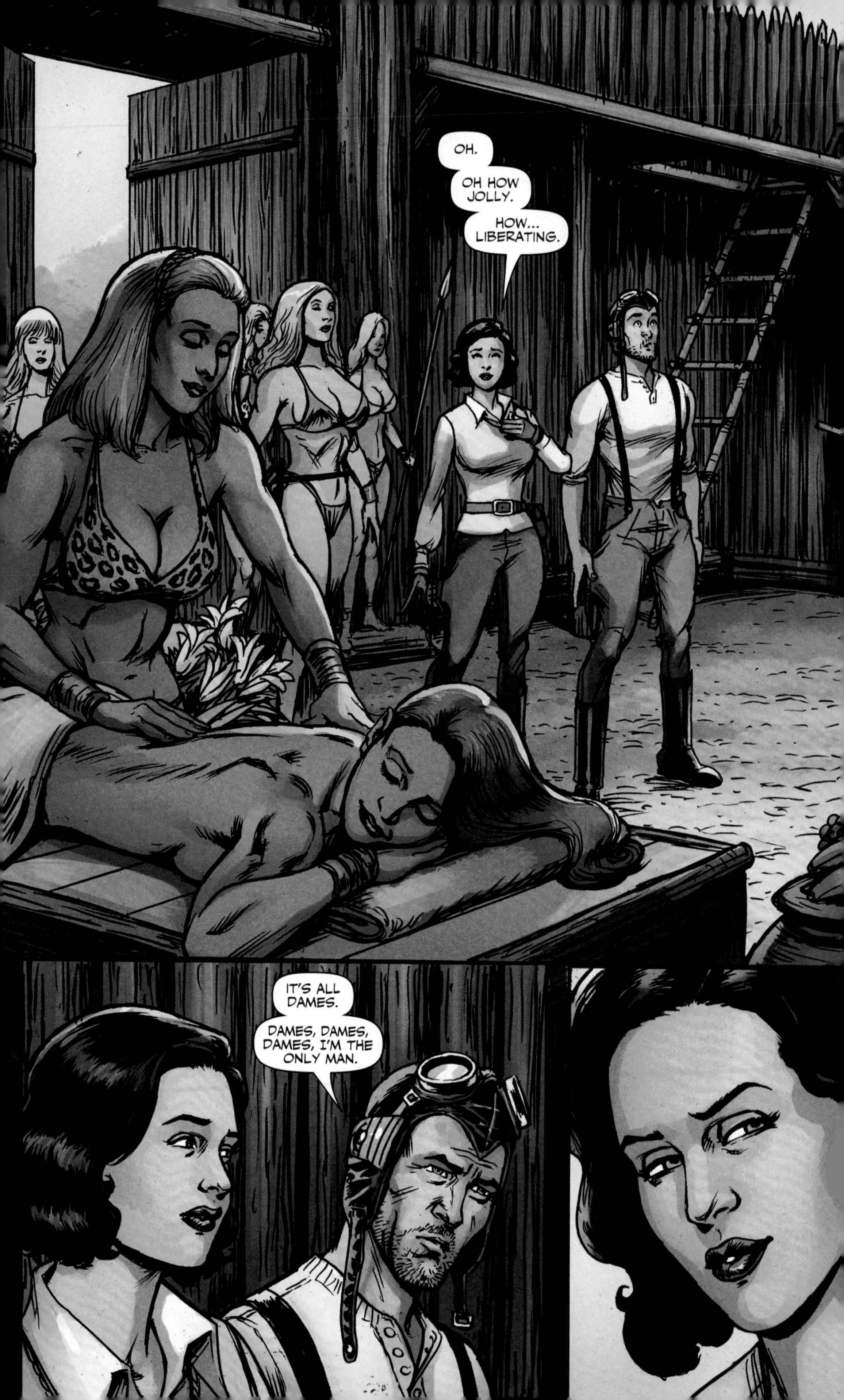
OH.
OH HOW JOLLY.
HOW... LIBERATING.
IT'S ALL DAMES.
DAMES, DAMES, DAMES, I'M THE ONLY MAN.

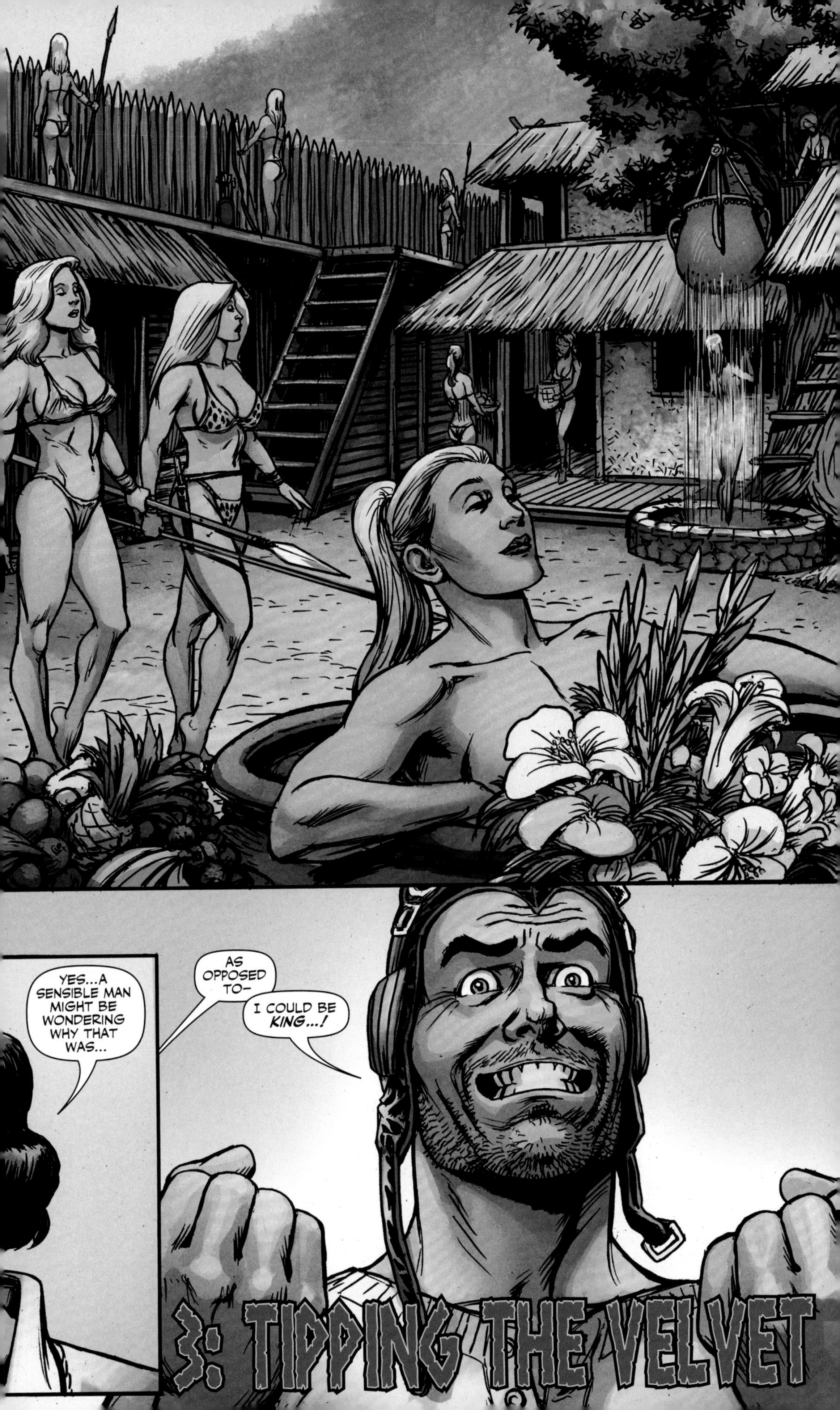
YES...A SENSIBLE MAN MIGHT BE WONDERING WHY THAT WAS...
AS OPPOSED TO–
I COULD BE *KING*...!
3: TIPPING THE VELVET

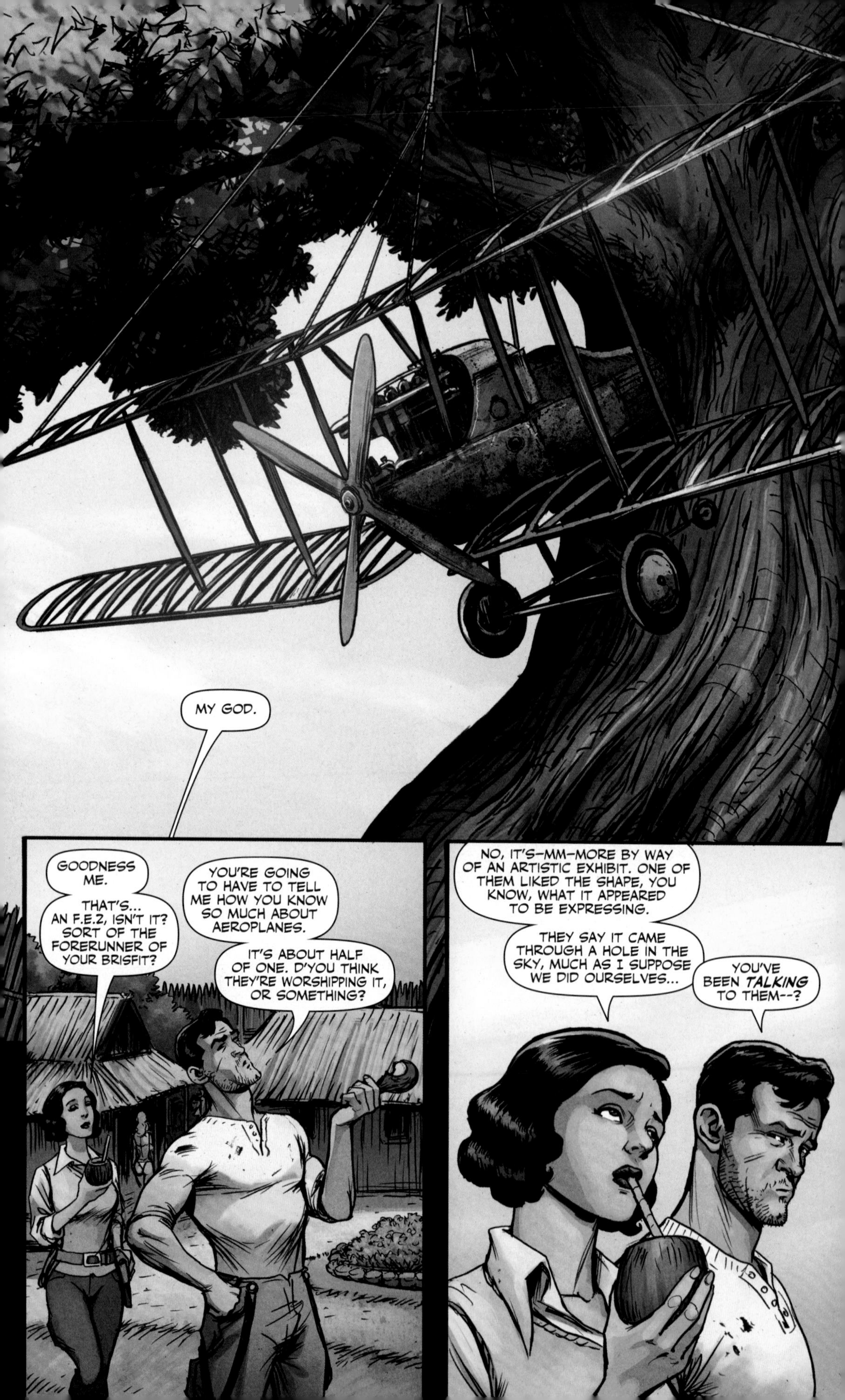
MY GOD.
GOODNESS ME.
THAT'S... AN F.E.2, ISN'T IT? SORT OF THE FORERUNNER OF YOUR BRISFIT?
YOU'RE GOING TO HAVE TO TELL ME HOW YOU KNOW SO MUCH ABOUT AEROPLANES.
IT'S ABOUT HALF OF ONE. D'YOU THINK THEY'RE WORSHIPPING IT, OR SOMETHING?
NO, IT'S--MM--MORE BY WAY OF AN ARTISTIC EXHIBIT. ONE OF THEM LIKED THE SHAPE, YOU KNOW, WHAT IT APPEARED TO BE EXPRESSING.
THEY SAY IT CAME THROUGH A HOLE IN THE SKY, MUCH AS I SUPPOSE WE DID OURSELVES...
YOU'VE BEEN *TALKING* TO THEM--?

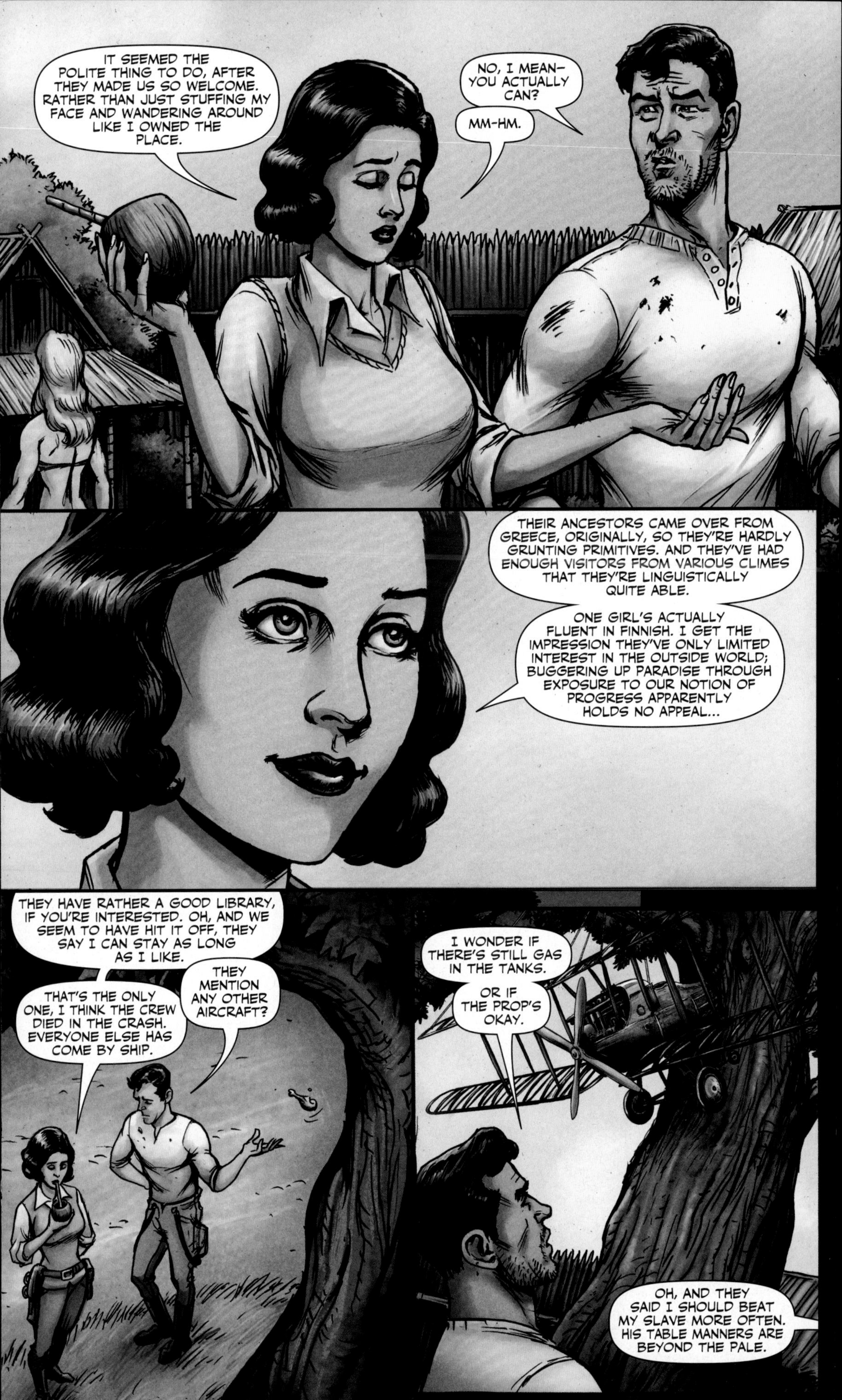
IT SEEMED THE POLITE THING TO DO, AFTER THEY MADE US SO WELCOME. RATHER THAN JUST STUFFING MY FACE AND WANDERING AROUND LIKE I OWNED THE PLACE.
NO, I MEAN— YOU ACTUALLY CAN?
MM-HM.
THEIR ANCESTORS CAME OVER FROM GREECE, ORIGINALLY, SO THEY'RE HARDLY GRUNTING PRIMITIVES. AND THEY'VE HAD ENOUGH VISITORS FROM VARIOUS CLIMES THAT THEY'RE LINGUISTICALLY QUITE ABLE.
ONE GIRL'S ACTUALLY FLUENT IN FINNISH. I GET THE IMPRESSION THEY'VE ONLY LIMITED INTEREST IN THE OUTSIDE WORLD; BUGGERING UP PARADISE THROUGH EXPOSURE TO OUR NOTION OF PROGRESS APPARENTLY HOLDS NO APPEAL...
THEY HAVE RATHER A GOOD LIBRARY, IF YOU'RE INTERESTED. OH, AND WE SEEM TO HAVE HIT IT OFF, THEY SAY I CAN STAY AS LONG AS I LIKE.
THEY MENTION ANY OTHER AIRCRAFT?
THAT'S THE ONLY ONE, I THINK THE CREW DIED IN THE CRASH. EVERYONE ELSE HAS COME BY SHIP.
I WONDER IF THERE'S STILL GAS IN THE TANKS.
OR IF THE PROP'S OKAY.
OH, AND THEY SAID I SHOULD BEAT MY SLAVE MORE OFTEN. HIS TABLE MANNERS ARE BEYOND THE PALE.

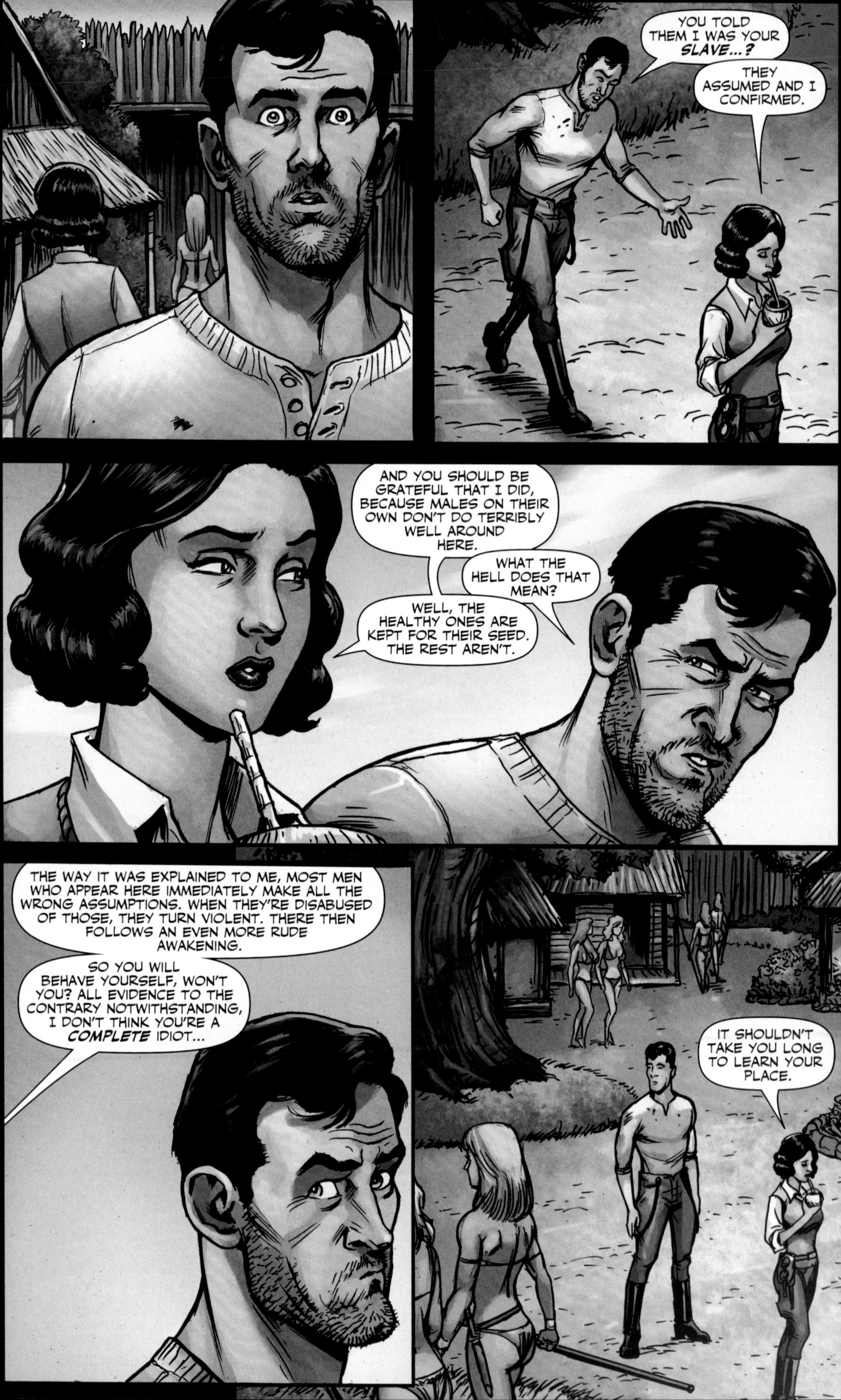

YOU TOLD THEM I WAS YOUR SLAVE...?
THEY ASSUMED AND I CONFIRMED.
AND YOU SHOULD BE GRATEFUL THAT I DID, BECAUSE MALES ON THEIR OWN DON'T DO TERRIBLY WELL AROUND HERE.
WHAT THE HELL DOES THAT MEAN?
WELL, THE HEALTHY ONES ARE KEPT FOR THEIR SEED. THE REST AREN'T.
THE WAY IT WAS EXPLAINED TO ME, MOST MEN WHO APPEAR HERE IMMEDIATELY MAKE ALL THE WRONG ASSUMPTIONS. WHEN THEY'RE DISABUSED OF THOSE, THEY TURN VIOLENT. THERE THEN FOLLOWS AN EVEN MORE RUDE AWAKENING.
SO YOU WILL BEHAVE YOURSELF, WON'T YOU? ALL EVIDENCE TO THE CONTRARY NOTWITHSTANDING, I DON'T THINK YOU'RE A COMPLETE IDIOT...
IT SHOULDN'T TAKE YOU LONG TO LEARN YOUR PLACE.

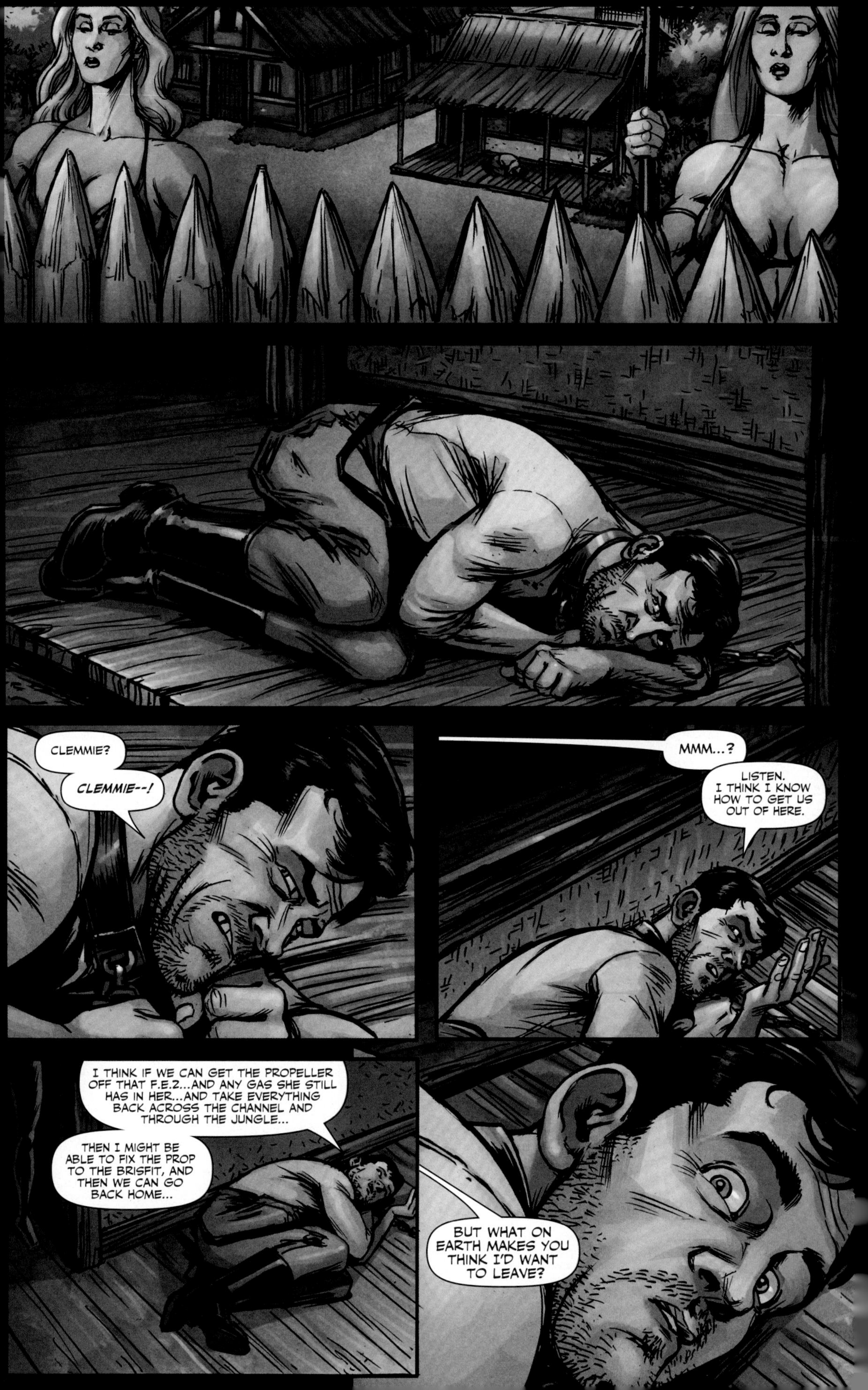
CLEMMIE?
CLEMMIE--!
MMM...?
LISTEN. I THINK I KNOW HOW TO GET US OUT OF HERE.
I THINK IF WE CAN GET THE PROPELLER OFF THAT F.E.2...AND ANY GAS SHE STILL HAS IN HER...AND TAKE EVERYTHING BACK ACROSS THE CHANNEL AND THROUGH THE JUNGLE...
THEN I MIGHT BE ABLE TO FIX THE PROP TO THE BRISFIT, AND THEN WE CAN GO BACK HOME...
BUT WHAT ON EARTH MAKES YOU THINK I'D WANT TO LEAVE?

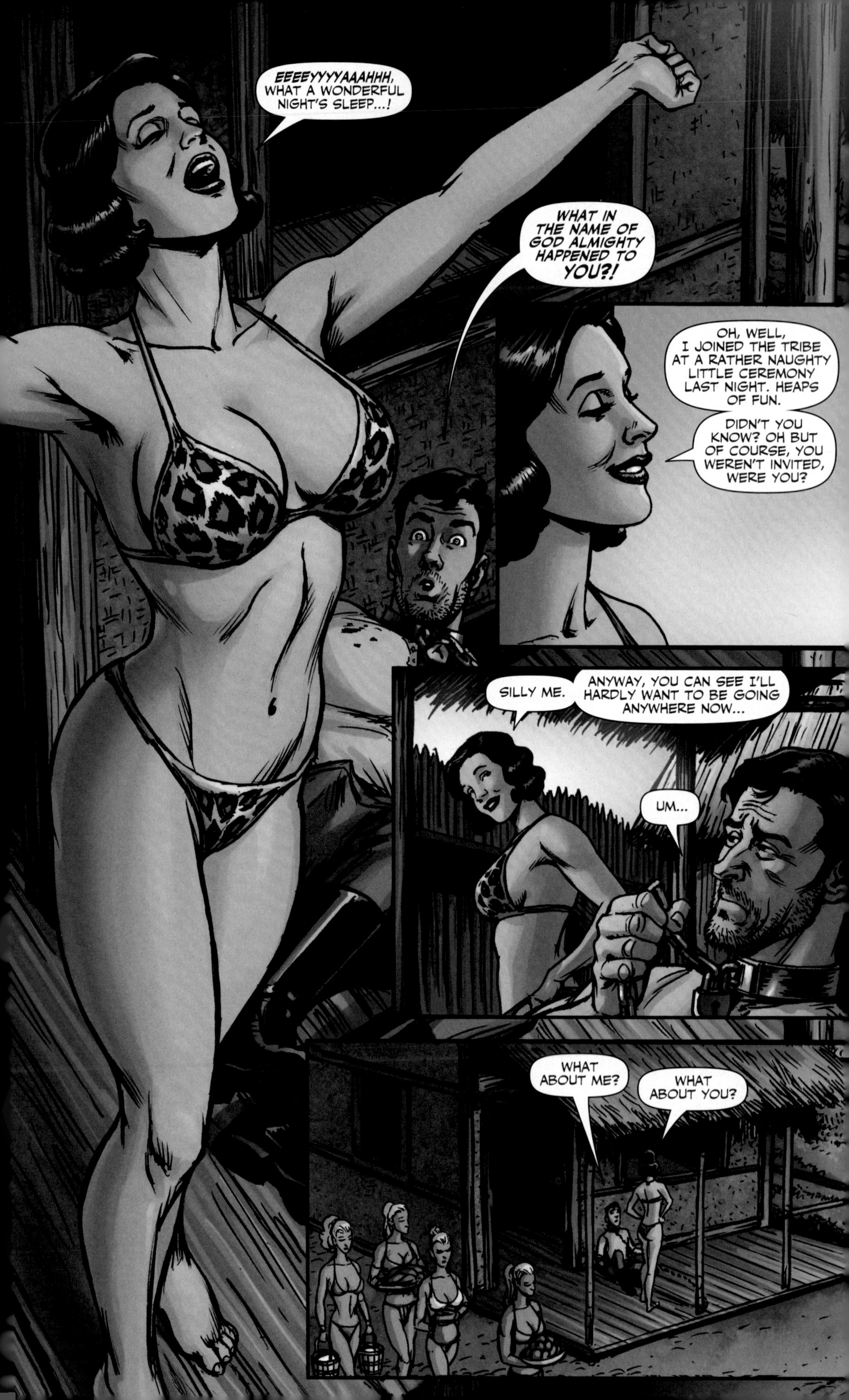
EEEEYYYYAAAHHH, WHAT A WONDERFUL NIGHT'S SLEEP...!
WHAT IN THE NAME OF GOD ALMIGHTY HAPPENED TO YOU?!
OH, WELL, I JOINED THE TRIBE AT A RATHER NAUGHTY LITTLE CEREMONY LAST NIGHT. HEAPS OF FUN.
DIDN'T YOU KNOW? OH BUT OF COURSE, YOU WEREN'T INVITED, WERE YOU?
SILLY ME.
ANYWAY, YOU CAN SEE I'LL HARDLY WANT TO BE GOING ANYWHERE NOW...
UM...
WHAT ABOUT ME?
WHAT ABOUT YOU?

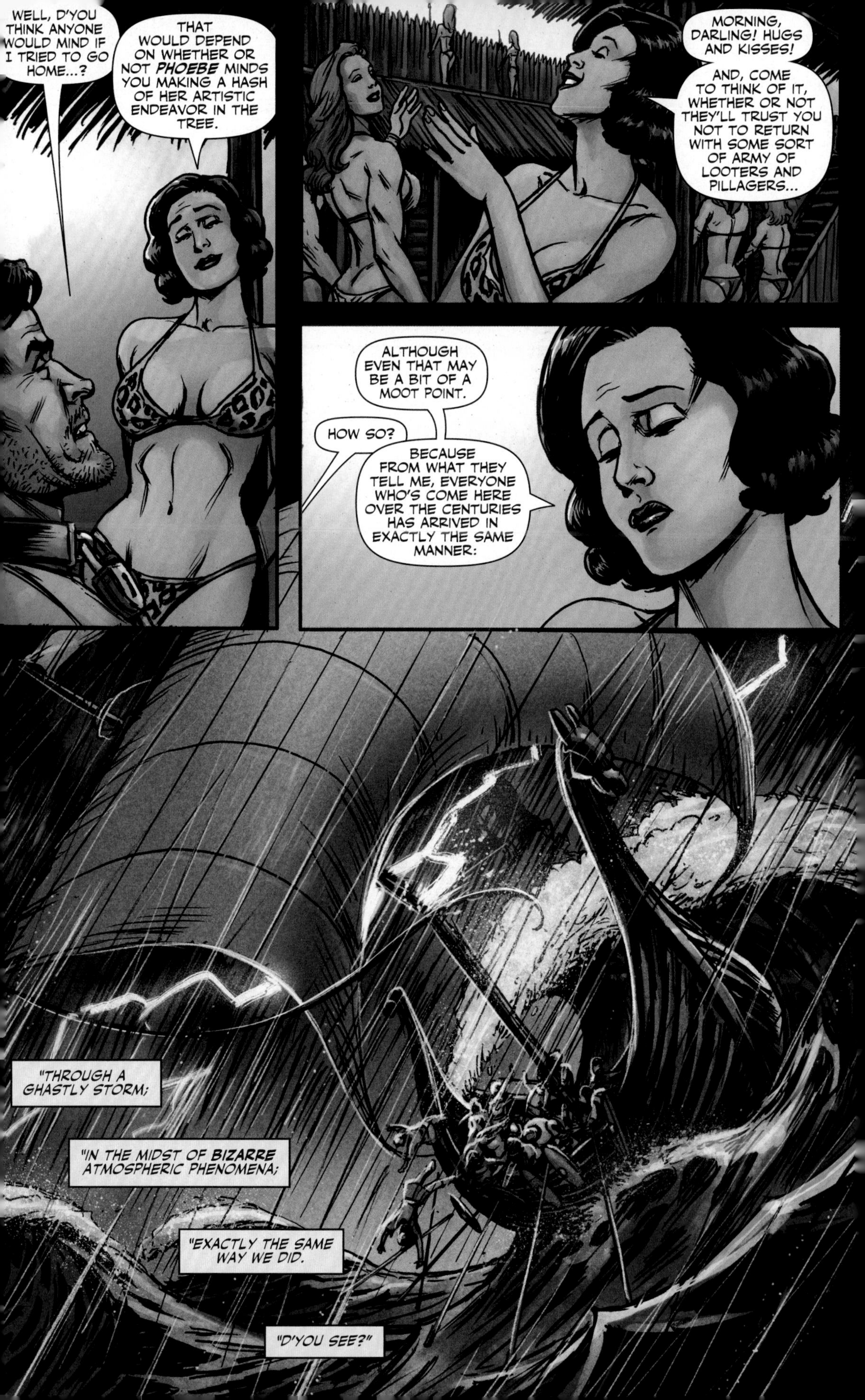

WELL, D'YOU THINK ANYONE WOULD MIND IF I TRIED TO GO HOME...?
THAT WOULD DEPEND ON WHETHER OR NOT PHOEBE MINDS YOU MAKING A HASH OF HER ARTISTIC ENDEAVOR IN THE TREE.
MORNING, DARLING! HUGS AND KISSES!
AND, COME TO THINK OF IT, WHETHER OR NOT THEY'LL TRUST YOU NOT TO RETURN WITH SOME SORT OF ARMY OF LOOTERS AND PILLAGERS...
ALTHOUGH EVEN THAT MAY BE A BIT OF A MOOT POINT.
HOW SO?
BECAUSE FROM WHAT THEY TELL ME, EVERYONE WHO'S COME HERE OVER THE CENTURIES HAS ARRIVED IN EXACTLY THE SAME MANNER:
"THROUGH A GHASTLY STORM;
"IN THE MIDST OF BIZARRE ATMOSPHERIC PHENOMENA;
"EXACTLY THE SAME WAY WE DID.
"D'YOU SEE?"

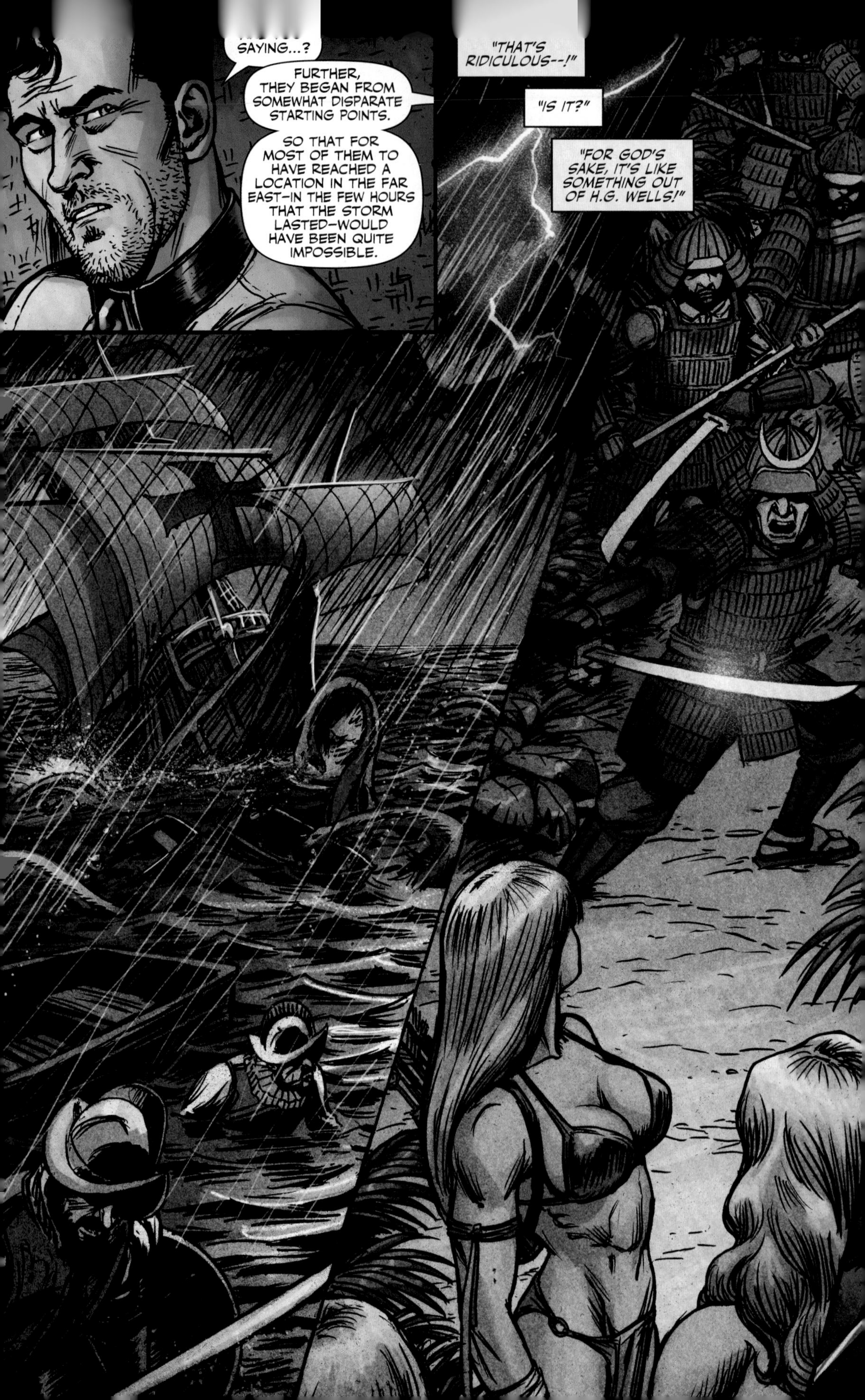
SAYING...?
FURTHER, THEY BEGAN FROM SOMEWHAT DISPARATE STARTING POINTS.
SO THAT FOR MOST OF THEM TO HAVE REACHED A LOCATION IN THE FAR EAST--IN THE FEW HOURS THAT THE STORM LASTED--WOULD HAVE BEEN QUITE IMPOSSIBLE.
"THAT'S RIDICULOUS--!"
"IS IT?"
"FOR GOD'S SAKE, IT'S LIKE SOMETHING OUT OF H.G. WELLS!"

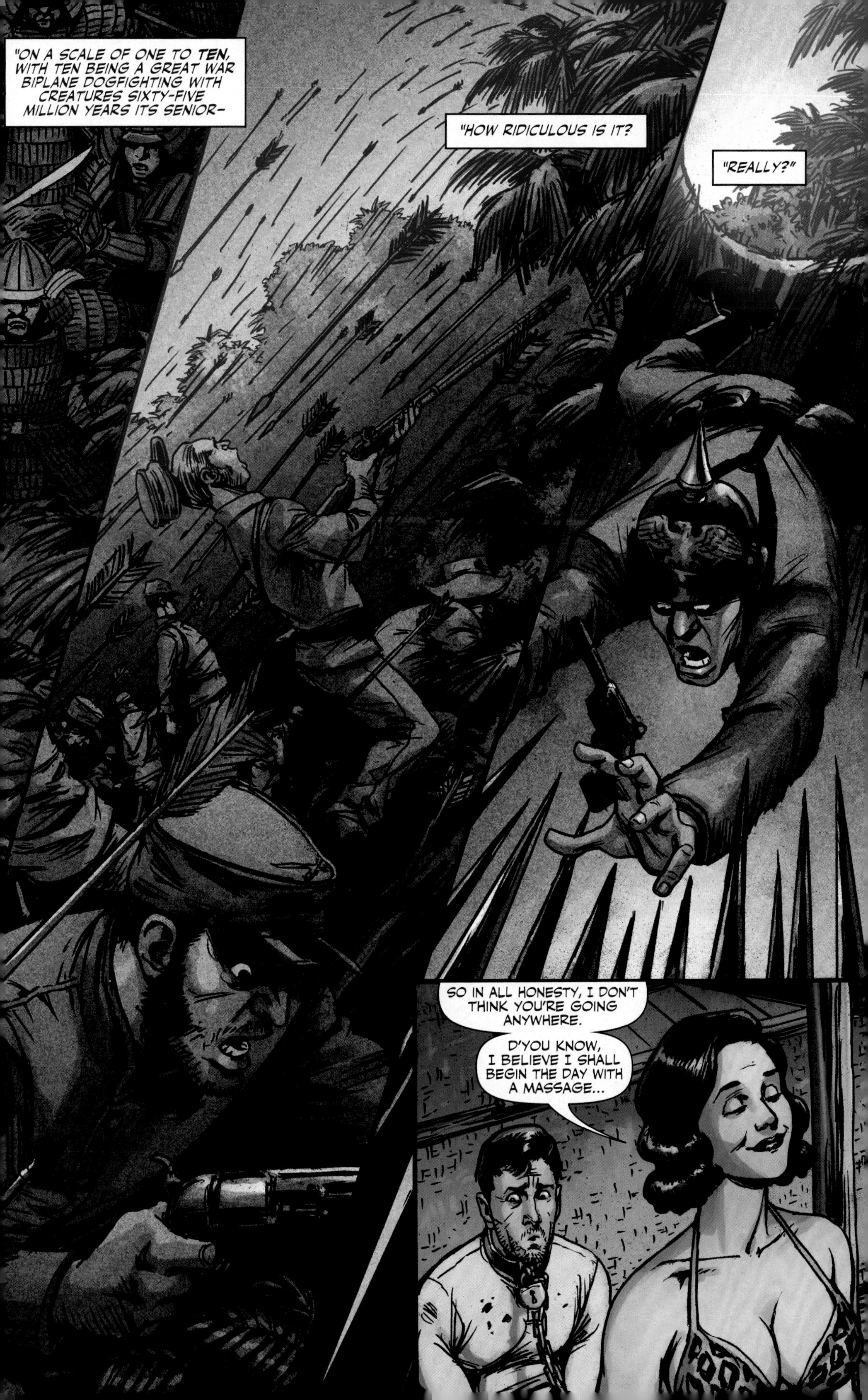
"ON A SCALE OF ONE TO TEN, WITH TEN BEING A GREAT WAR BIPLANE DOGFIGHTING WITH CREATURES SIXTY-FIVE MILLION YEARS ITS SENIOR-
"HOW RIDICULOUS IS IT?
"REALLY?"
SO IN ALL HONESTY, I DON'T THINK YOU'RE GOING ANYWHERE.
D'YOU KNOW, I BELIEVE I SHALL BEGIN THE DAY WITH A MASSAGE...

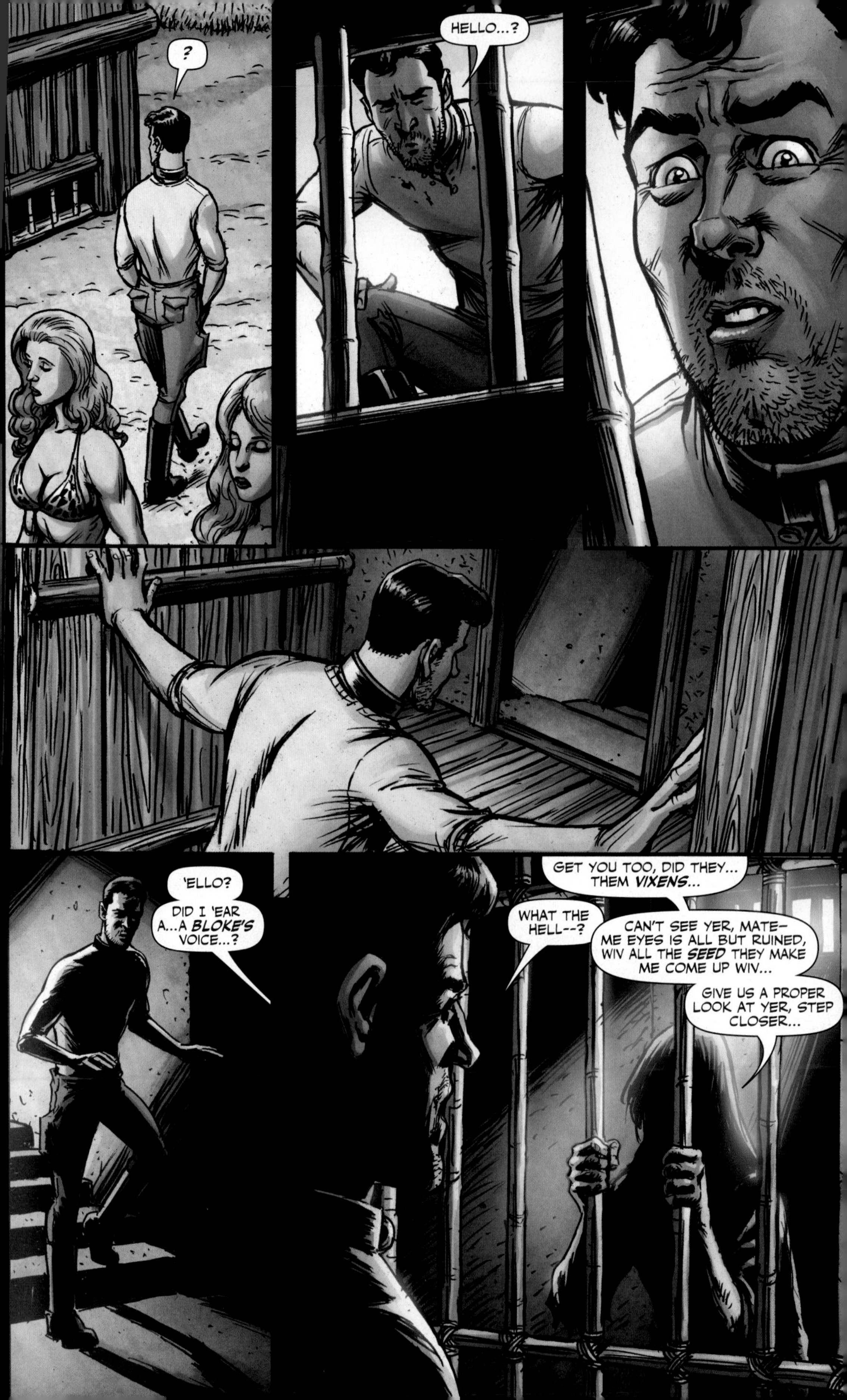
?
HELLO...?
'ELLO?
DID I 'EAR A...A BLOKE'S VOICE...?
WHAT THE HELL--?
GET YOU TOO, DID THEY... THEM VIXENS...
CAN'T SEE YER, MATE-- ME EYES IS ALL BUT RUINED, WIV ALL THE SEED THEY MAKE ME COME UP WIV...
GIVE US A PROPER LOOK AT YER, STEP CLOSER...

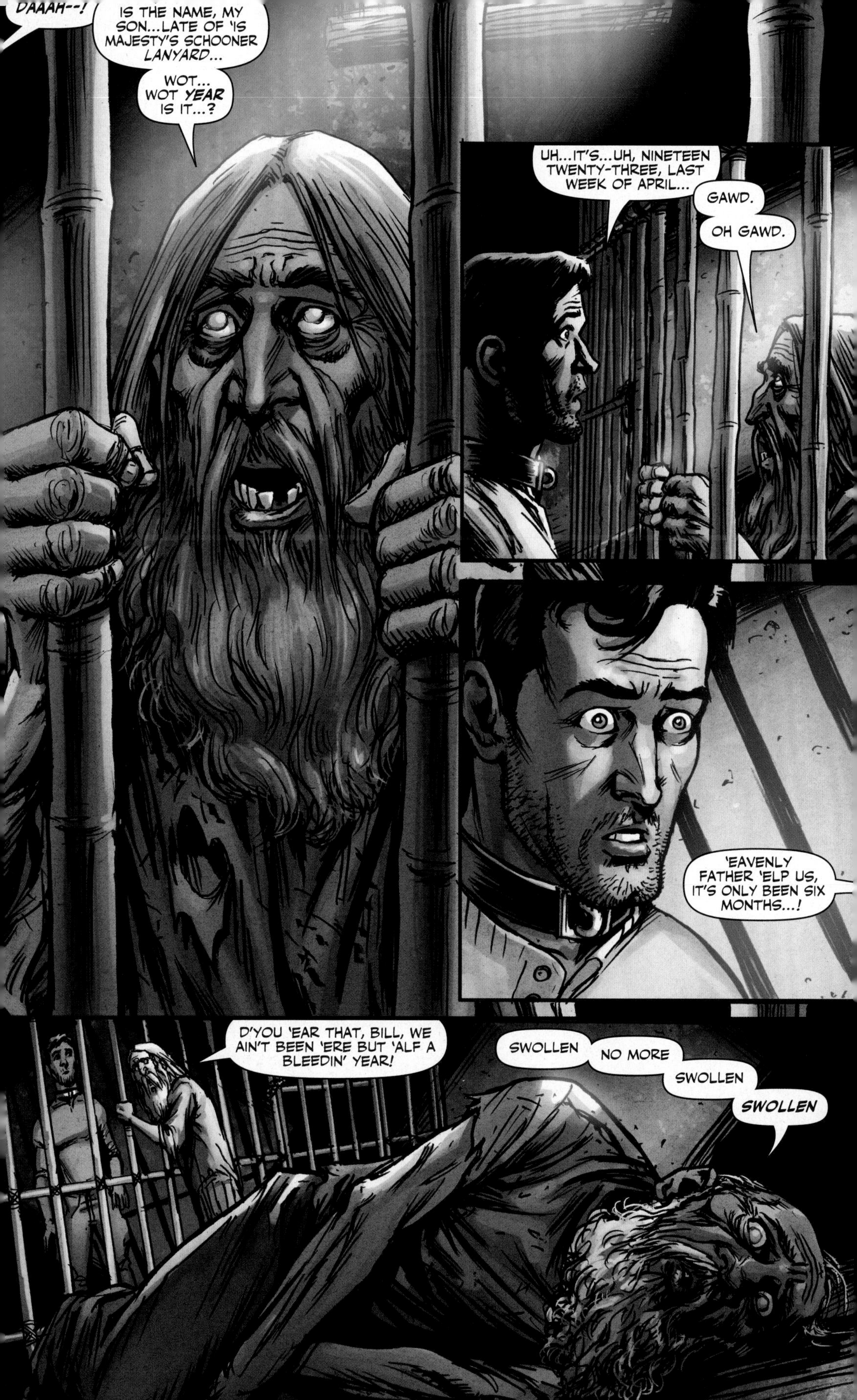
DAAAH--!
IS THE NAME, MY SON...LATE OF 'IS MAJESTY'S SCHOONER *LANYARD*...
WOT... WOT *YEAR* IS IT...?
UH...IT'S...UH, NINETEEN TWENTY-THREE, LAST WEEK OF APRIL...
GAWD.
OH GAWD.
'EAVENLY FATHER 'ELP US, IT'S ONLY BEEN SIX MONTHS...!
D'YOU 'EAR THAT, BILL, WE AIN'T BEEN 'ERE BUT 'ALF A BLEEDIN' YEAR!
SWOLLEN
NO MORE
SWOLLEN
SWOLLEN

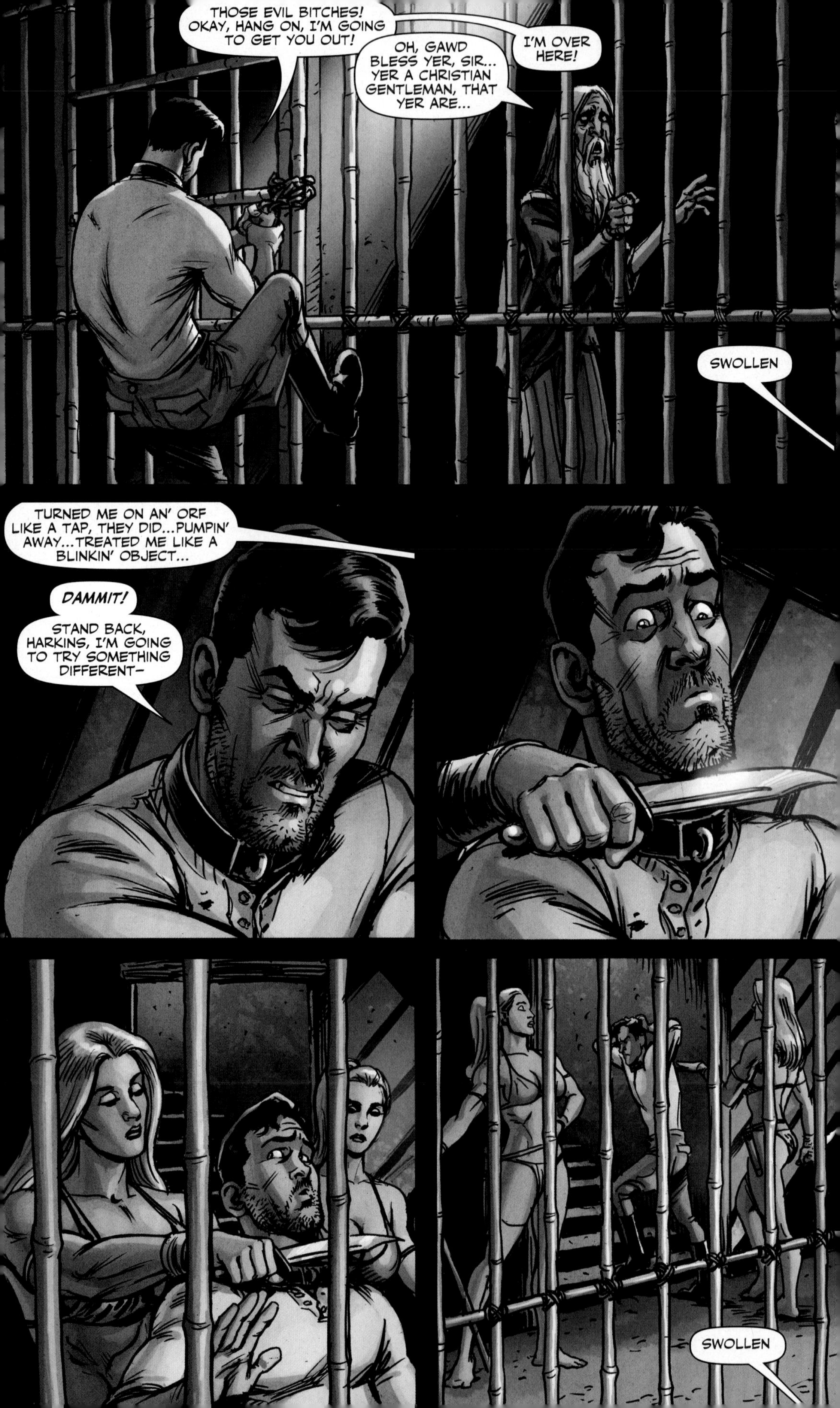
THOSE EVIL BITCHES! OKAY, HANG ON, I'M GOING TO GET YOU OUT!
I'M OVER HERE!
OH, GAWD BLESS YER, SIR... YER A CHRISTIAN GENTLEMAN, THAT YER ARE...
SWOLLEN
TURNED ME ON AN' ORF LIKE A TAP, THEY DID...PUMPIN' AWAY...TREATED ME LIKE A BLINKIN' OBJECT...
DAMMIT!
STAND BACK, HARKINS, I'M GOING TO TRY SOMETHING DIFFERENT–
SWOLLEN

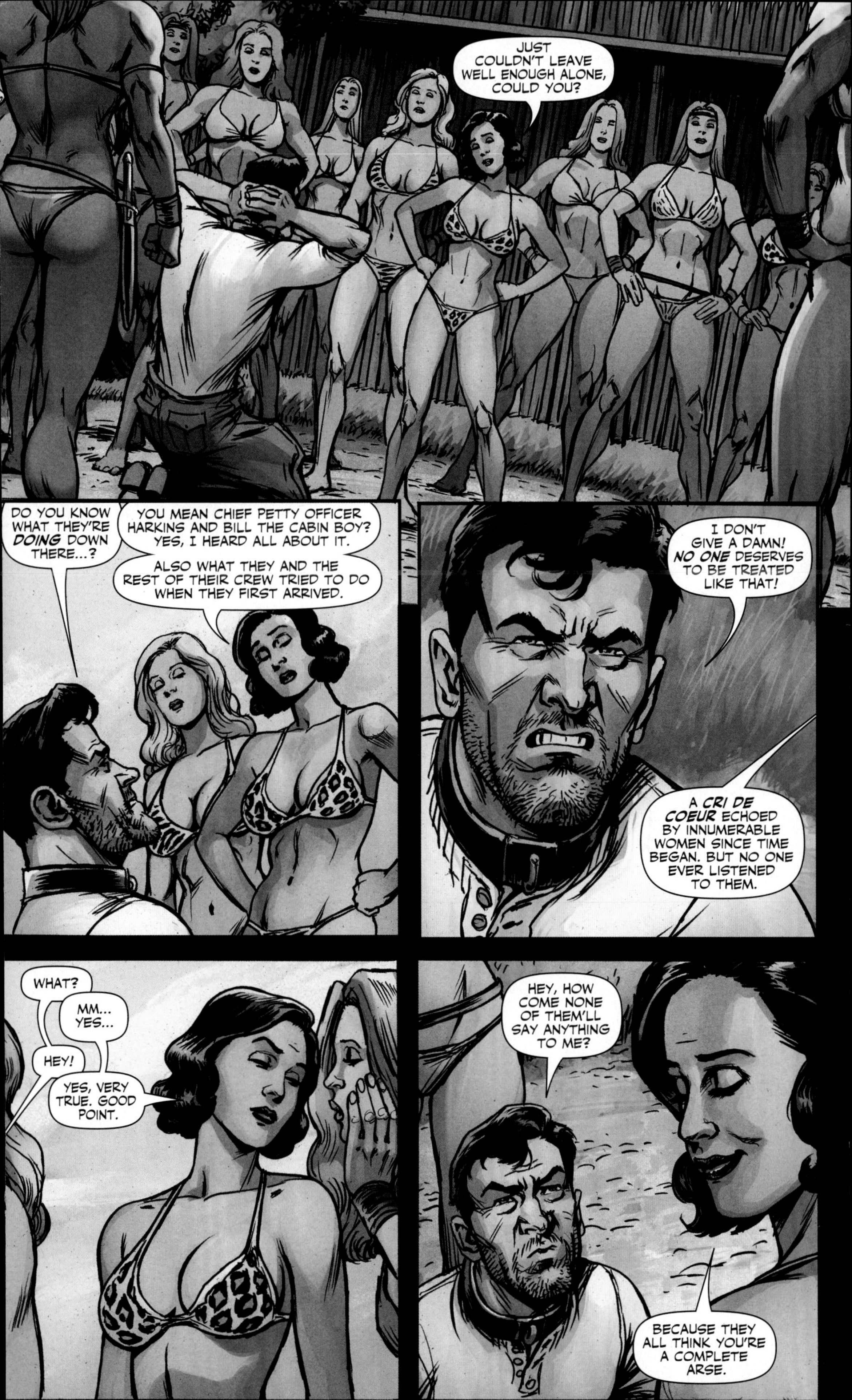
JUST COULDN'T LEAVE WELL ENOUGH ALONE, COULD YOU?
DO YOU KNOW WHAT THEY'RE *DOING* DOWN THERE...?
YOU MEAN CHIEF PETTY OFFICER HARKINS AND BILL THE CABIN BOY? YES, I HEARD ALL ABOUT IT.
ALSO WHAT THEY AND THE REST OF THEIR CREW TRIED TO DO WHEN THEY FIRST ARRIVED.
I DON'T GIVE A DAMN! *NO ONE* DESERVES TO BE TREATED LIKE THAT!
A *CRI DE COEUR* ECHOED BY INNUMERABLE WOMEN SINCE TIME BEGAN. BUT NO ONE EVER LISTENED TO THEM.
WHAT?
MM... YES...
HEY!
YES, VERY TRUE. GOOD POINT.
HEY, HOW COME NONE OF THEM'LL SAY ANYTHING TO ME?
BECAUSE THEY ALL THINK YOU'RE A COMPLETE ARSE.

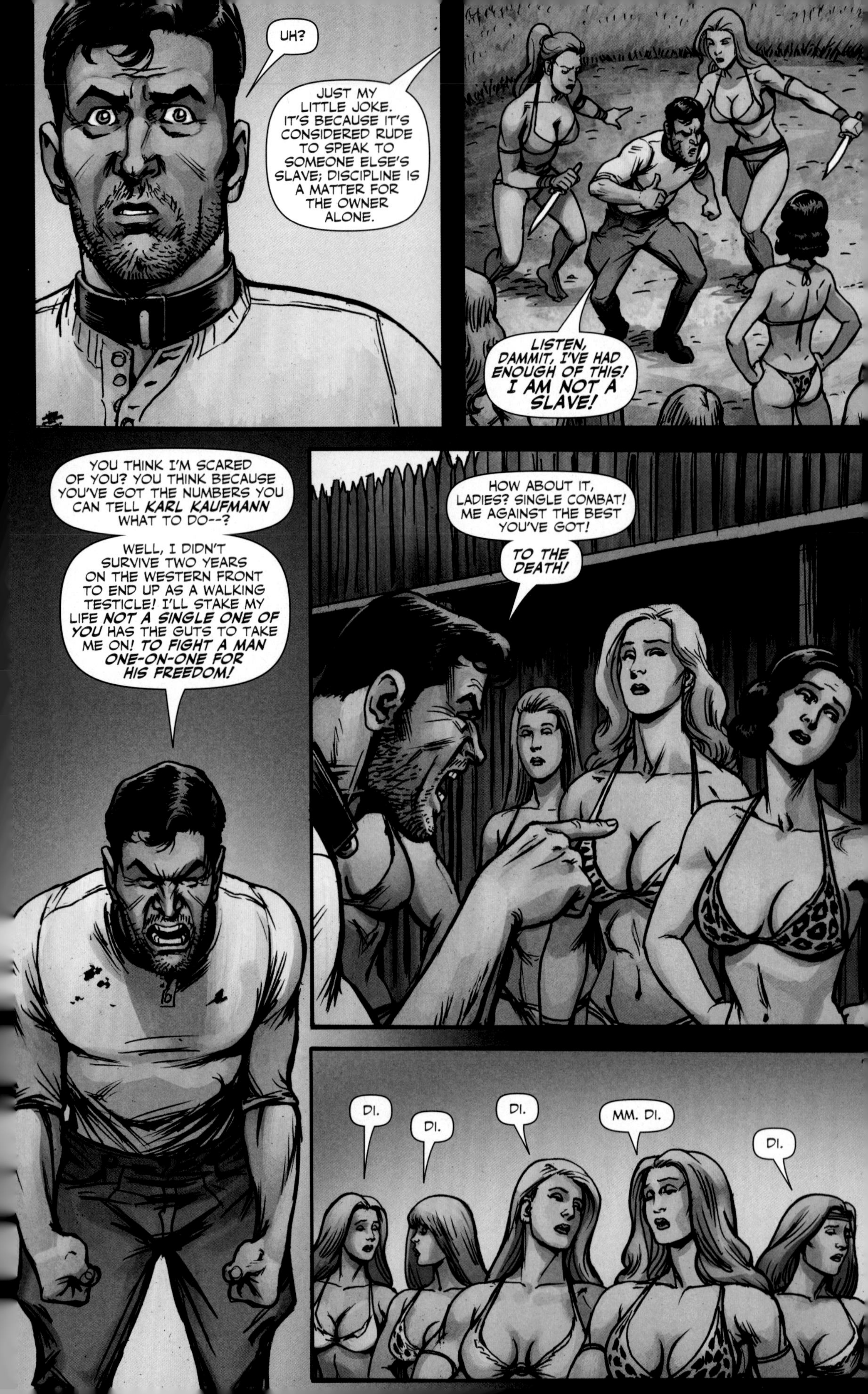
UH?
JUST MY LITTLE JOKE. IT'S BECAUSE IT'S CONSIDERED RUDE TO SPEAK TO SOMEONE ELSE'S SLAVE; DISCIPLINE IS A MATTER FOR THE OWNER ALONE.
LISTEN, DAMMIT, I'VE HAD ENOUGH OF THIS! I AM NOT A SLAVE!
YOU THINK I'M SCARED OF YOU? YOU THINK BECAUSE YOU'VE GOT THE NUMBERS YOU CAN TELL KARL KAUFMANN WHAT TO DO--?
WELL, I DIDN'T SURVIVE TWO YEARS ON THE WESTERN FRONT TO END UP AS A WALKING TESTICLE! I'LL STAKE MY LIFE NOT A SINGLE ONE OF YOU HAS THE GUTS TO TAKE ME ON! TO FIGHT A MAN ONE-ON-ONE FOR HIS FREEDOM!
HOW ABOUT IT, LADIES? SINGLE COMBAT! ME AGAINST THE BEST YOU'VE GOT!
TO THE DEATH!
DI.
DI.
DI.
MM. DI.
DI.

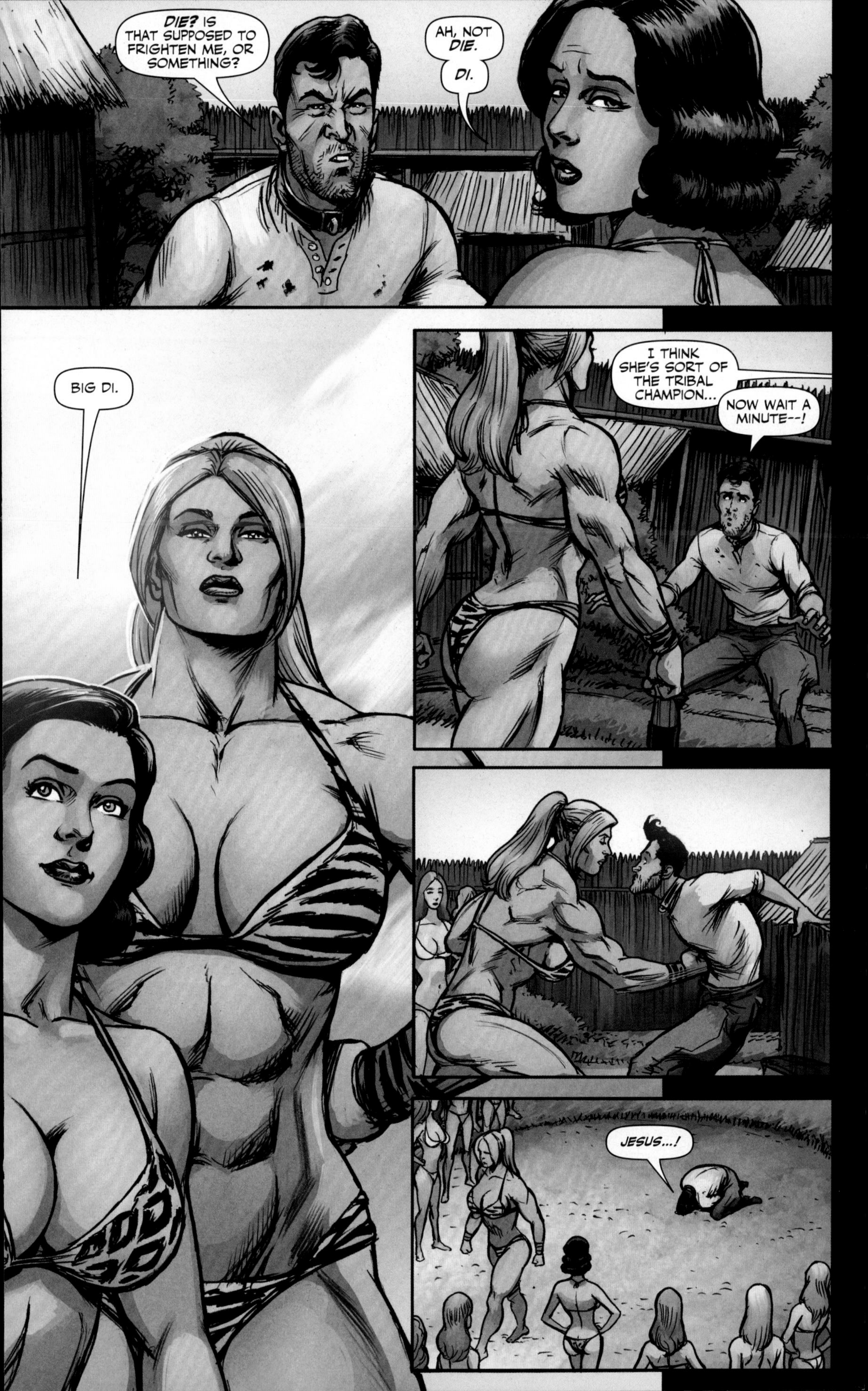
DIE? IS THAT SUPPOSED TO FRIGHTEN ME, OR SOMETHING?
AH, NOT DIE.
DI.
BIG DI.
I THINK SHE'S SORT OF THE TRIBAL CHAMPION...
NOW WAIT A MINUTE--!
JESUS...!

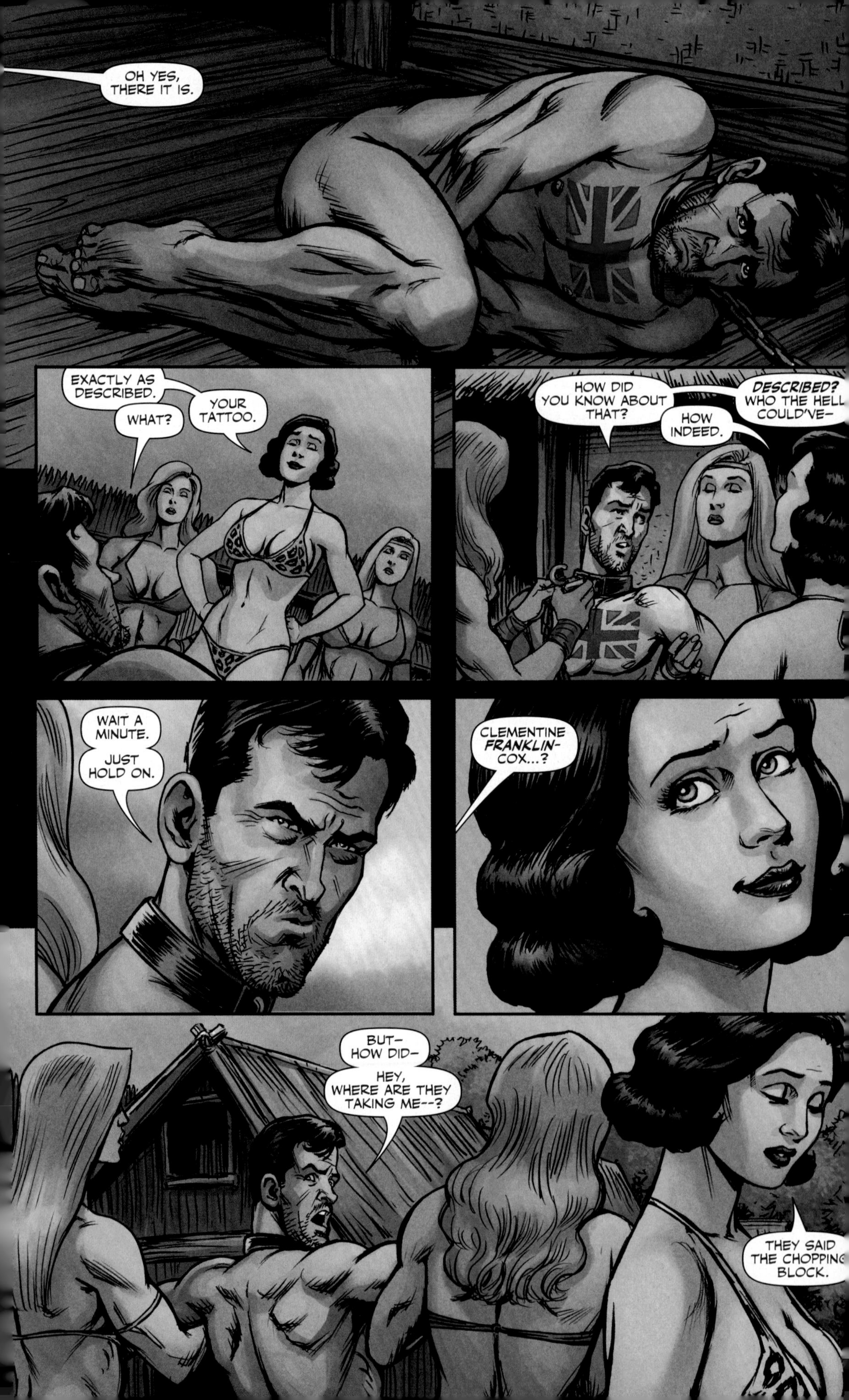
OH YES, THERE IT IS.
EXACTLY AS DESCRIBED.
WHAT?
YOUR TATTOO.
HOW DID YOU KNOW ABOUT THAT?
HOW INDEED.
DESCRIBED? WHO THE HELL COULD'VE–
WAIT A MINUTE.
JUST HOLD ON.
CLEMENTINE FRANKLIN-COX...?
BUT– HOW DID–
HEY, WHERE ARE THEY TAKING ME--?
THEY SAID THE CHOPPING BLOCK.

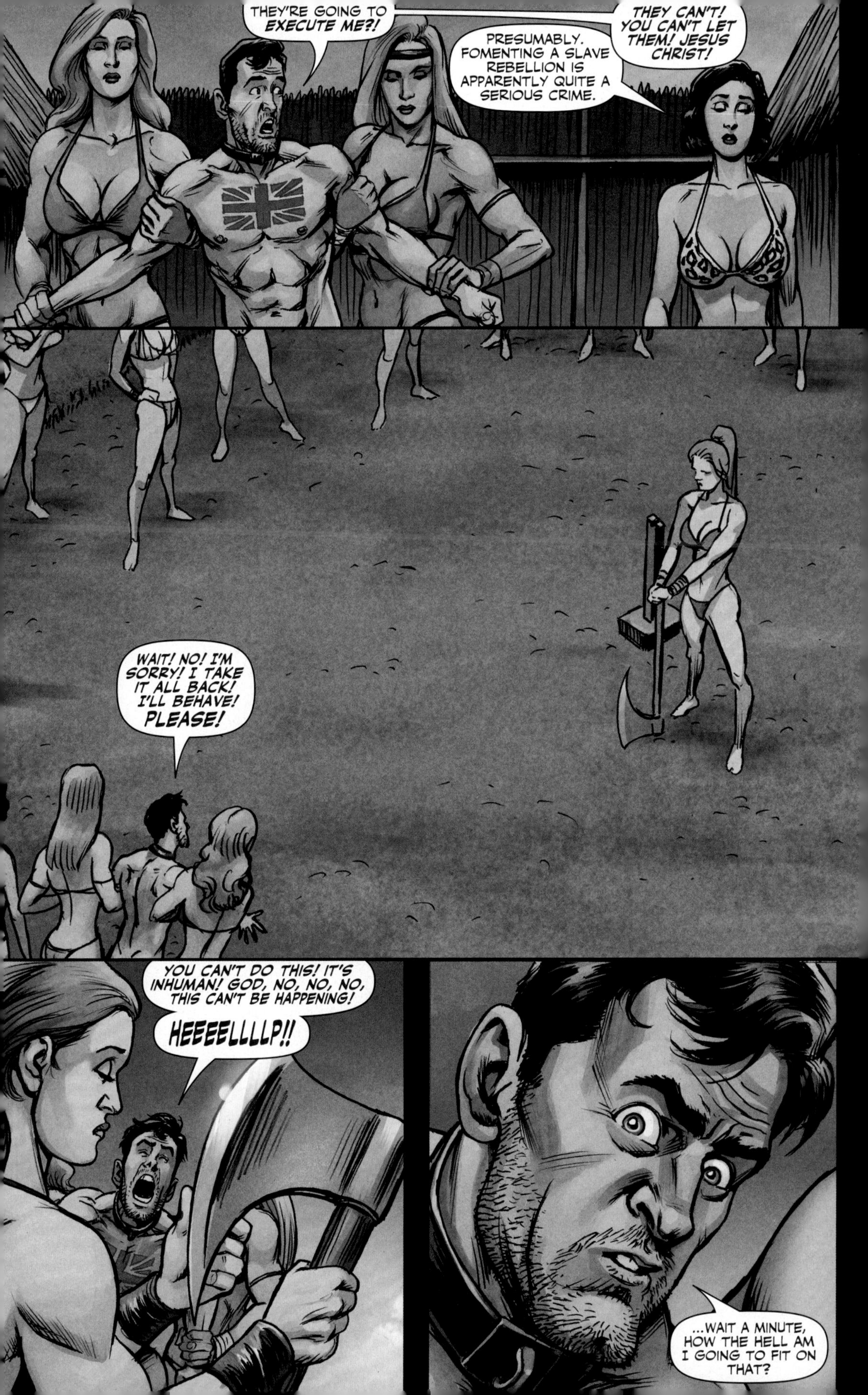
THEY'RE GOING TO EXECUTE ME?!
PRESUMABLY. FOMENTING A SLAVE REBELLION IS APPARENTLY QUITE A SERIOUS CRIME.
THEY CAN'T! YOU CAN'T LET THEM! JESUS CHRIST!
WAIT! NO! I'M SORRY! I TAKE IT ALL BACK! I'LL BEHAVE! PLEASE!
YOU CAN'T DO THIS! IT'S INHUMAN! GOD, NO, NO, NO, THIS CAN'T BE HAPPENING!
HEEEELLLLP!!
...WAIT A MINUTE, HOW THE HELL AM I GOING TO FIT ON THAT?

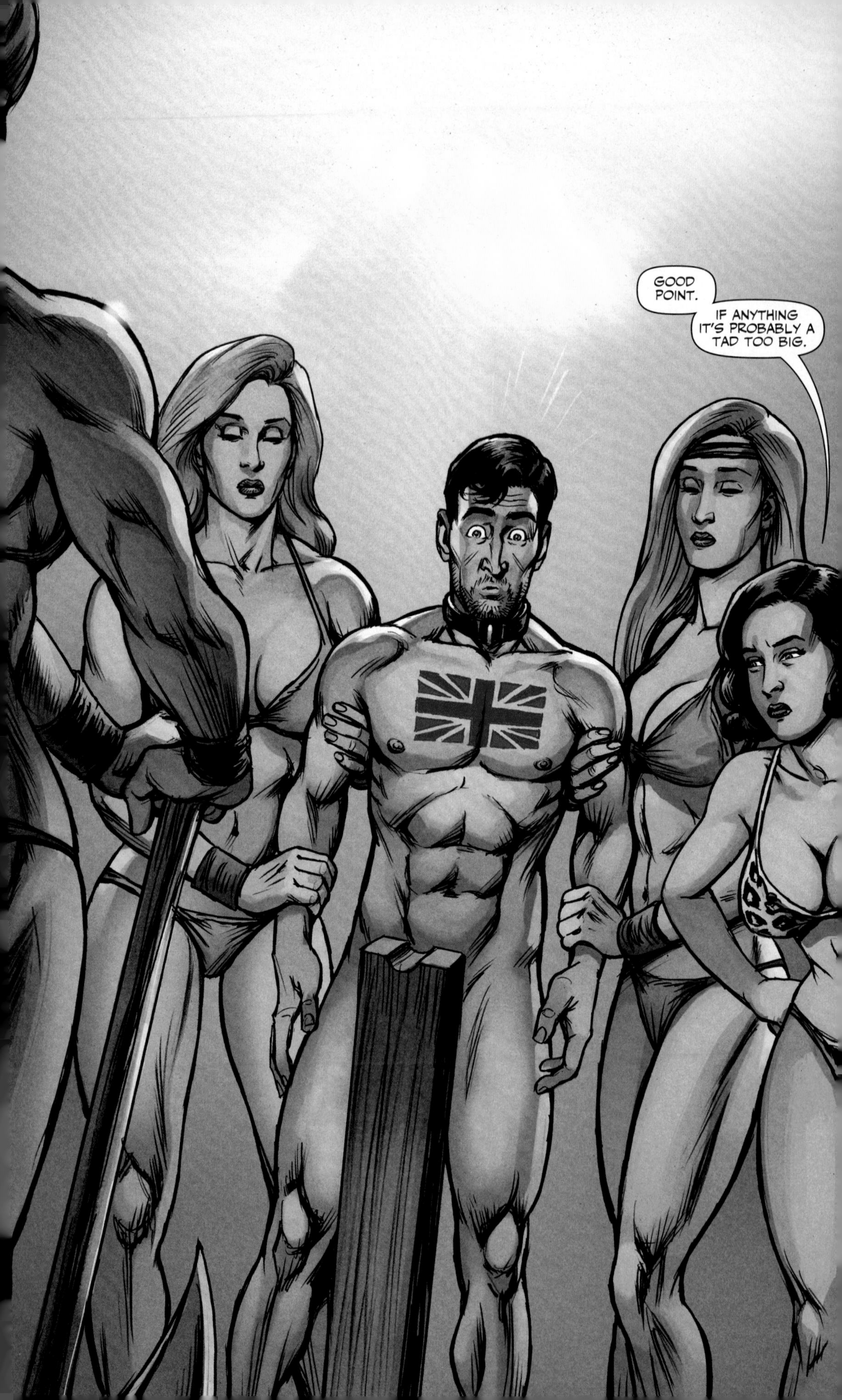
GOOD POINT.
IF ANYTHING IT'S PROBABLY A TAD TOO BIG.

CLEMENTINE BY RUSS BRAUN

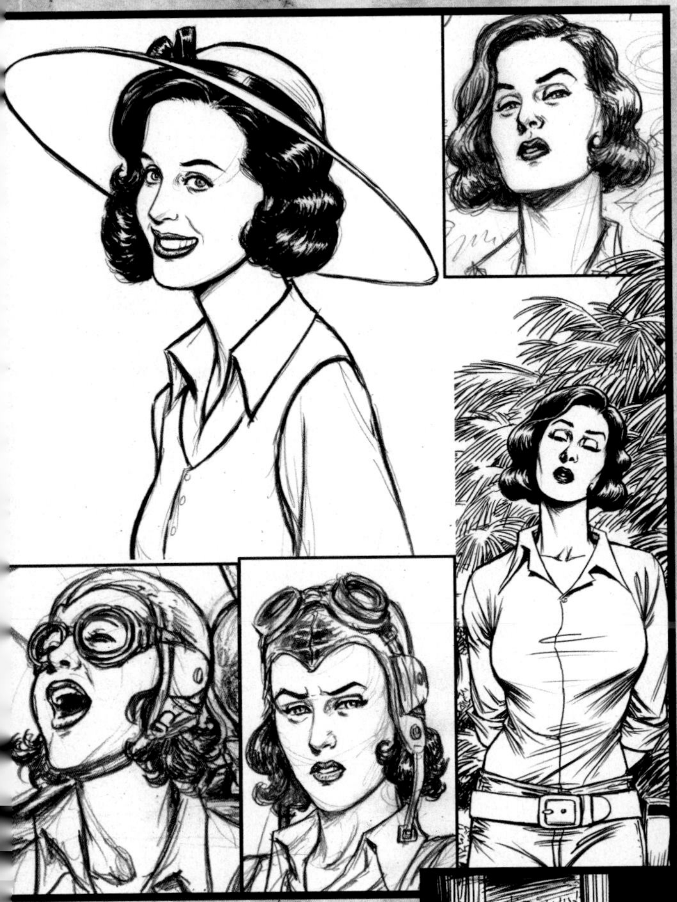

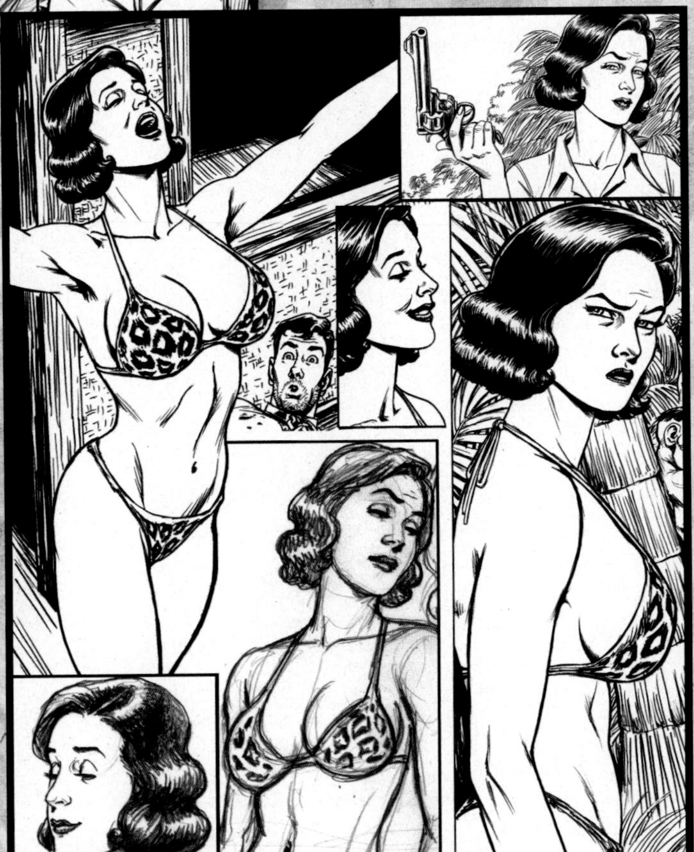

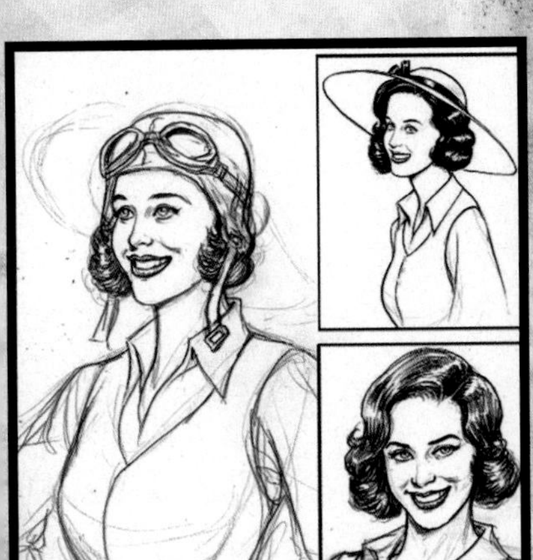

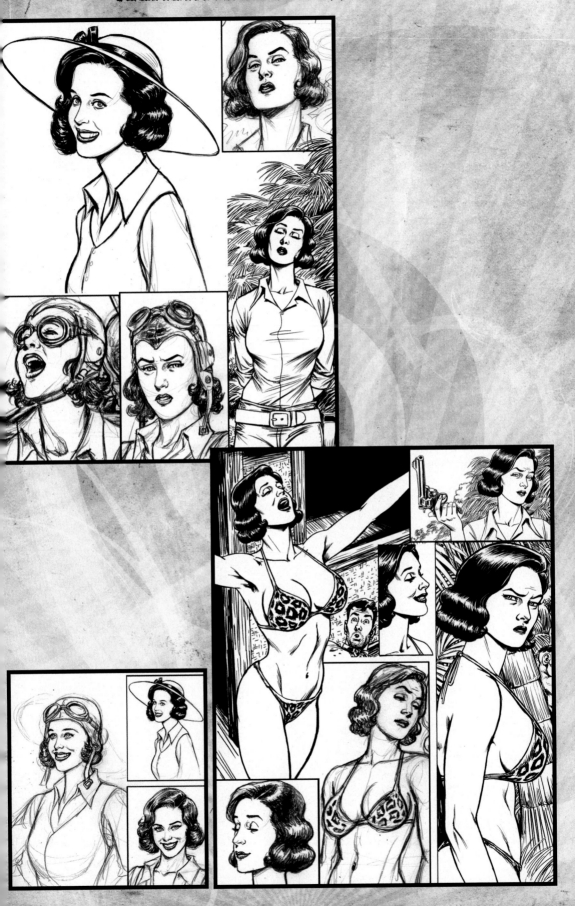

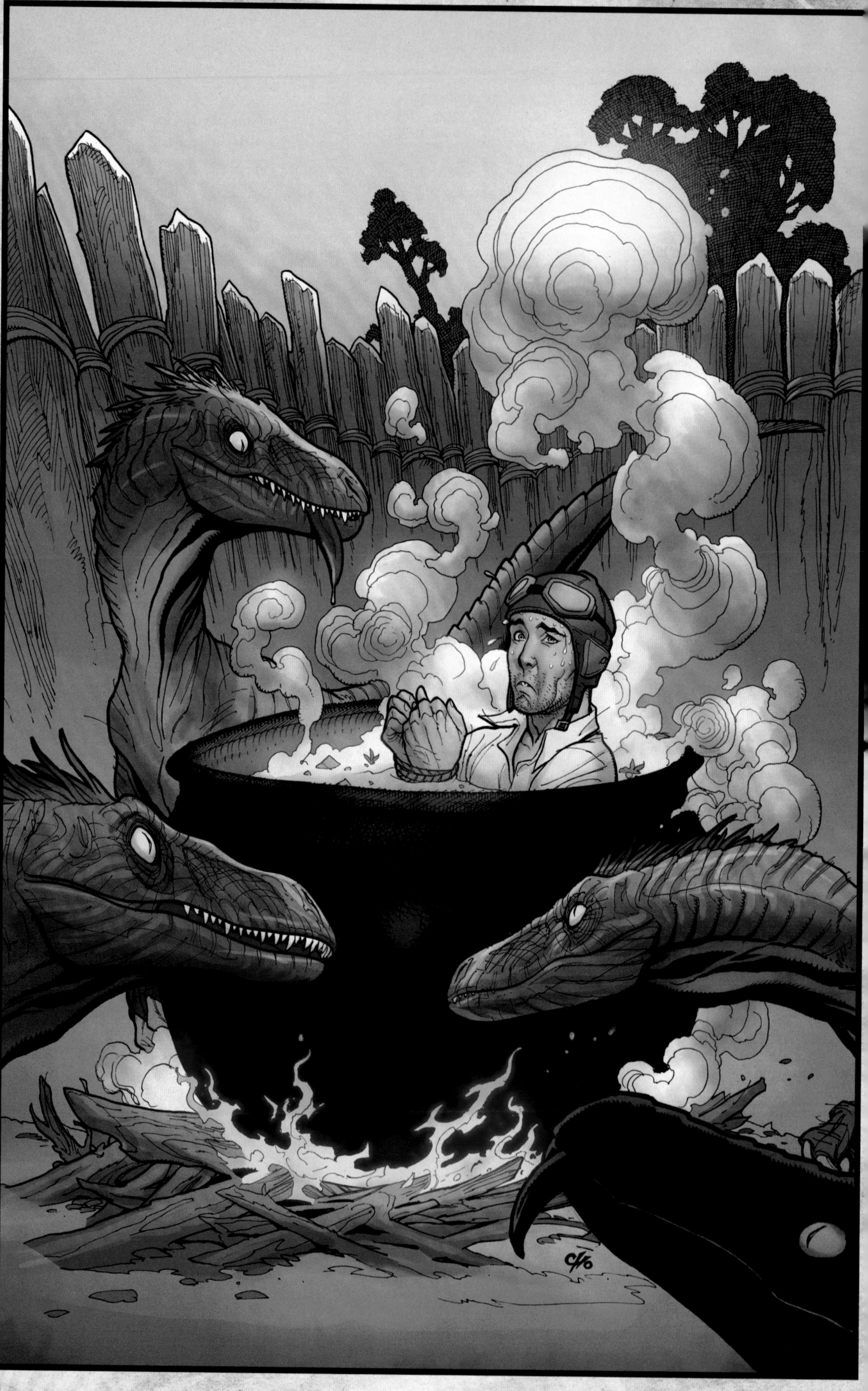

★ 4 ★

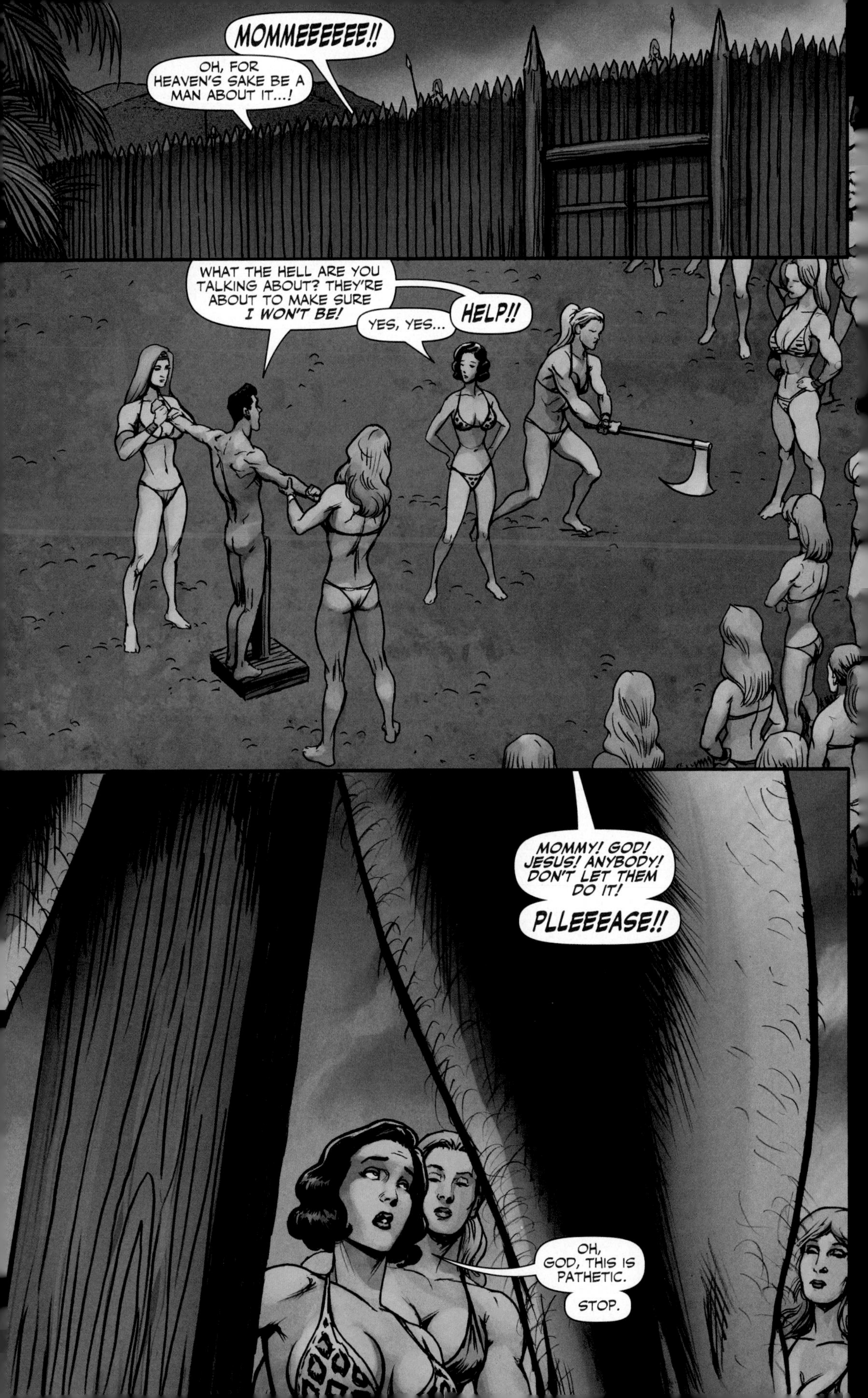
MOMMEEEEEE!!
OH, FOR HEAVEN'S SAKE BE A MAN ABOUT IT...!
WHAT THE HELL ARE YOU TALKING ABOUT? THEY'RE ABOUT TO MAKE SURE *I WON'T BE!*
HELP!!
YES, YES...
MOMMY! GOD! JESUS! ANYBODY! DON'T LET THEM DO IT!
PLLEEEASE!!
OH, GOD, THIS IS PATHETIC.
STOP.

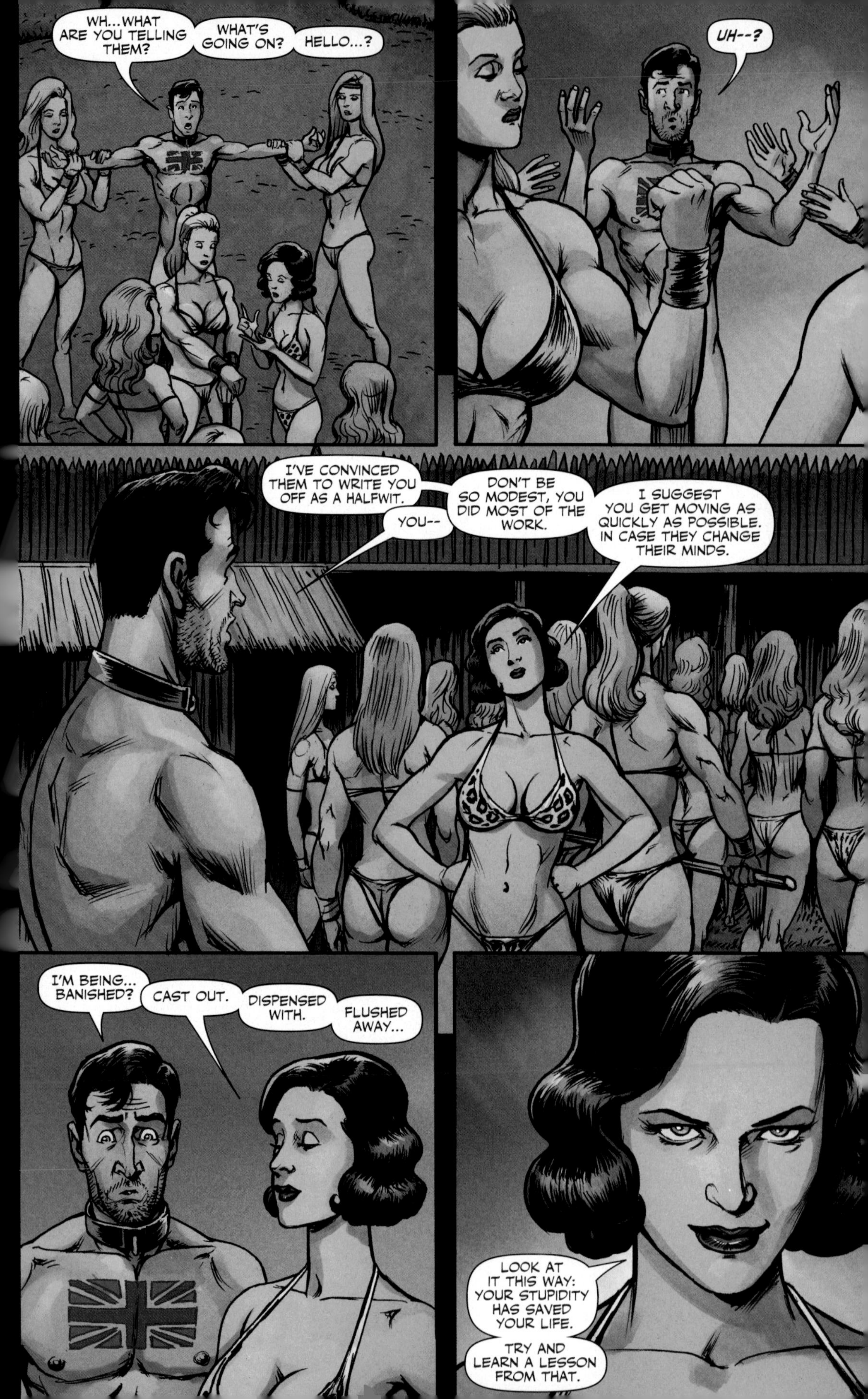
WH...WHAT ARE YOU TELLING THEM?
WHAT'S GOING ON?
HELLO...?
UH--?
I'VE CONVINCED THEM TO WRITE YOU OFF AS A HALFWIT.
YOU--
DON'T BE SO MODEST, YOU DID MOST OF THE WORK.
I SUGGEST YOU GET MOVING AS QUICKLY AS POSSIBLE. IN CASE THEY CHANGE THEIR MINDS.
I'M BEING... BANISHED?
CAST OUT.
DISPENSED WITH.
FLUSHED AWAY...
LOOK AT IT THIS WAY: YOUR STUPIDITY HAS SAVED YOUR LIFE.
TRY AND LEARN A LESSON FROM THAT.

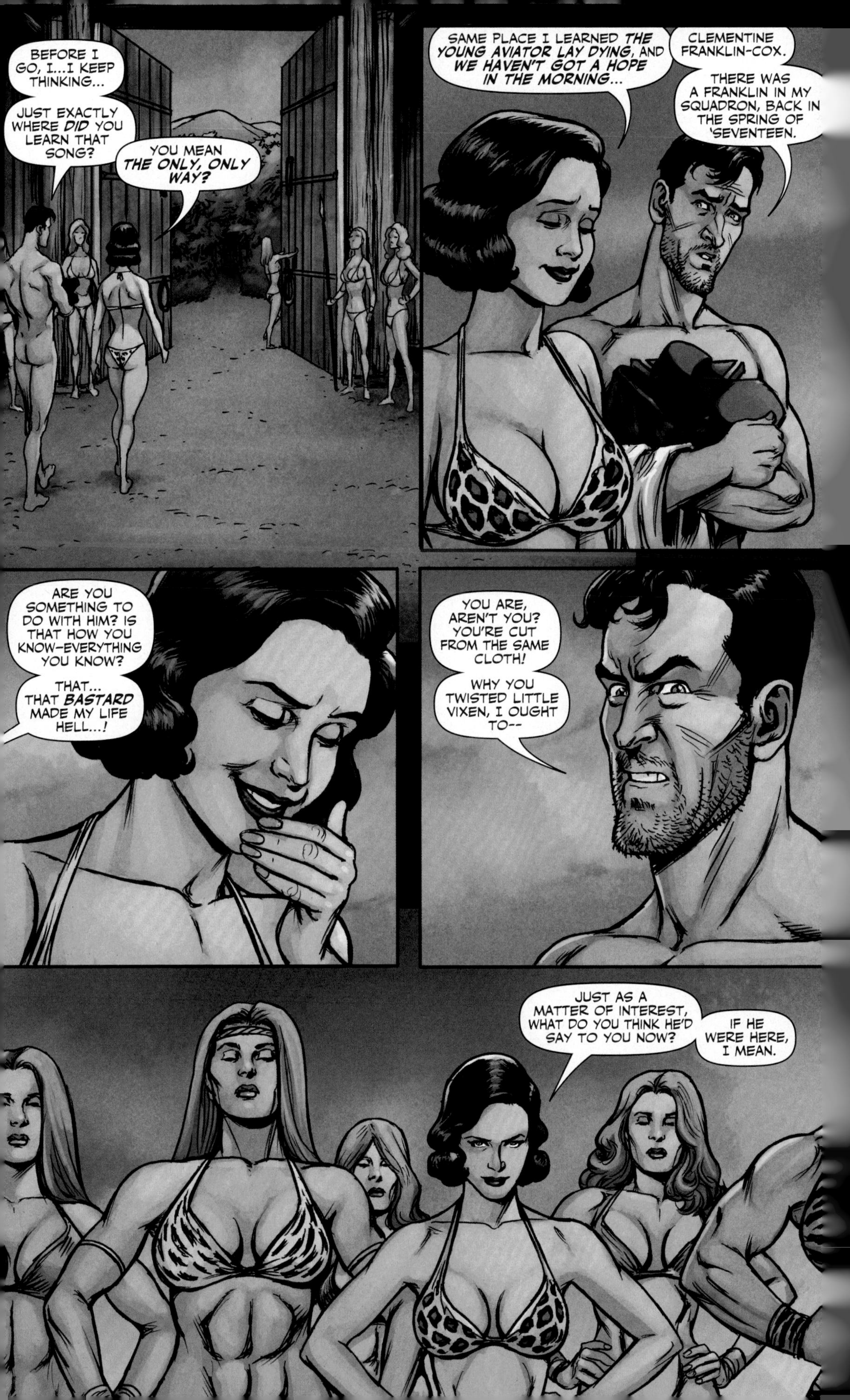
BEFORE I GO, I...I KEEP THINKING...
JUST EXACTLY WHERE DID YOU LEARN THAT SONG?
YOU MEAN THE ONLY, ONLY WAY?
SAME PLACE I LEARNED THE YOUNG AVIATOR LAY DYING, AND WE HAVEN'T GOT A HOPE IN THE MORNING...
CLEMENTINE FRANKLIN-COX.
THERE WAS A FRANKLIN IN MY SQUADRON, BACK IN THE SPRING OF 'SEVENTEEN.
ARE YOU SOMETHING TO DO WITH HIM? IS THAT HOW YOU KNOW--EVERYTHING YOU KNOW?
THAT... THAT BASTARD MADE MY LIFE HELL...!
YOU ARE, AREN'T YOU? YOU'RE CUT FROM THE SAME CLOTH!
WHY YOU TWISTED LITTLE VIXEN, I OUGHT TO--
JUST AS A MATTER OF INTEREST, WHAT DO YOU THINK HE'D SAY TO YOU NOW?
IF HE WERE HERE, I MEAN.

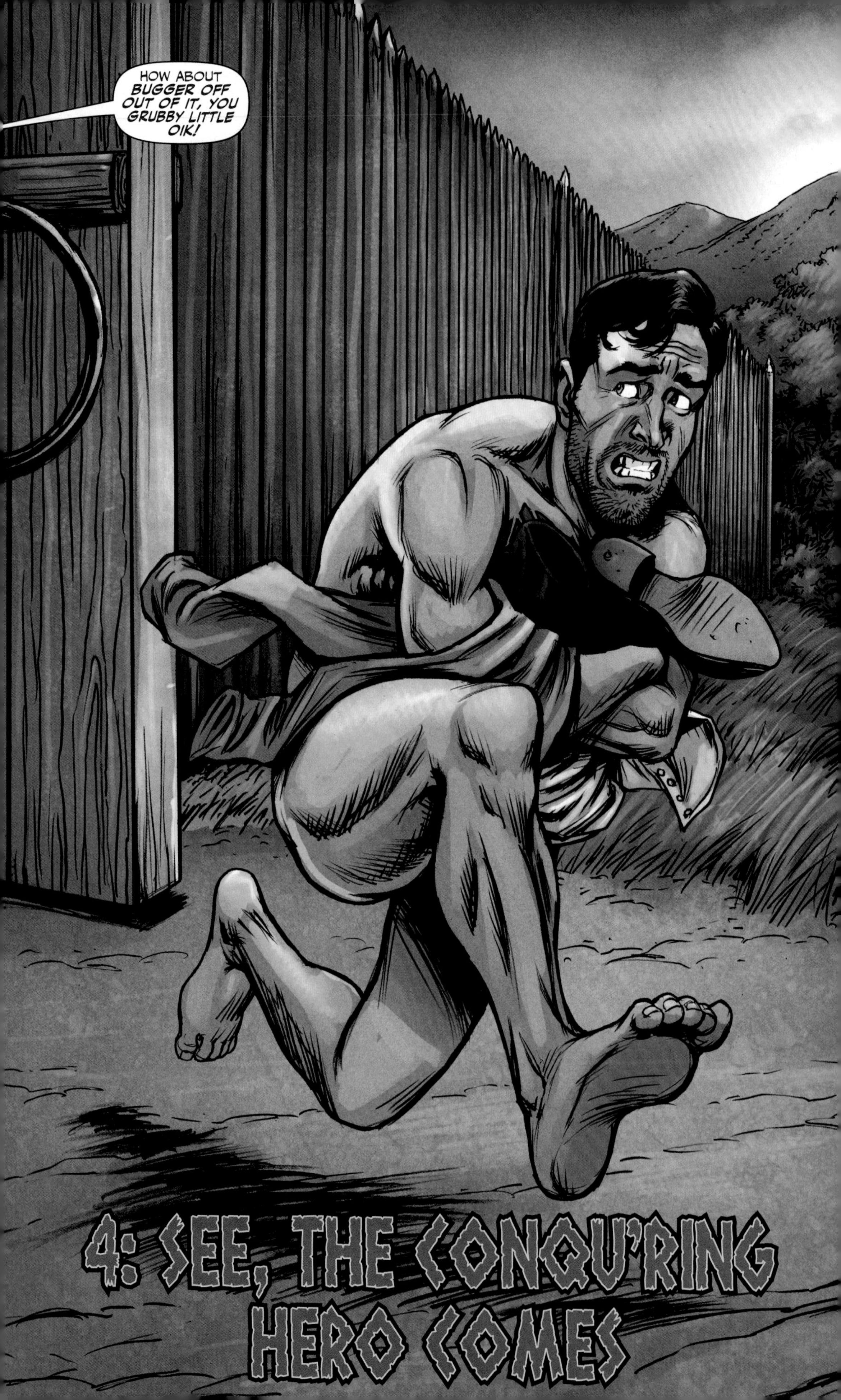
HOW ABOUT BUGGER OFF OUT OF IT, YOU GRUBBY LITTLE OIK!
4: SEE, THE CONQU'RING HERO COMES

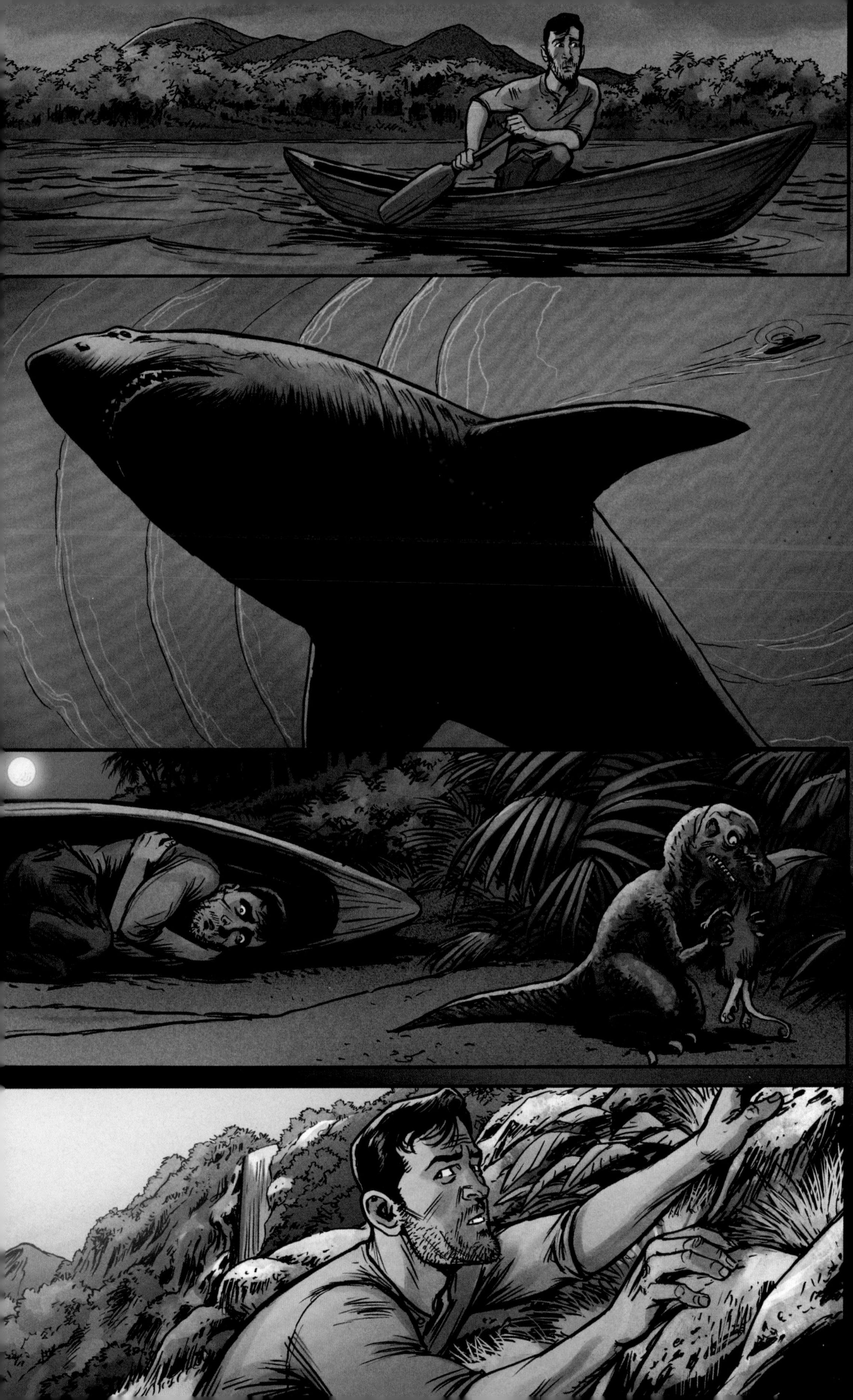

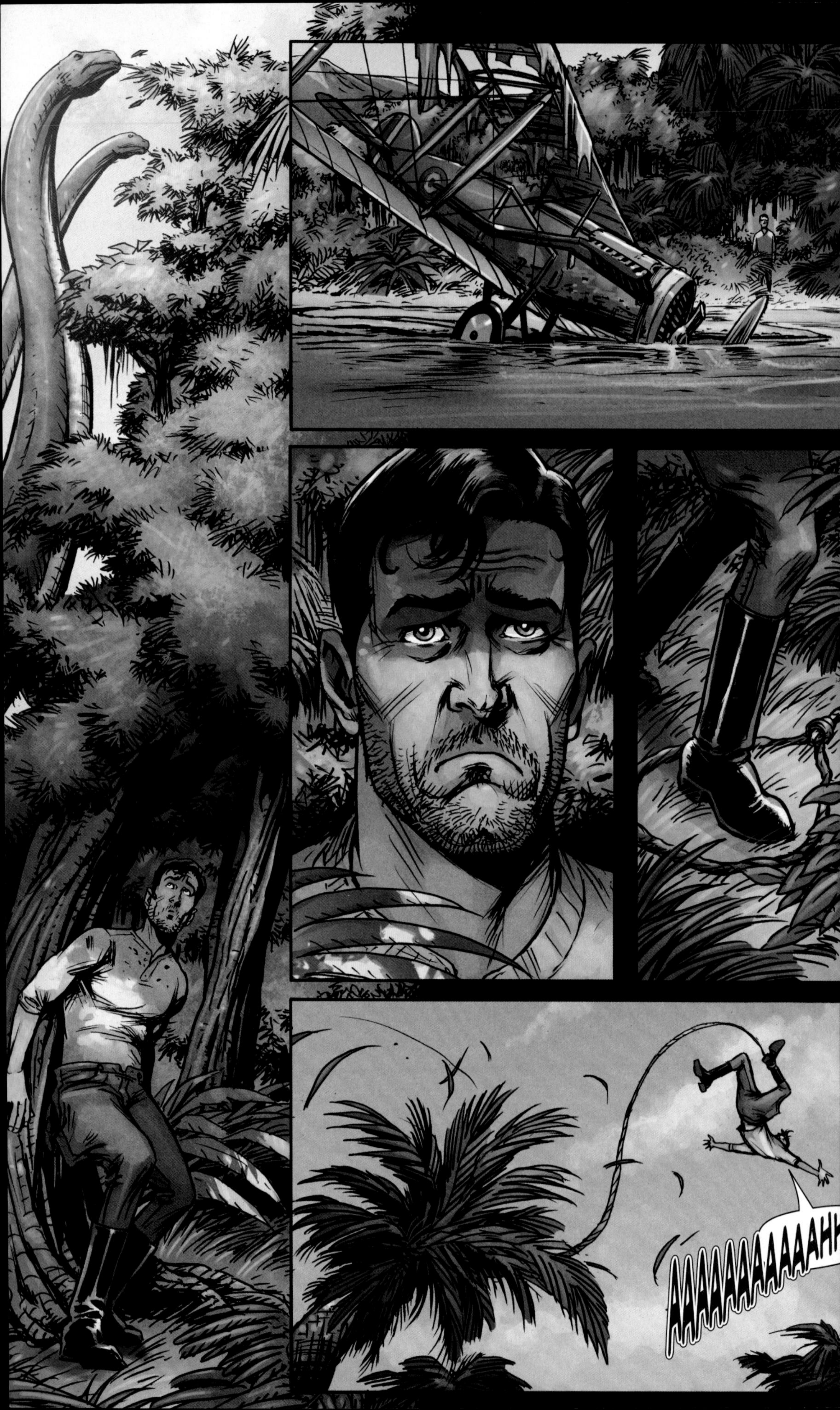

AAAAAAAAAAAAH

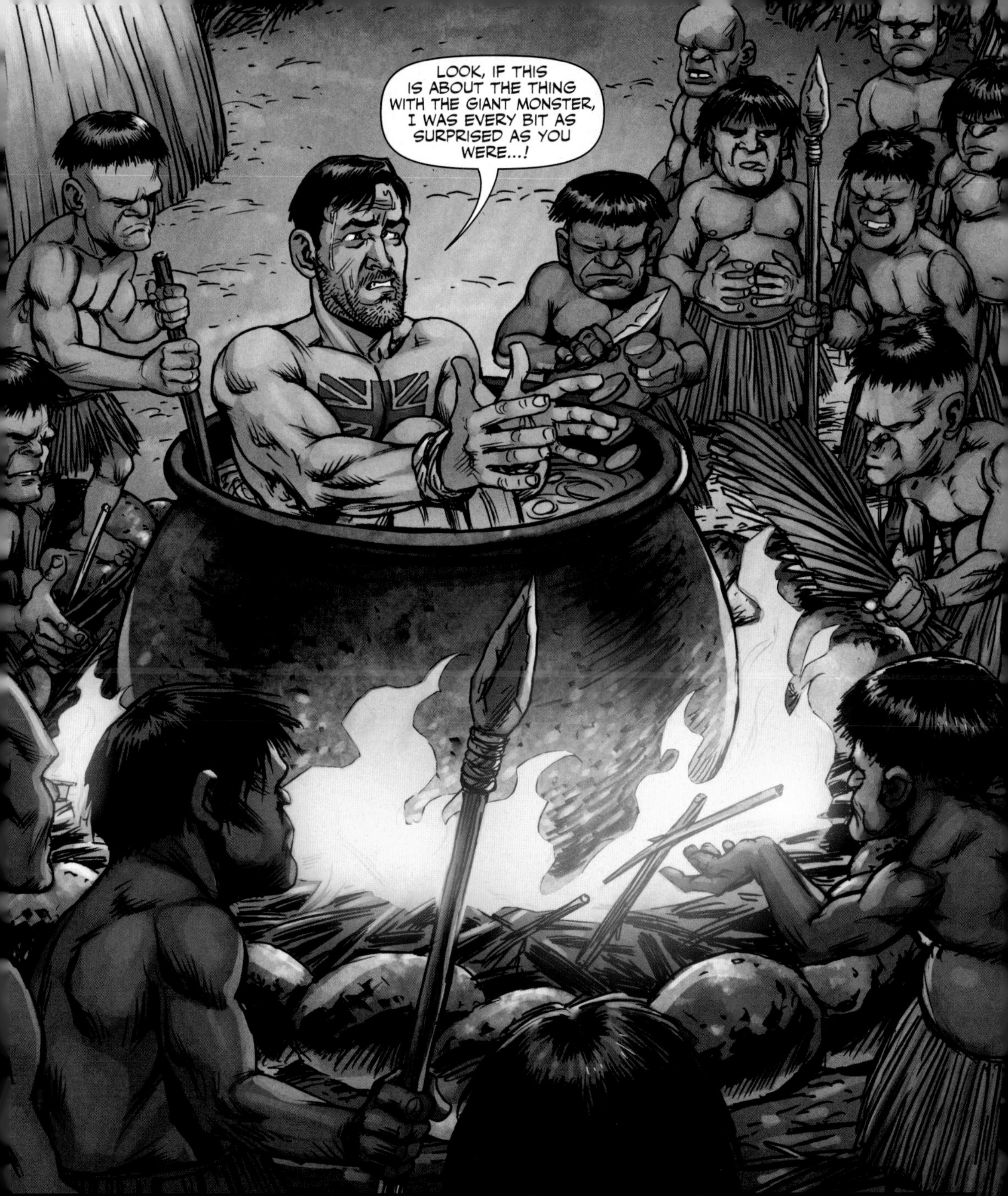
LOOK, IF THIS IS ABOUT THE THING WITH THE GIANT MONSTER, I WAS EVERY BIT AS SURPRISED AS YOU WERE...!

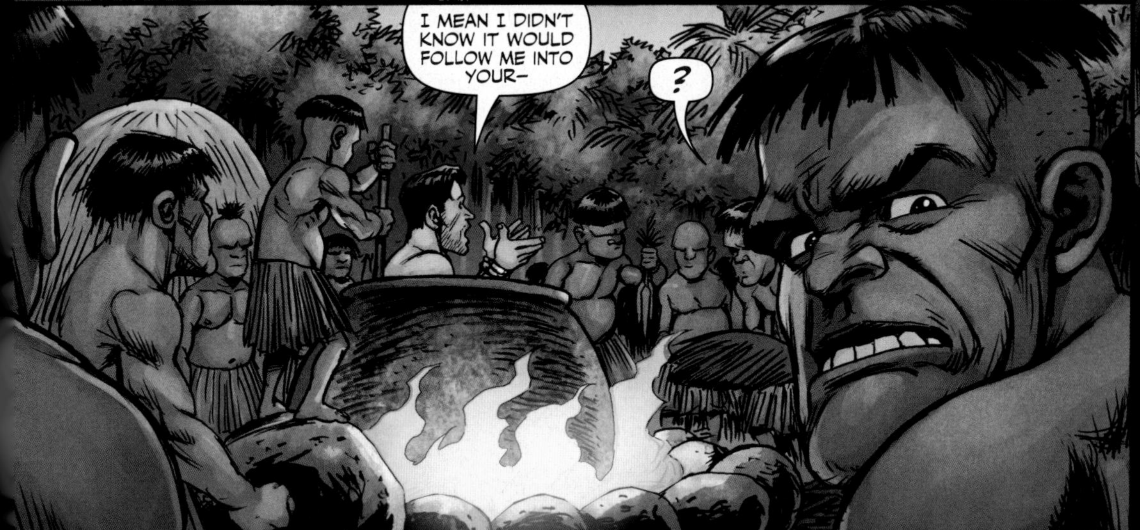
I MEAN I DIDN'T KNOW IT WOULD FOLLOW ME INTO YOUR–
?

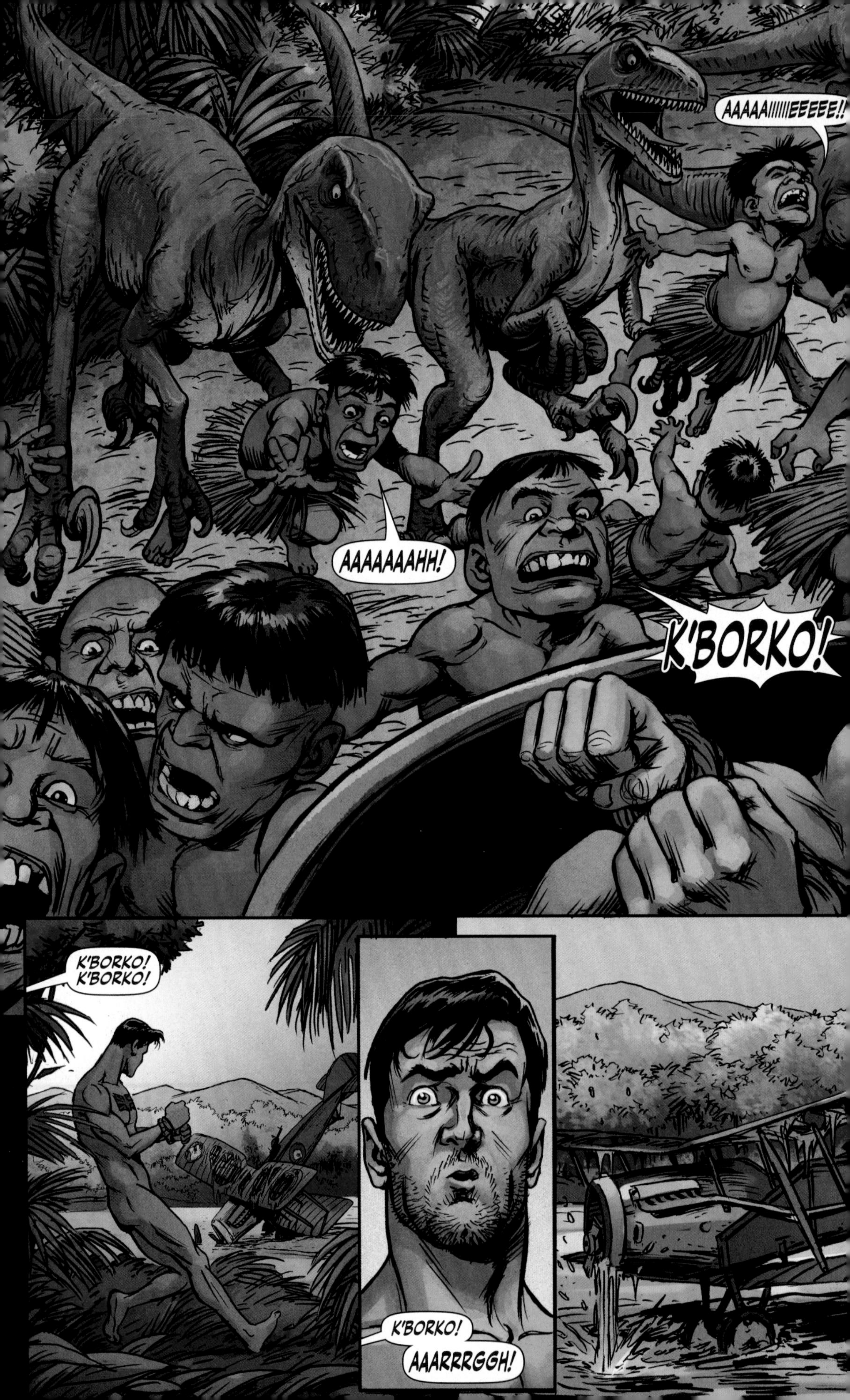
AAAAAIIIIIIEEEEE!!
AAAAAAAHH!
K'BORKO!
K'BORKO! K'BORKO!
K'BORKO! AAARRRGGH!

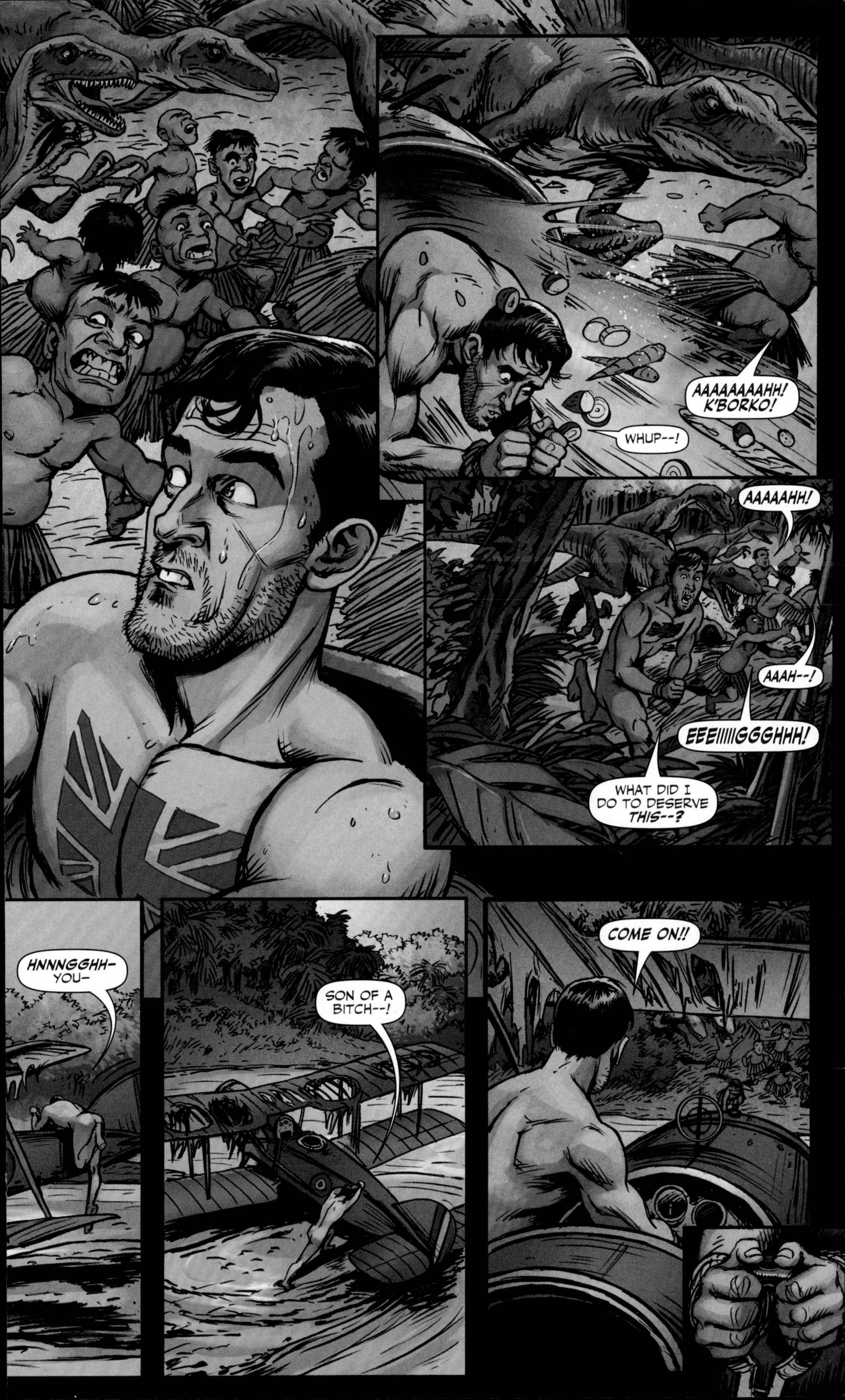
AAAAAAAAAH! K'BORKO!
WHUP--!
AAAAAHH!
AAAH--!
EEEIIIIIIGGGHHH!
WHAT DID I DO TO DESERVE THIS--?
HNNNGGHH-YOU-
SON OF A BITCH--!
COME ON!!

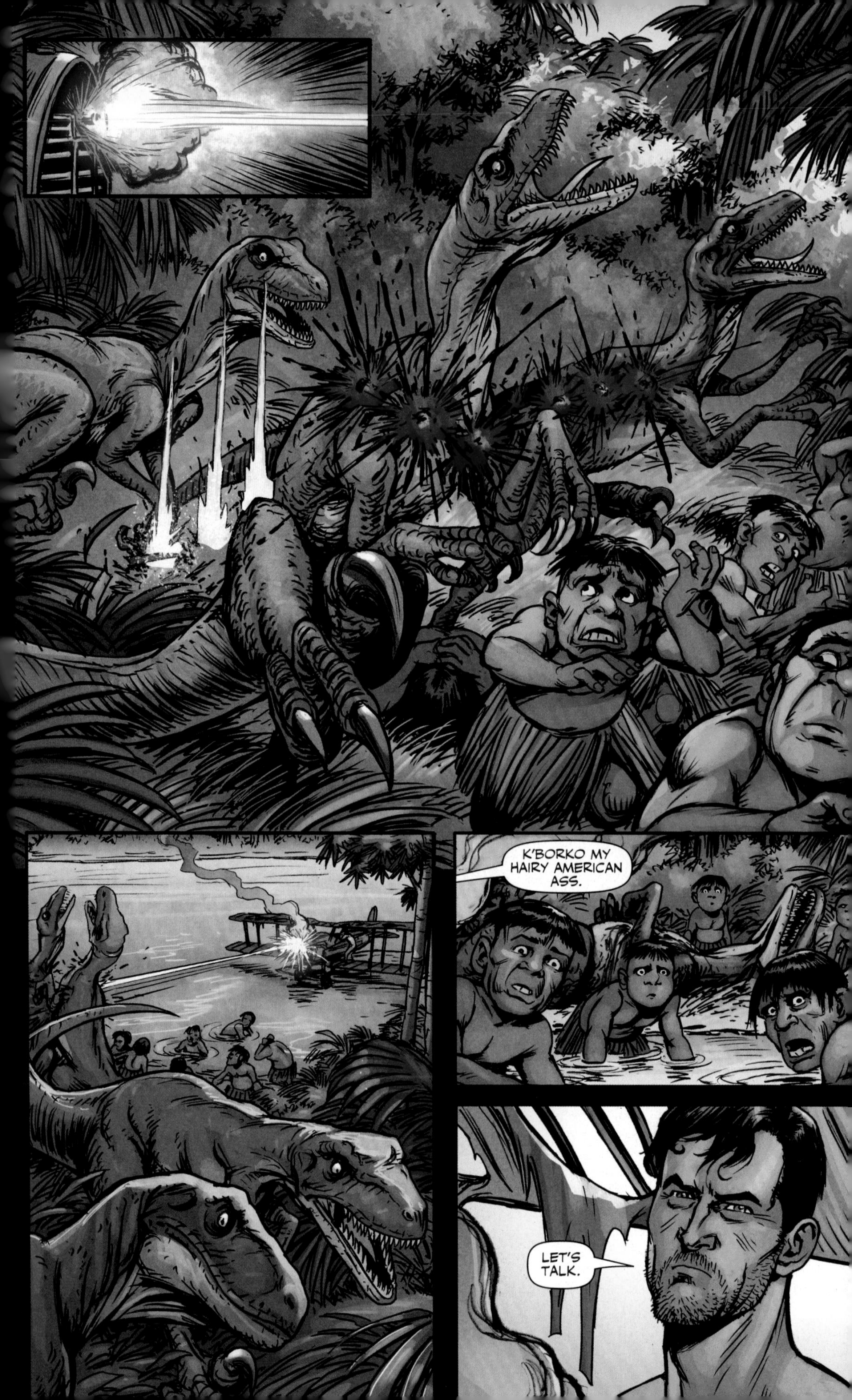
K'BORKO MY HAIRY AMERICAN ASS.
LET'S TALK.

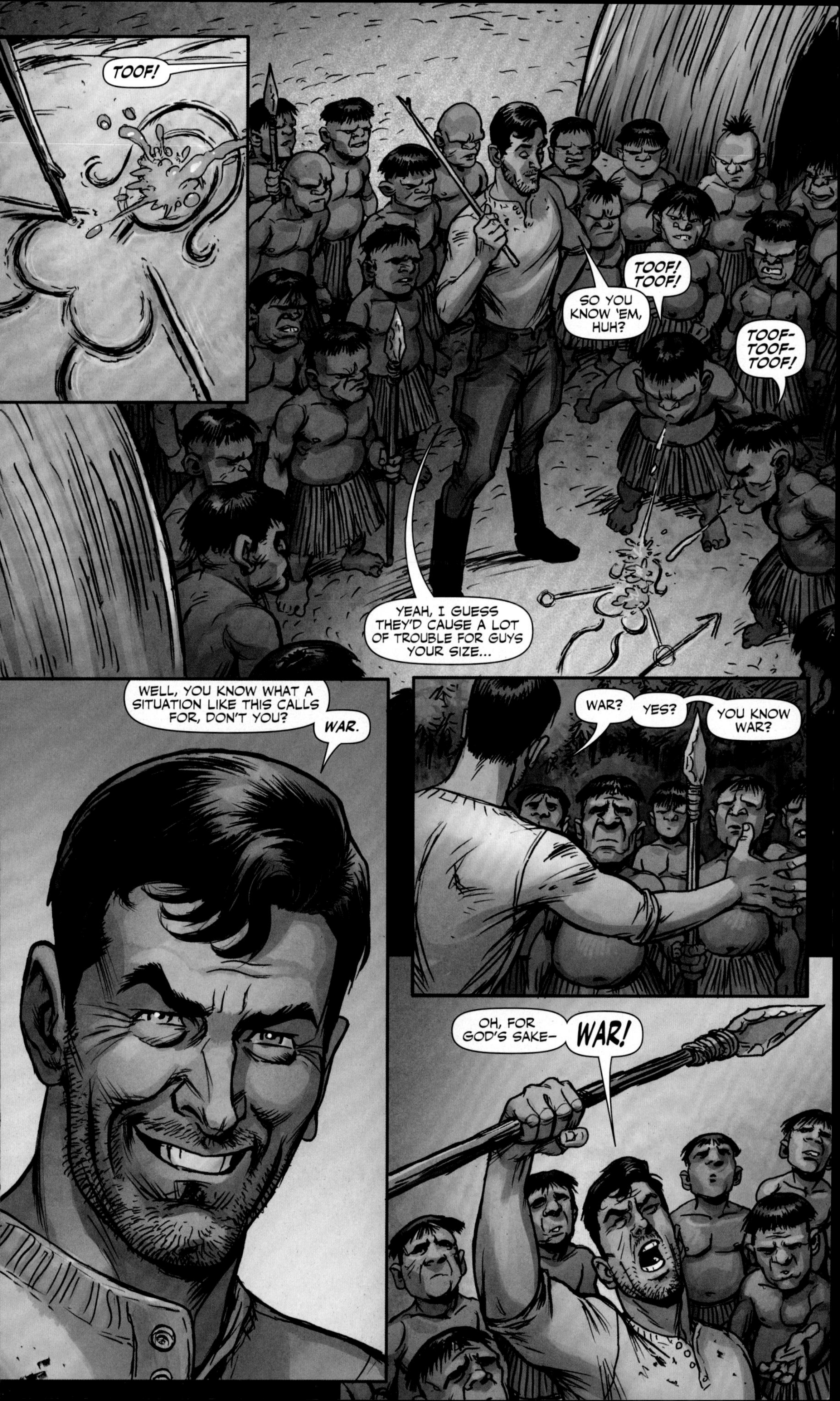
TOOF!
SO YOU KNOW 'EM, HUH?
TOOF! TOOF!
TOOF-TOOF-TOOF!
YEAH, I GUESS THEY'D CAUSE A LOT OF TROUBLE FOR GUYS YOUR SIZE...
WELL, YOU KNOW WHAT A SITUATION LIKE THIS CALLS FOR, DON'T YOU?
WAR.
WAR?
YES?
YOU KNOW WAR?
OH, FOR GOD'S SAKE–
WAR!

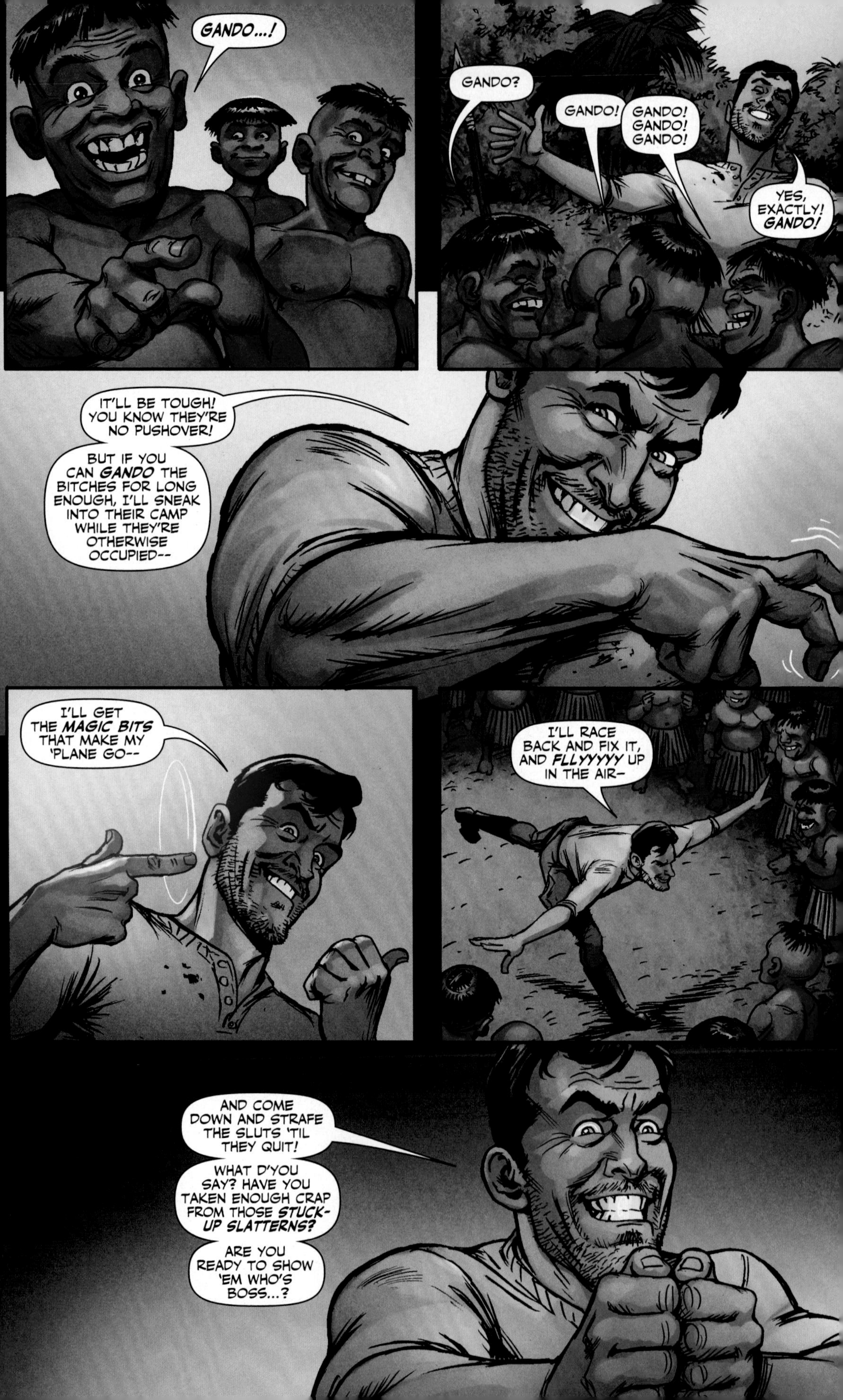
GANDO...!
GANDO?
GANDO!
GANDO! GANDO! GANDO!
YES, EXACTLY! GANDO!
IT'LL BE TOUGH! YOU KNOW THEY'RE NO PUSHOVER!
BUT IF YOU CAN GANDO THE BITCHES FOR LONG ENOUGH, I'LL SNEAK INTO THEIR CAMP WHILE THEY'RE OTHERWISE OCCUPIED--
I'LL GET THE MAGIC BITS THAT MAKE MY 'PLANE GO--
I'LL RACE BACK AND FIX IT, AND FLLYYYYY UP IN THE AIR-
AND COME DOWN AND STRAFE THE SLUTS 'TIL THEY QUIT!
WHAT D'YOU SAY? HAVE YOU TAKEN ENOUGH CRAP FROM THOSE STUCK-UP SLATTERNS?
ARE YOU READY TO SHOW 'EM WHO'S BOSS...?

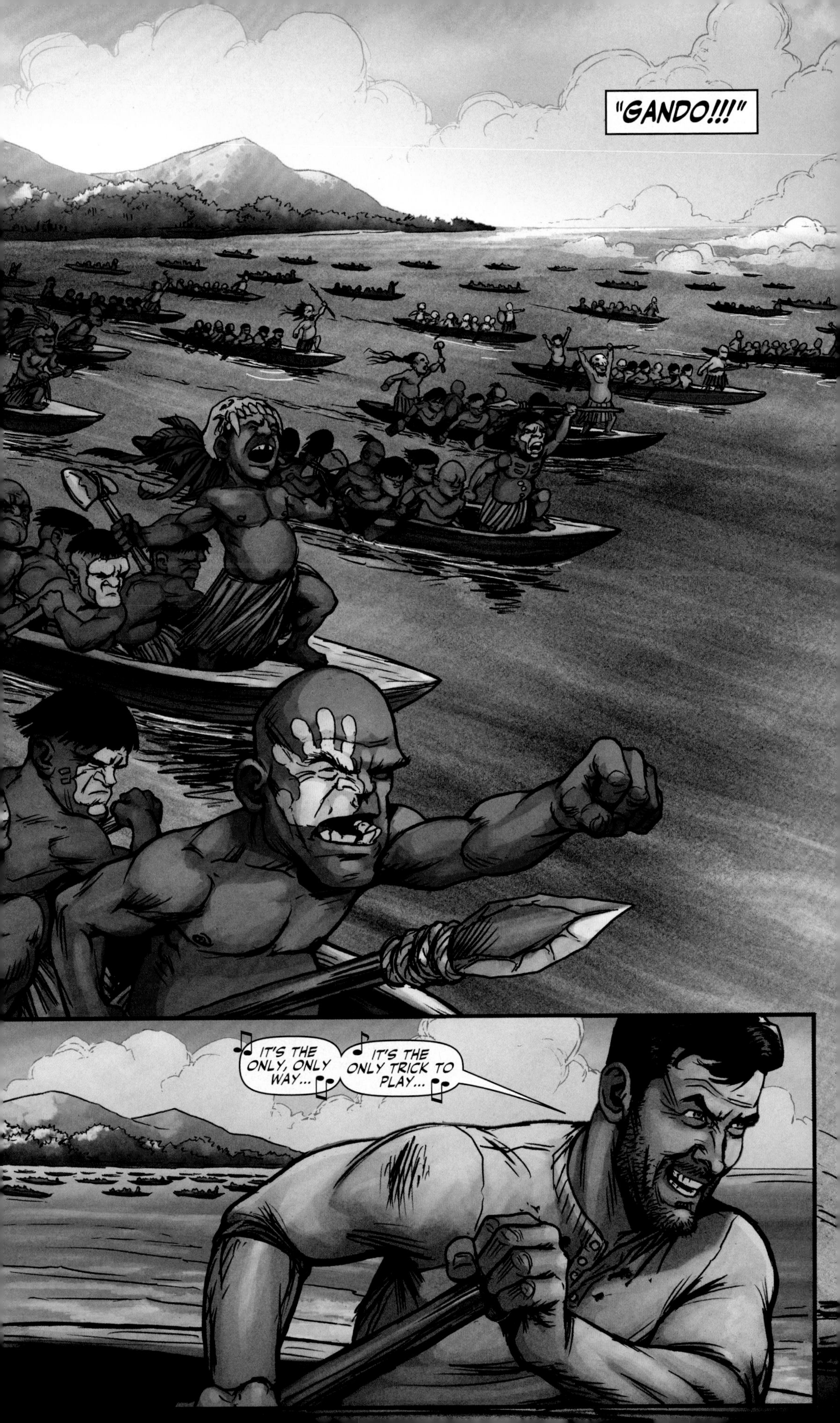
"GANDO!!!"
IT'S THE ONLY, ONLY WAY...
IT'S THE ONLY TRICK TO PLAY...

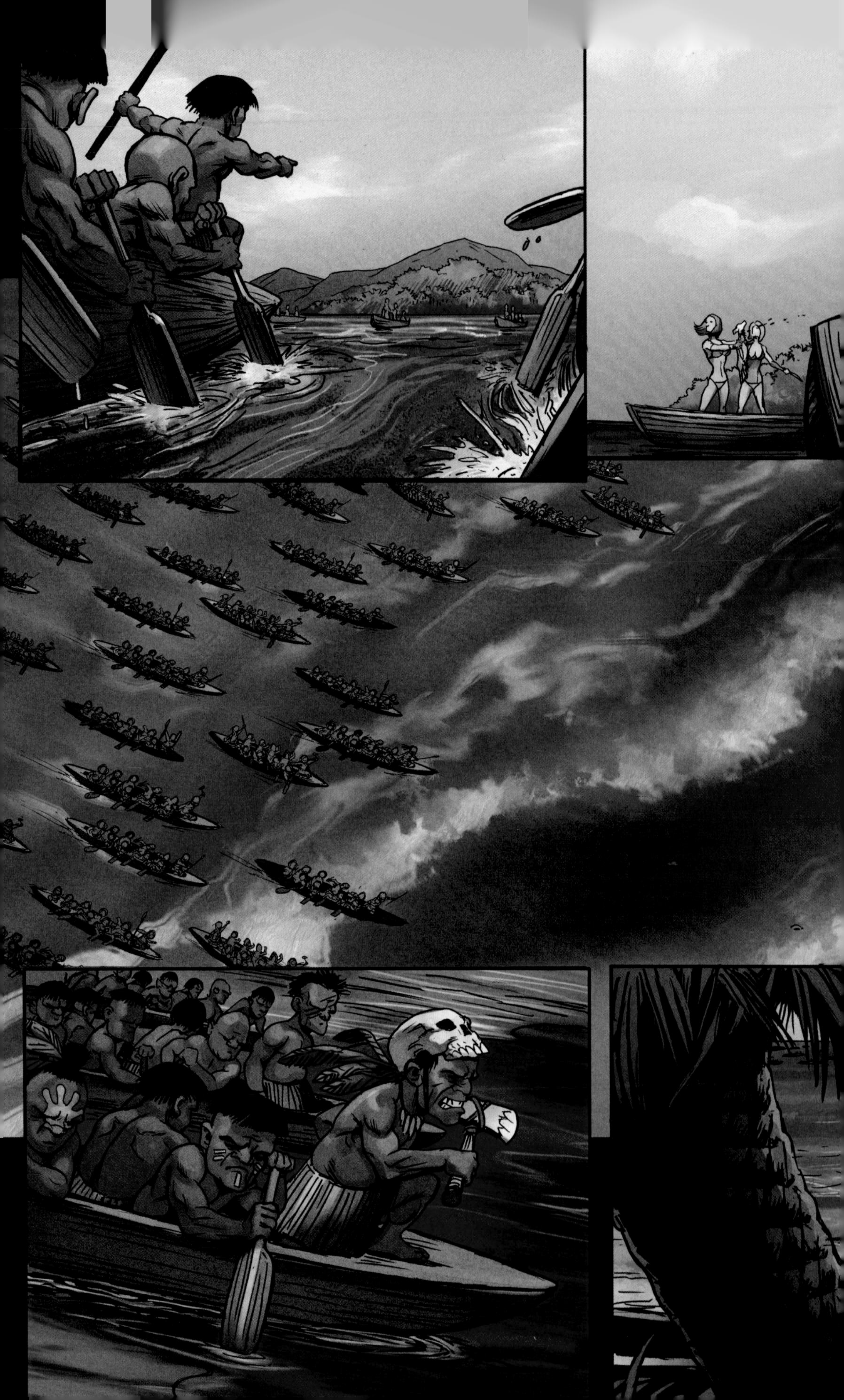

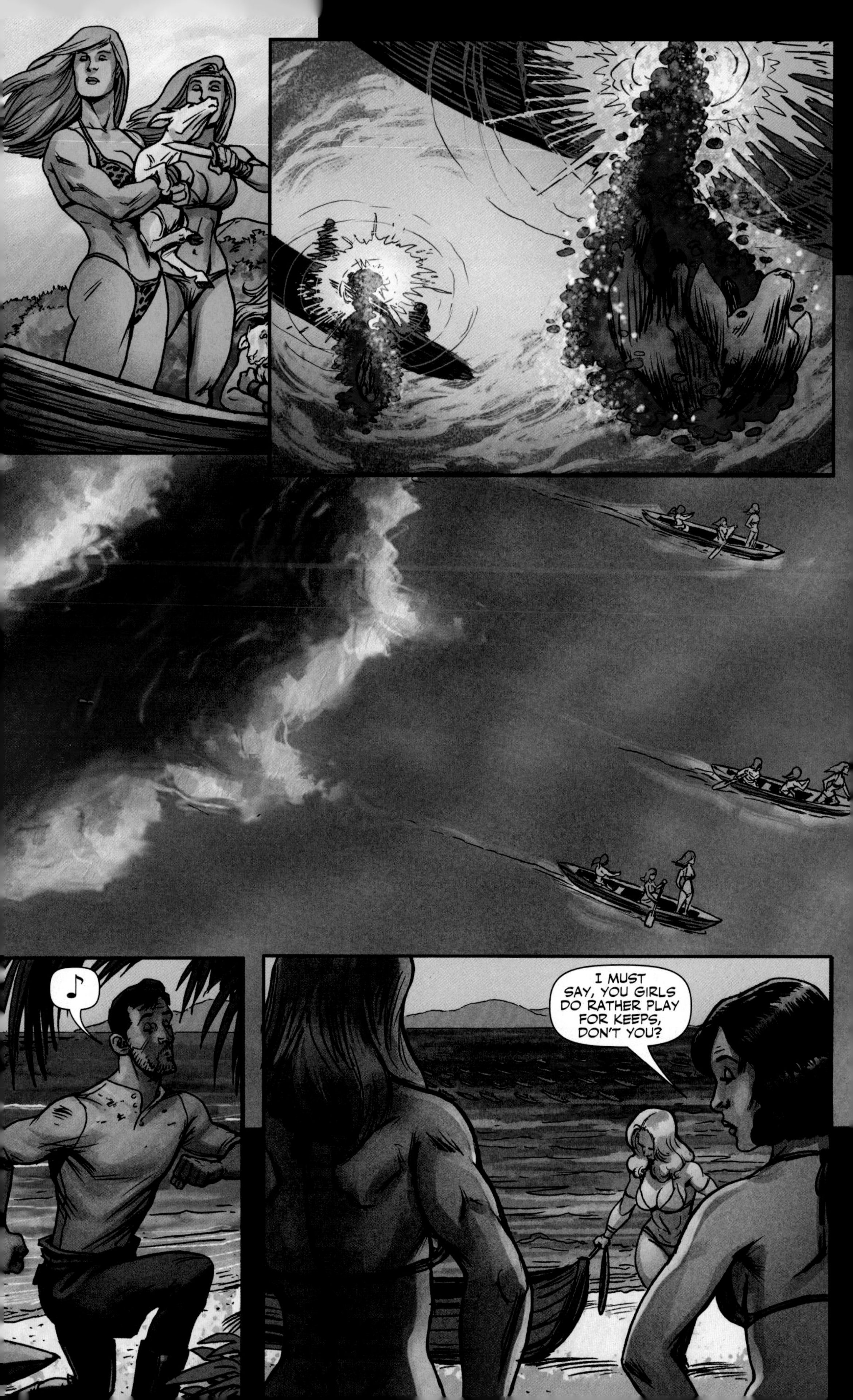
♪
I MUST SAY, YOU GIRLS DO RATHER PLAY FOR KEEPS, DON'T YOU?

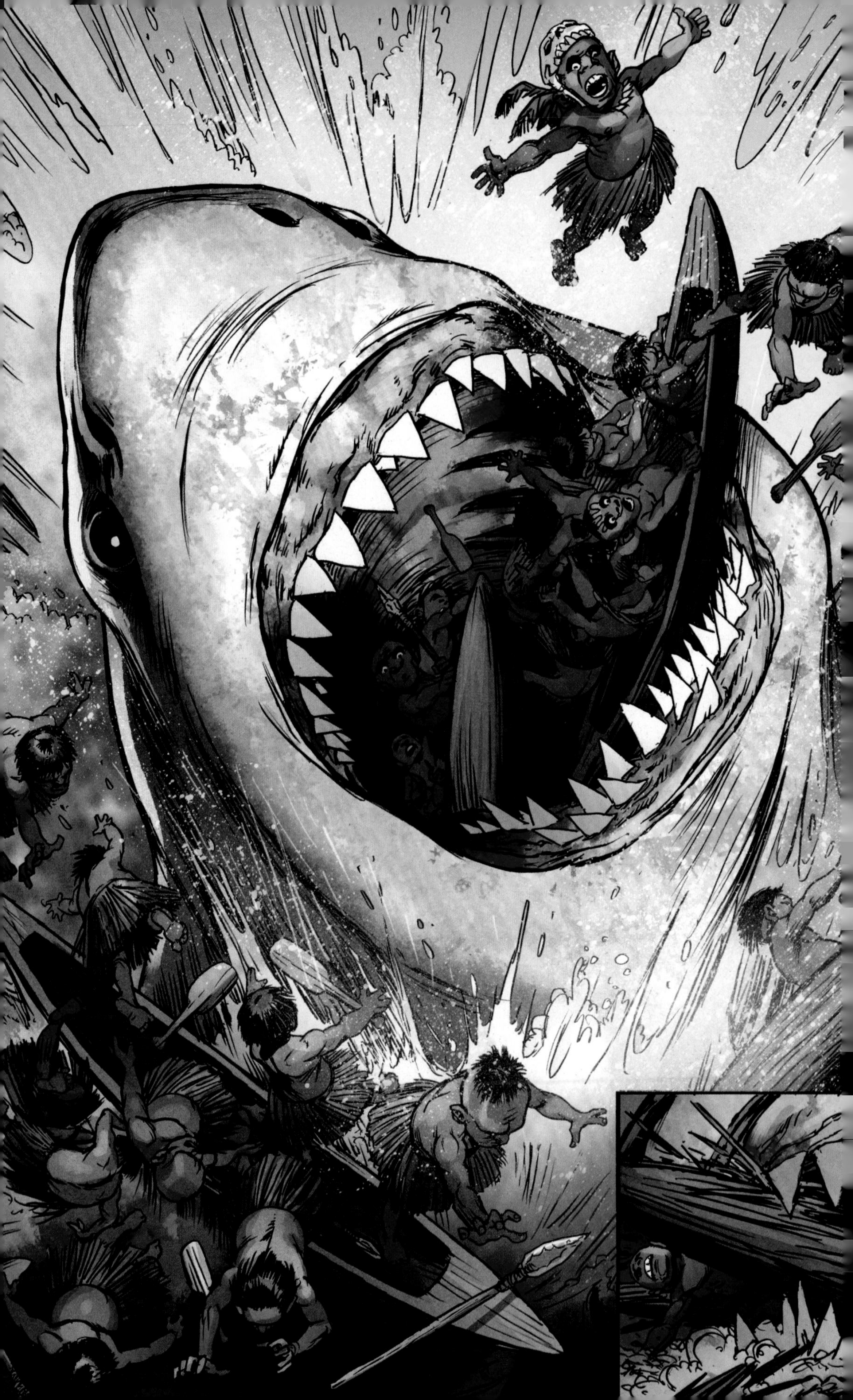

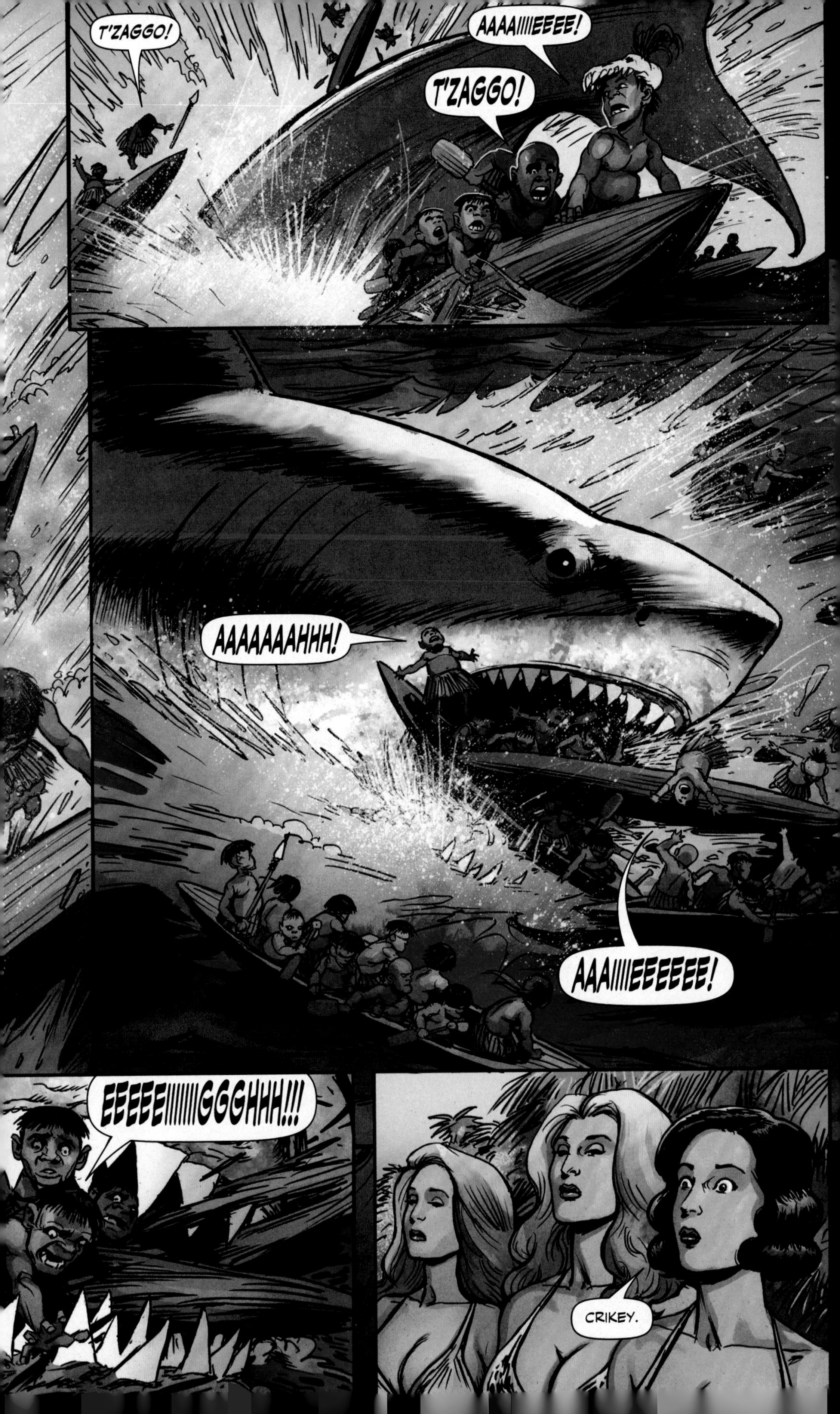
T'ZAGGO!
AAAAIIIIIEEEE!
T'ZAGGO!
AAAAAAAHHH!
AAAIIIIIEEEEEE!
EEEEEIIIIIIIIGGGHHH!!!
CRIKEY.

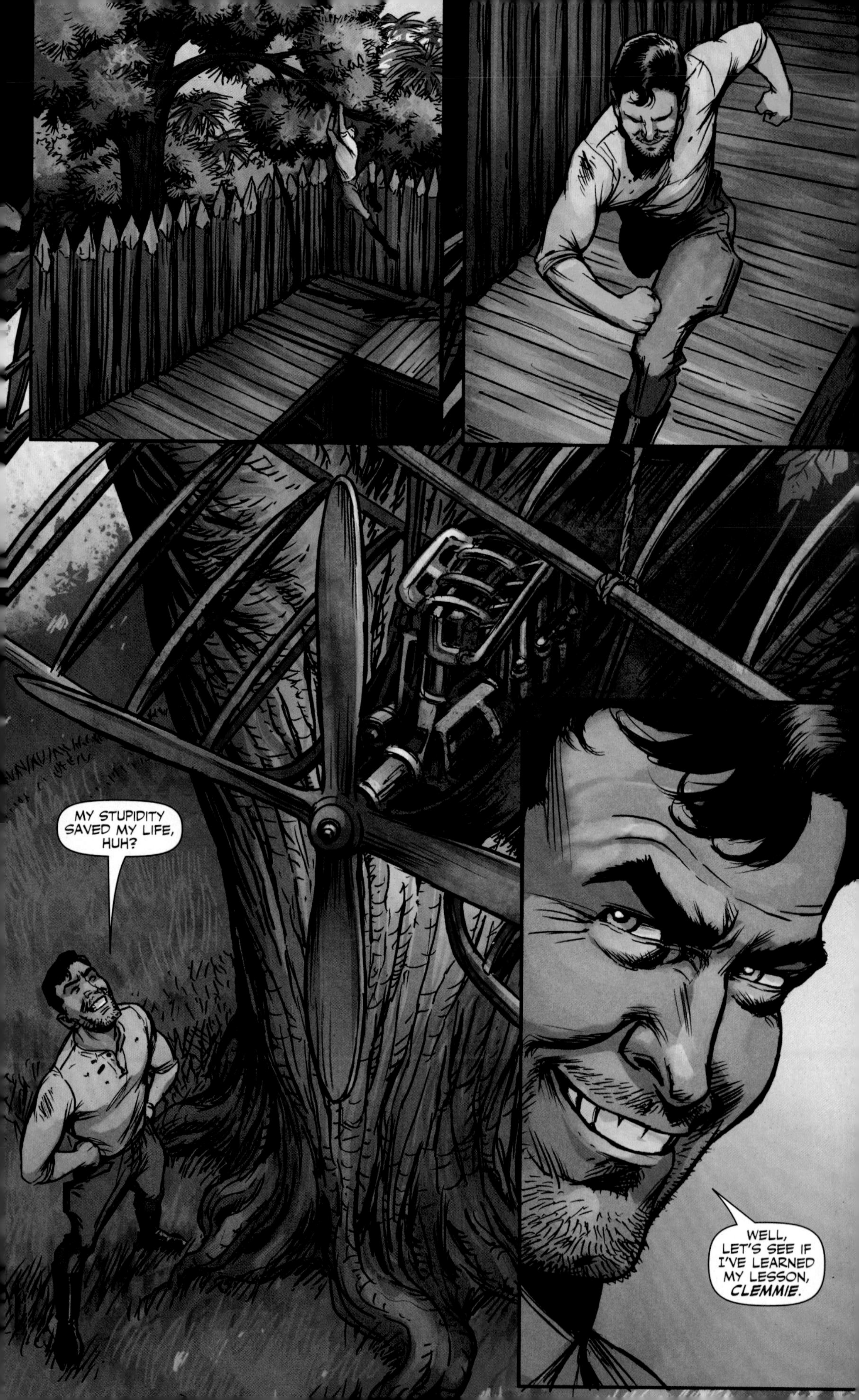
MY STUPIDITY SAVED MY LIFE, HUH?
WELL, LET'S SEE IF I'VE LEARNED MY LESSON, *CLEMMIE*.

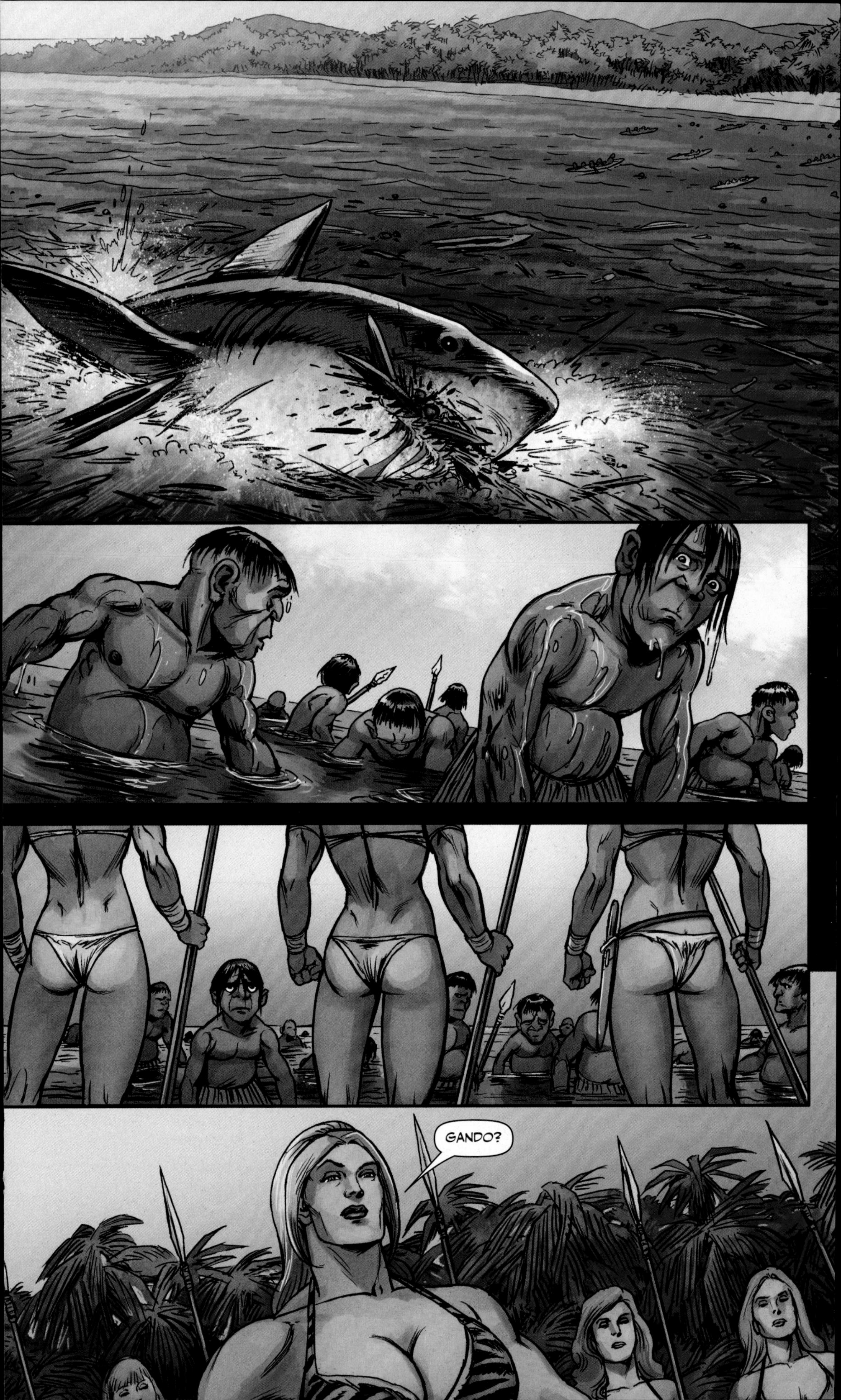
GANDO?

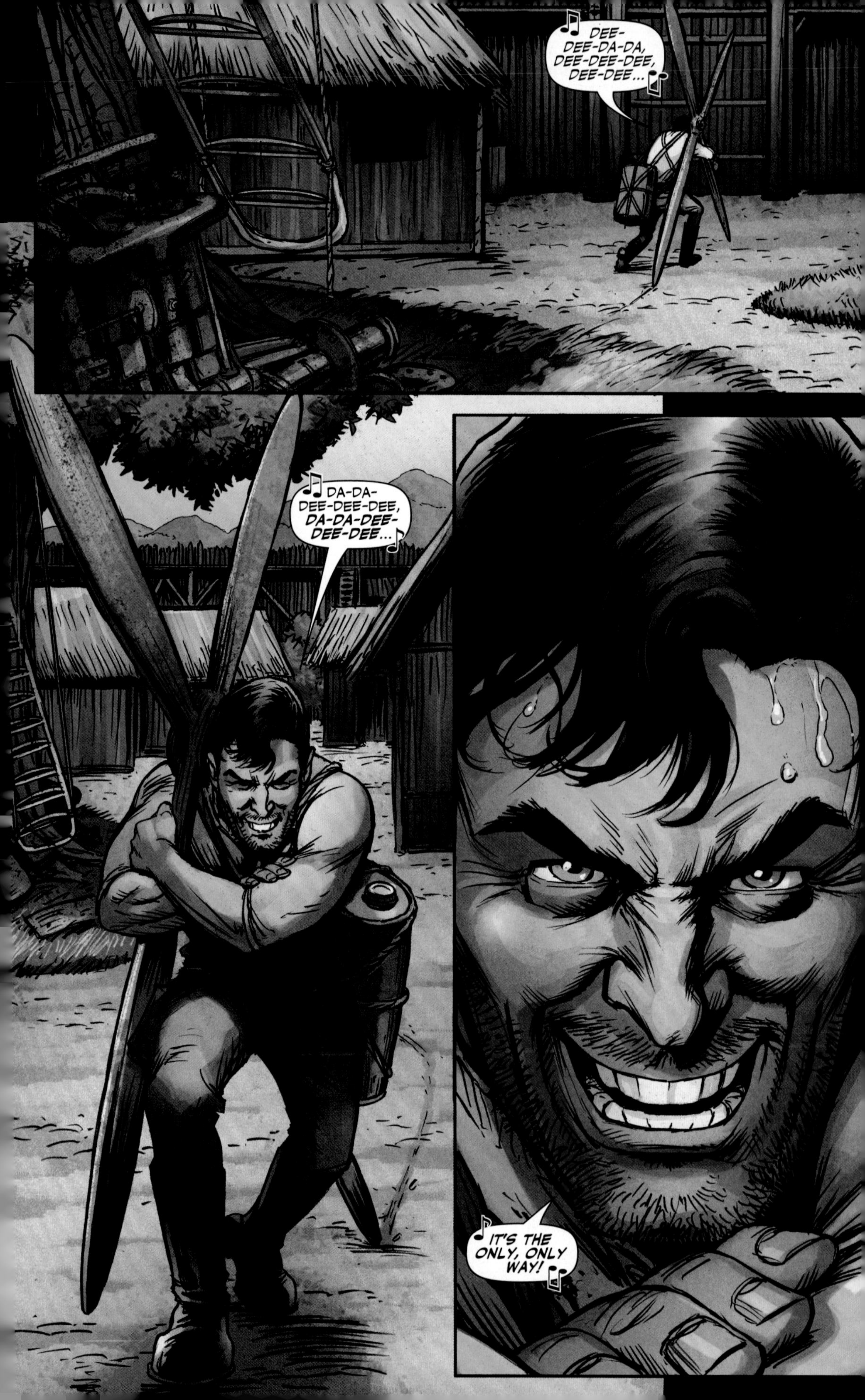
DEE-DEE-DA-DA, DEE-DEE-DEE, DEE-DEE...
DA-DA-DEE-DEE-DEE, DA-DA-DEE-DEE-DEE...
IT'S THE ONLY, ONLY WAY!

#2 PAGES 4-5 PROCESS BY RUSS BRAUN

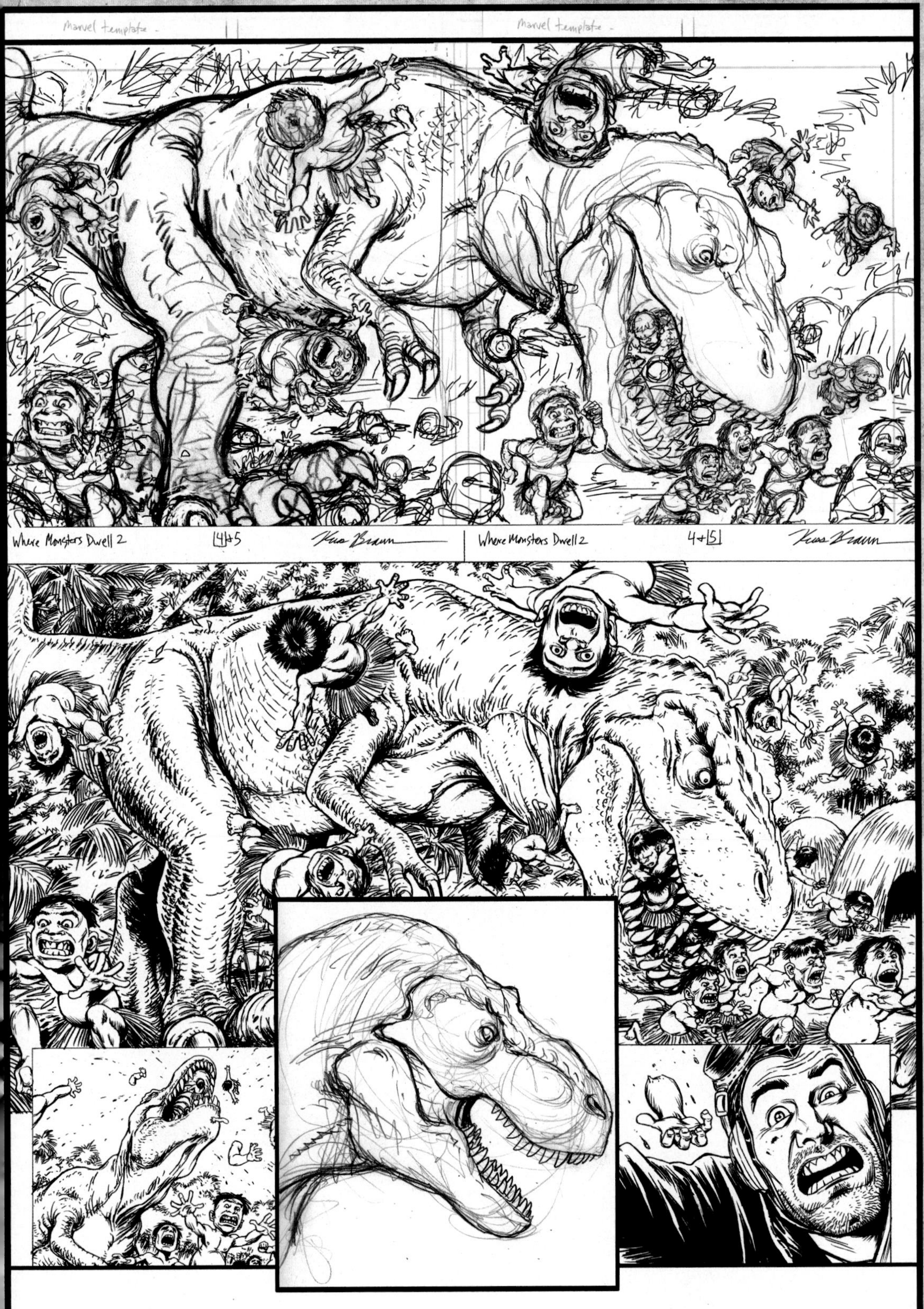
Marvel template -
Marvel template -
Where Monsters Dwell 2
4+5
Where Monsters Dwell 2
4+5

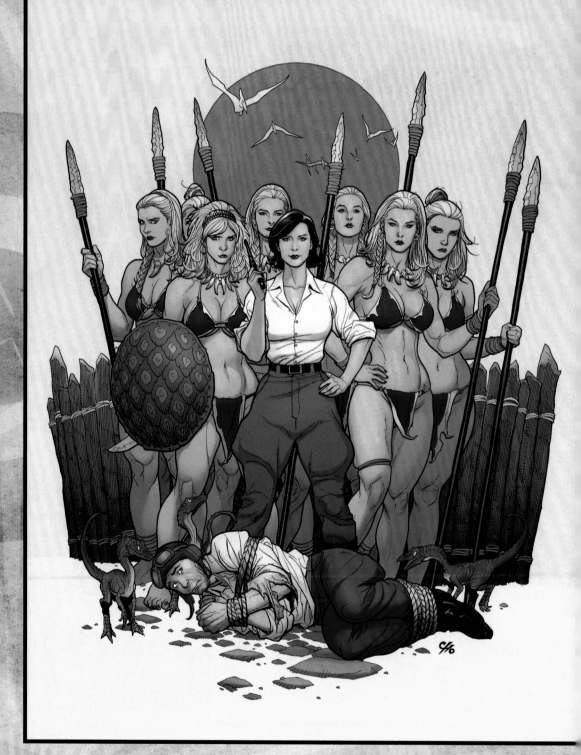

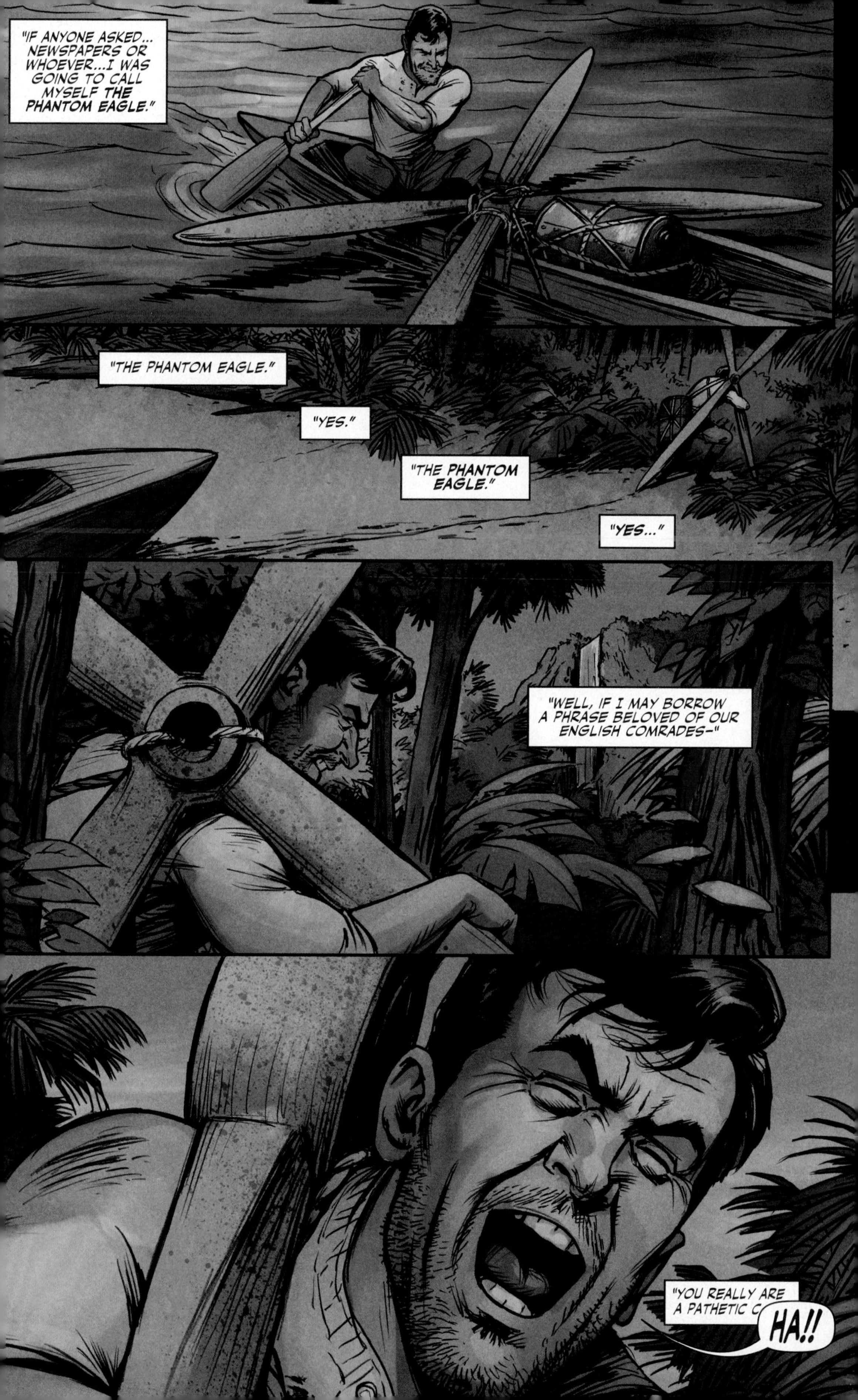
"IF ANYONE ASKED... NEWSPAPERS OR WHOEVER...I WAS GOING TO CALL MYSELF THE PHANTOM EAGLE."
"THE PHANTOM EAGLE."
"YES."
"THE PHANTOM EAGLE."
"YES..."
"WELL, IF I MAY BORROW A PHRASE BELOVED OF OUR ENGLISH COMRADES-"
"YOU REALLY ARE A PATHETIC C
HA!!

5: WHAT COMES

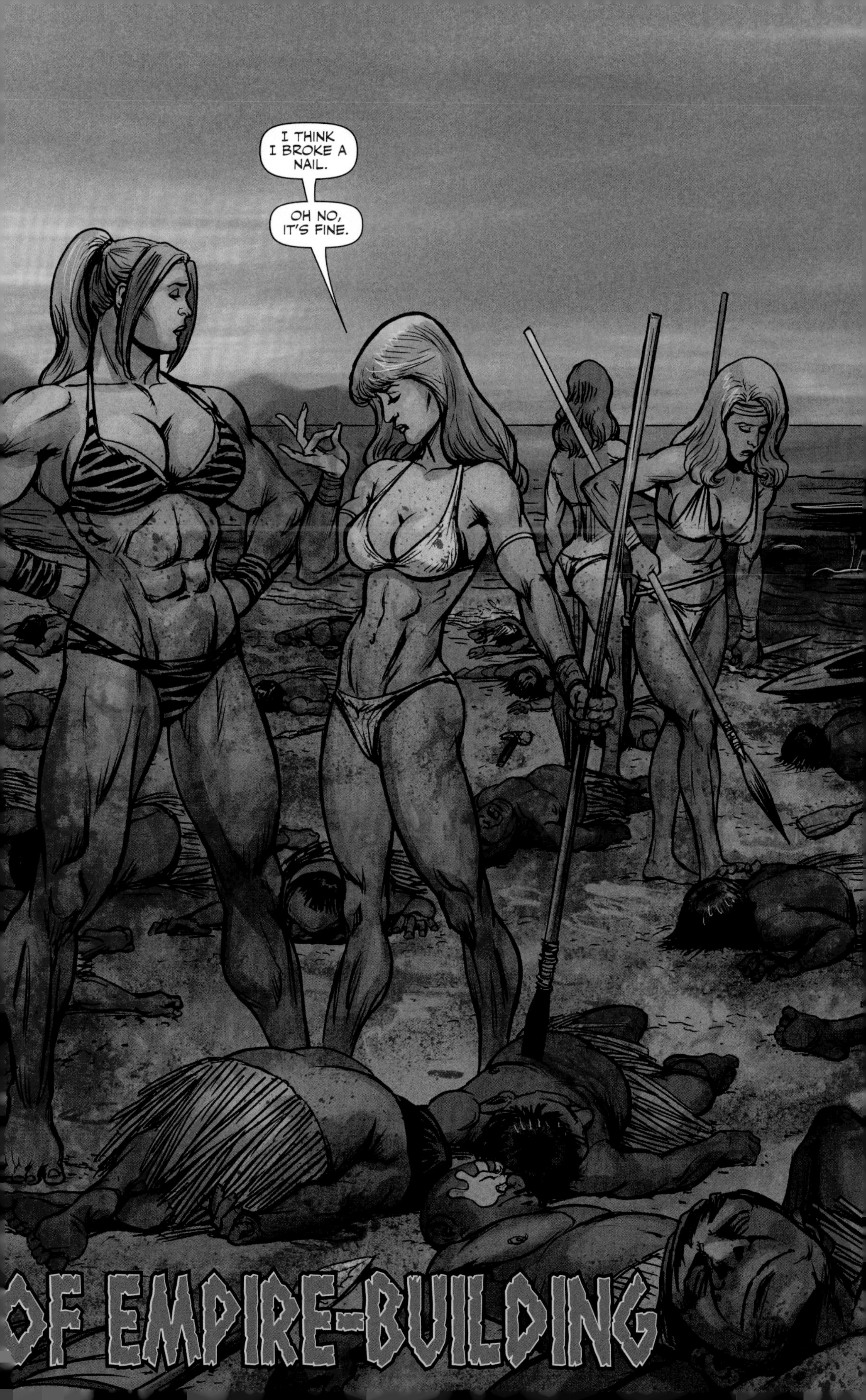
I THINK I BROKE A NAIL.
OH NO, IT'S FINE.
OF EMPIRE-BUILDING

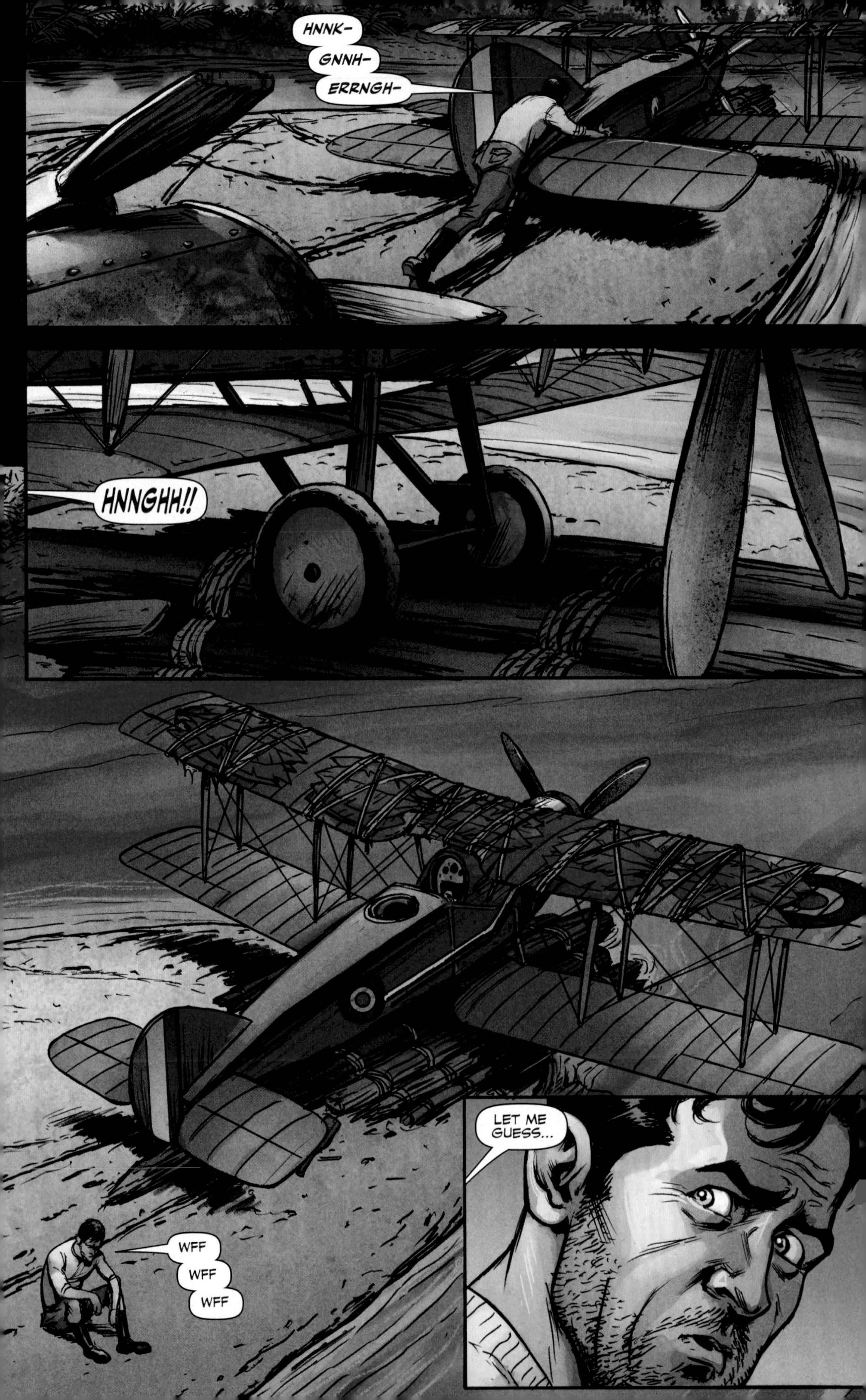
HNNK-
GNNH-
ERRNGH-
HNNGHH!!
WFF
WFF
WFF
LET ME GUESS...

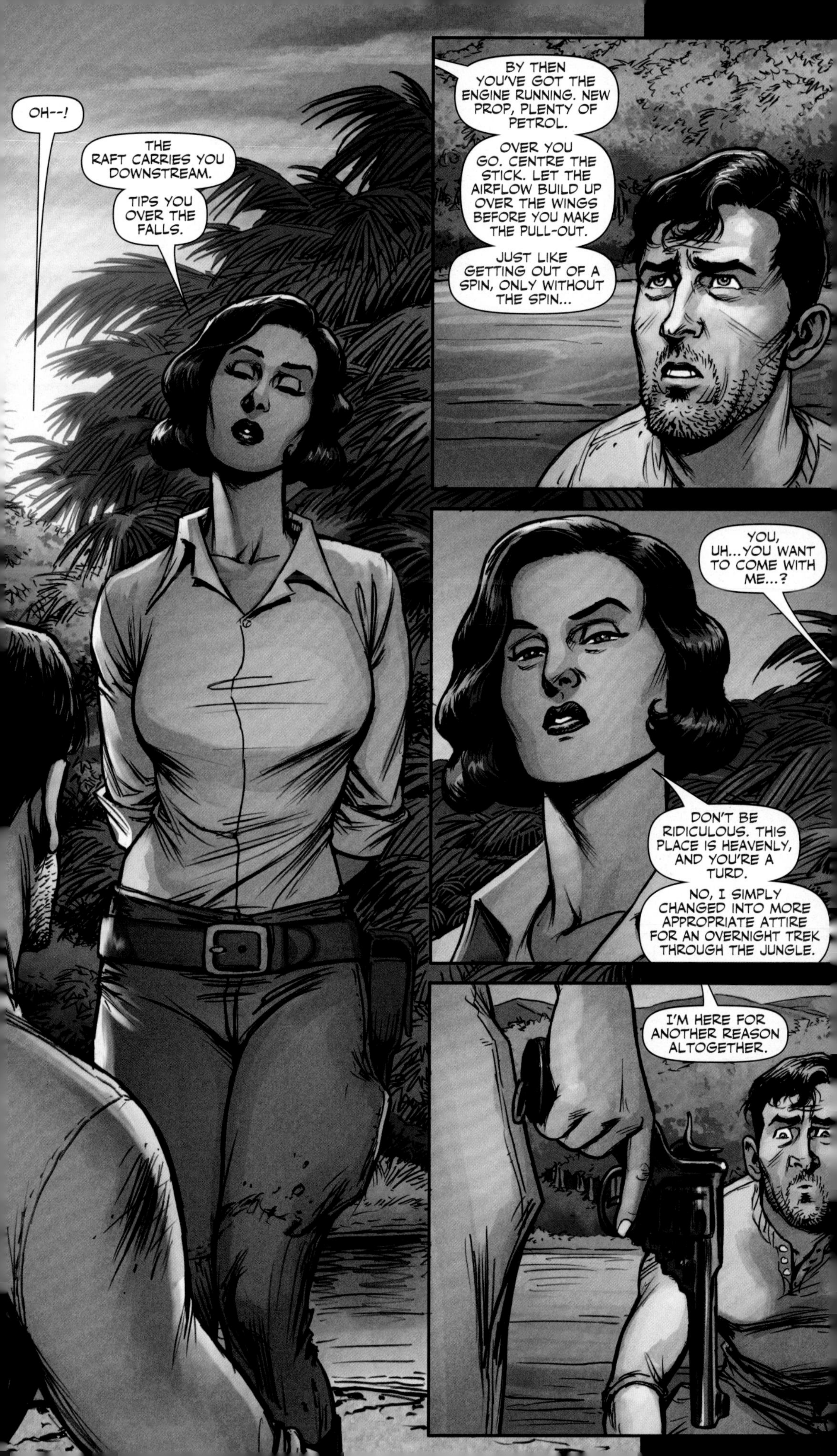

OH--!
THE RAFT CARRIES YOU DOWNSTREAM.
TIPS YOU OVER THE FALLS.
BY THEN YOU'VE GOT THE ENGINE RUNNING. NEW PROP, PLENTY OF PETROL.
OVER YOU GO. CENTRE THE STICK. LET THE AIRFLOW BUILD UP OVER THE WINGS BEFORE YOU MAKE THE PULL-OUT.
JUST LIKE GETTING OUT OF A SPIN, ONLY WITHOUT THE SPIN...
YOU, UH...YOU WANT TO COME WITH ME...?
DON'T BE RIDICULOUS. THIS PLACE IS HEAVENLY, AND YOU'RE A TURD.
NO, I SIMPLY CHANGED INTO MORE APPROPRIATE ATTIRE FOR AN OVERNIGHT TREK THROUGH THE JUNGLE.
I'M HERE FOR ANOTHER REASON ALTOGETHER.

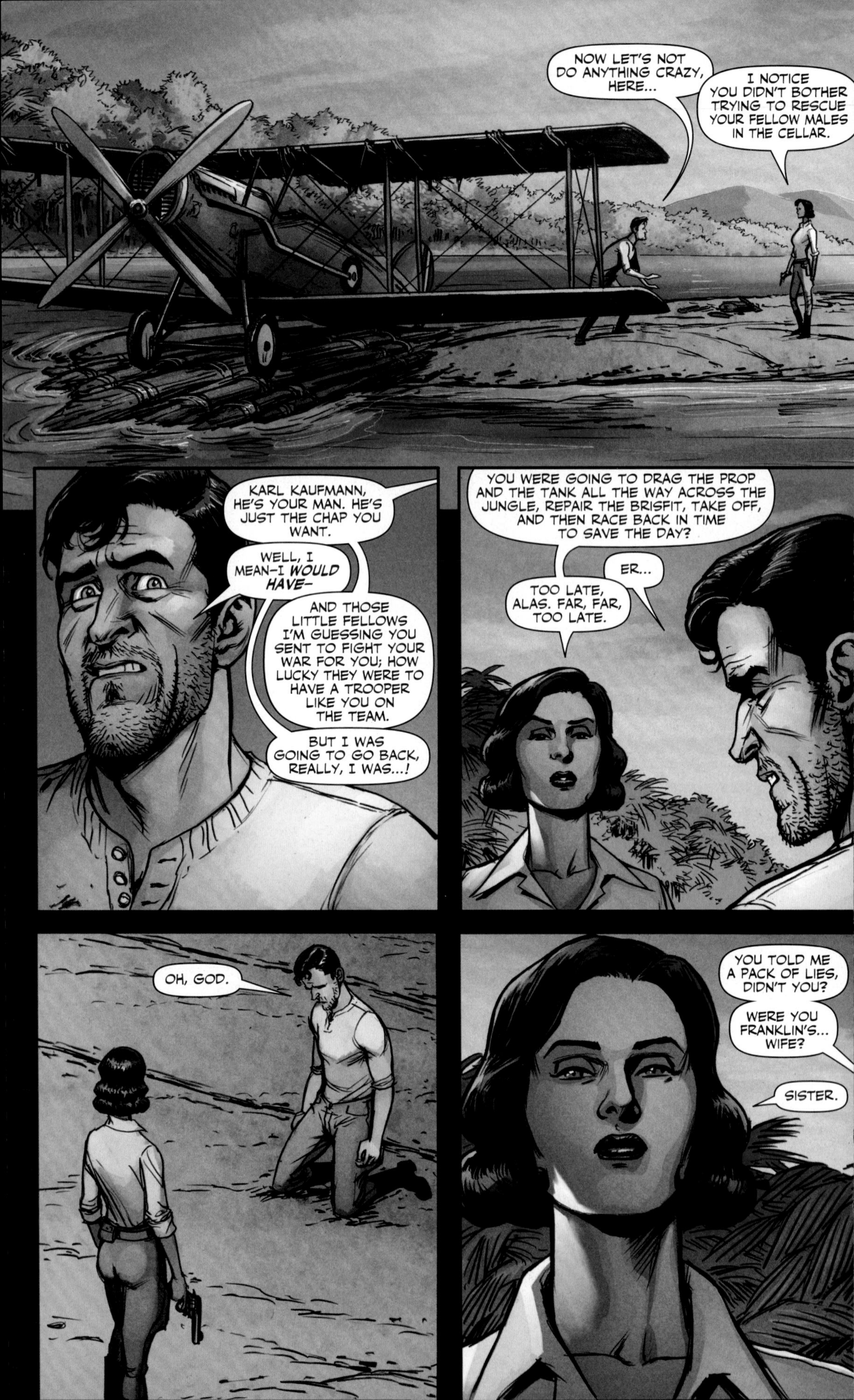
NOW LET'S NOT DO ANYTHING CRAZY, HERE...
I NOTICE YOU DIDN'T BOTHER TRYING TO RESCUE YOUR FELLOW MALES IN THE CELLAR.
KARL KAUFMANN, HE'S YOUR MAN. HE'S JUST THE CHAP YOU WANT.
WELL, I MEAN—I *WOULD HAVE*—
AND THOSE LITTLE FELLOWS I'M GUESSING YOU SENT TO FIGHT YOUR WAR FOR YOU; HOW LUCKY THEY WERE TO HAVE A TROOPER LIKE YOU ON THE TEAM.
BUT I WAS GOING TO GO BACK, REALLY, I WAS...!
YOU WERE GOING TO DRAG THE PROP AND THE TANK ALL THE WAY ACROSS THE JUNGLE, REPAIR THE BRISFIT, TAKE OFF, AND THEN RACE BACK IN TIME TO SAVE THE DAY?
ER...
TOO LATE, ALAS. FAR, FAR, TOO LATE.
OH, GOD.
YOU TOLD ME A PACK OF LIES, DIDN'T YOU?
WERE YOU FRANKLIN'S... WIFE?
SISTER.

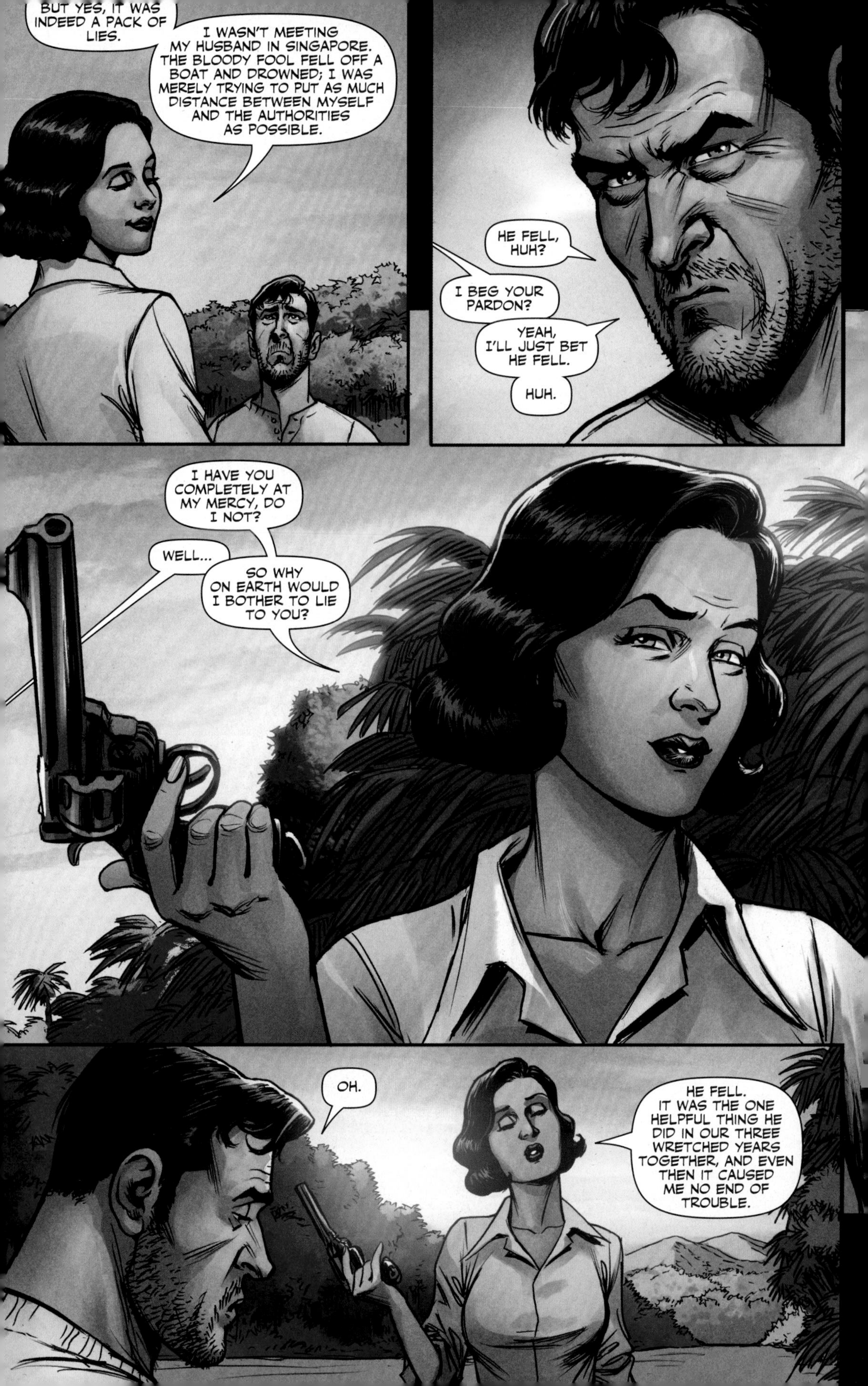
BUT YES, IT WAS INDEED A PACK OF LIES.
I WASN'T MEETING MY HUSBAND IN SINGAPORE. THE BLOODY FOOL FELL OFF A BOAT AND DROWNED; I WAS MERELY TRYING TO PUT AS MUCH DISTANCE BETWEEN MYSELF AND THE AUTHORITIES AS POSSIBLE.
HE FELL, HUH?
I BEG YOUR PARDON?
YEAH, I'LL JUST BET HE FELL.
HUH.
I HAVE YOU COMPLETELY AT MY MERCY, DO I NOT?
WELL...
SO WHY ON EARTH WOULD I BOTHER TO LIE TO YOU?
OH.
HE FELL. IT WAS THE ONE HELPFUL THING HE DID IN OUR THREE WRETCHED YEARS TOGETHER, AND EVEN THEN IT CAUSED ME NO END OF TROUBLE.

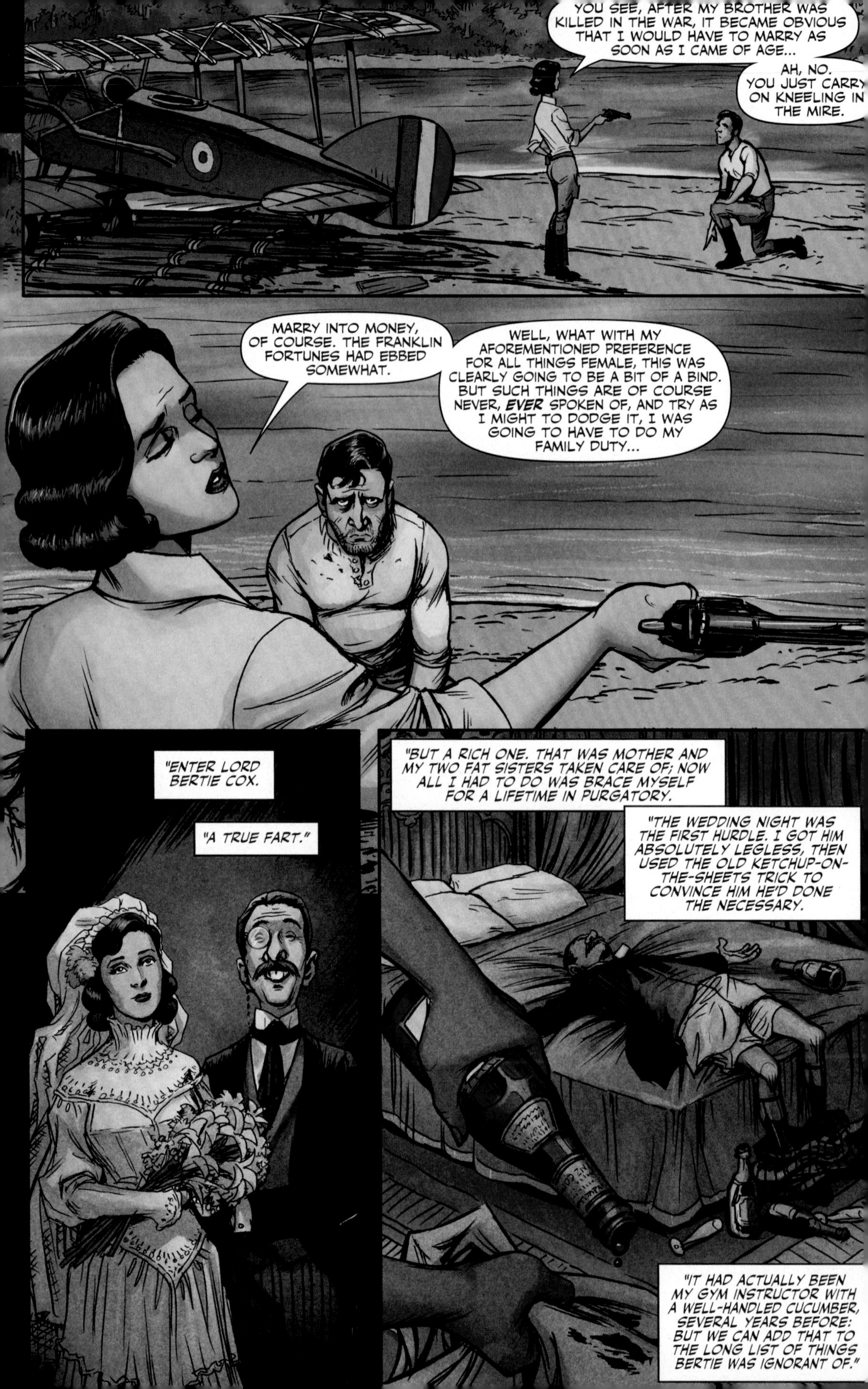
YOU SEE, AFTER MY BROTHER WAS KILLED IN THE WAR, IT BECAME OBVIOUS THAT I WOULD HAVE TO MARRY AS SOON AS I CAME OF AGE...
AH, NO. YOU JUST CARRY ON KNEELING IN THE MIRE.
MARRY INTO MONEY, OF COURSE. THE FRANKLIN FORTUNES HAD EBBED SOMEWHAT.
WELL, WHAT WITH MY AFOREMENTIONED PREFERENCE FOR ALL THINGS FEMALE, THIS WAS CLEARLY GOING TO BE A BIT OF A BIND. BUT SUCH THINGS ARE OF COURSE NEVER, ***EVER*** SPOKEN OF, AND TRY AS I MIGHT TO DODGE IT, I WAS GOING TO HAVE TO DO MY FAMILY DUTY...
"ENTER LORD BERTIE COX.
"A TRUE FART."
"BUT A RICH ONE. THAT WAS MOTHER AND MY TWO FAT SISTERS TAKEN CARE OF; NOW ALL I HAD TO DO WAS BRACE MYSELF FOR A LIFETIME IN PURGATORY.
"THE WEDDING NIGHT WAS THE FIRST HURDLE. I GOT HIM ABSOLUTELY LEGLESS, THEN USED THE OLD KETCHUP-ON-THE-SHEETS TRICK TO CONVINCE HIM HE'D DONE THE NECESSARY.
"IT HAD ACTUALLY BEEN MY GYM INSTRUCTOR WITH A WELL-HANDLED CUCUMBER, SEVERAL YEARS BEFORE: BUT WE CAN ADD THAT TO THE LONG LIST OF THINGS BERTIE WAS IGNORANT OF."

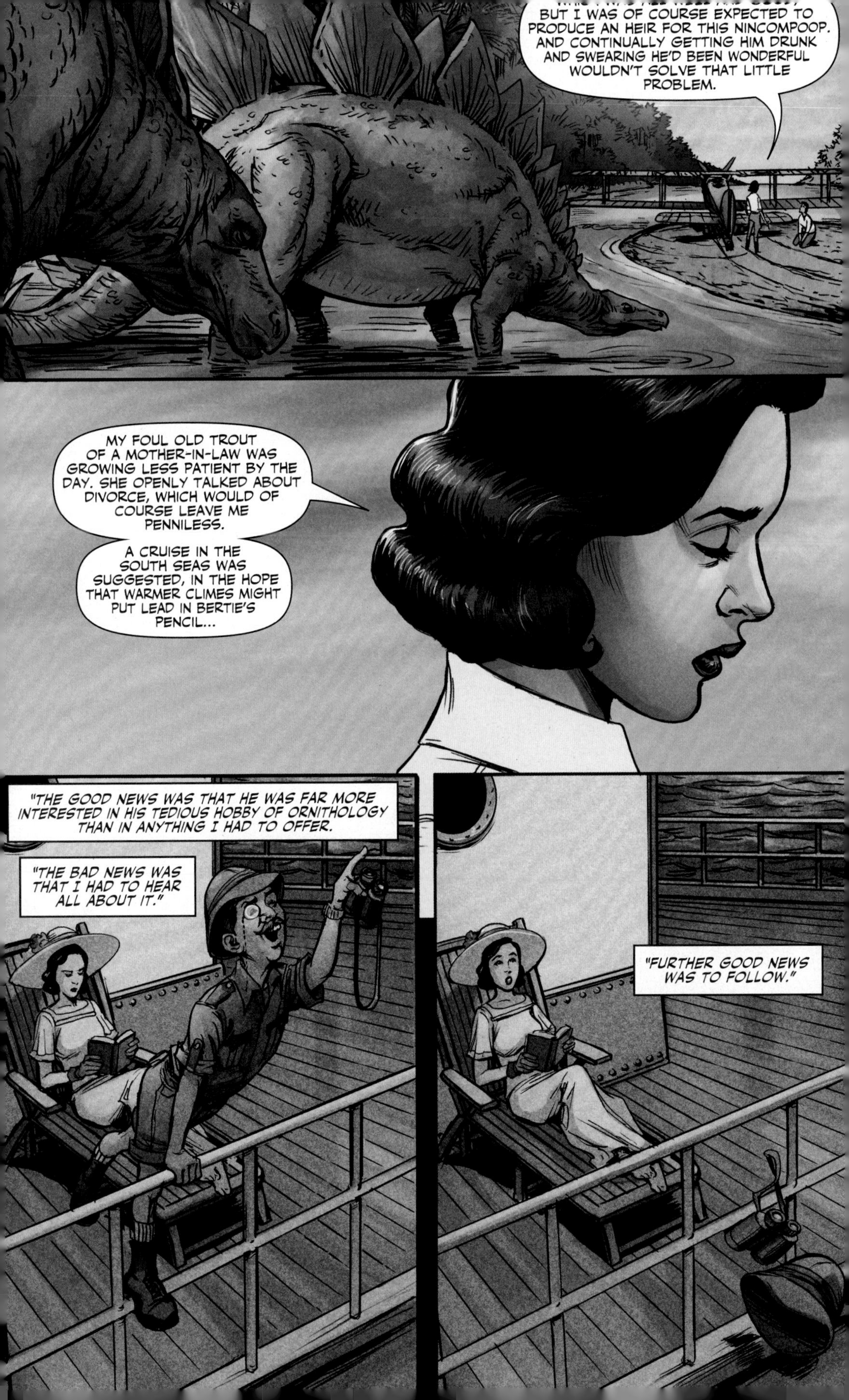
BUT I WAS OF COURSE EXPECTED TO PRODUCE AN HEIR FOR THIS NINCOMPOOP. AND CONTINUALLY GETTING HIM DRUNK AND SWEARING HE'D BEEN WONDERFUL WOULDN'T SOLVE THAT LITTLE PROBLEM.
MY FOUL OLD TROUT OF A MOTHER-IN-LAW WAS GROWING LESS PATIENT BY THE DAY. SHE OPENLY TALKED ABOUT DIVORCE, WHICH WOULD OF COURSE LEAVE ME PENNILESS.
A CRUISE IN THE SOUTH SEAS WAS SUGGESTED, IN THE HOPE THAT WARMER CLIMES MIGHT PUT LEAD IN BERTIE'S PENCIL...
"THE GOOD NEWS WAS THAT HE WAS FAR MORE INTERESTED IN HIS TEDIOUS HOBBY OF ORNITHOLOGY THAN IN ANYTHING I HAD TO OFFER.
"THE BAD NEWS WAS THAT I HAD TO HEAR ALL ABOUT IT."
"FURTHER GOOD NEWS WAS TO FOLLOW."

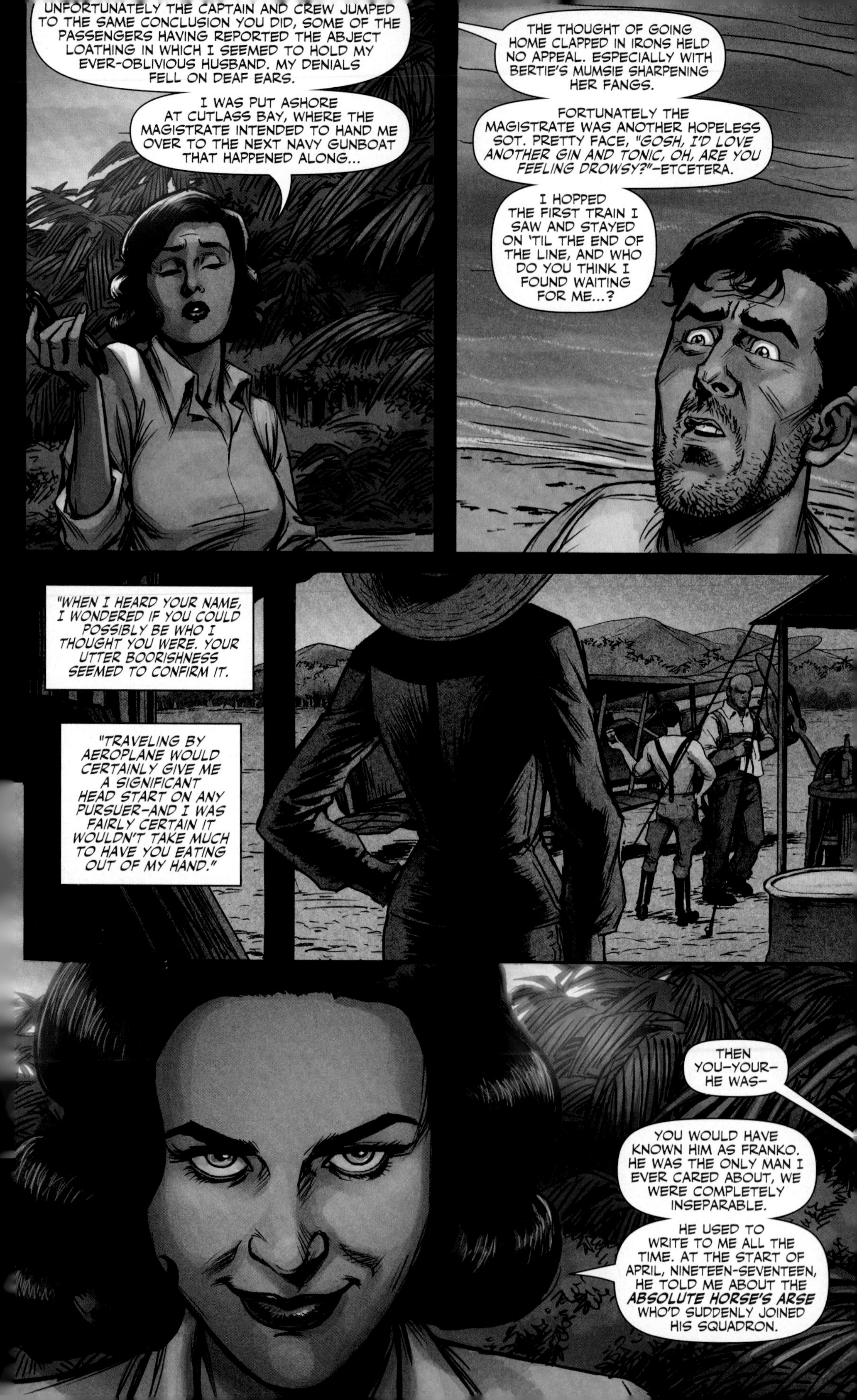
UNFORTUNATELY THE CAPTAIN AND CREW JUMPED TO THE SAME CONCLUSION YOU DID, SOME OF THE PASSENGERS HAVING REPORTED THE ABJECT LOATHING IN WHICH I SEEMED TO HOLD MY EVER-OBLIVIOUS HUSBAND. MY DENIALS FELL ON DEAF EARS.
I WAS PUT ASHORE AT CUTLASS BAY, WHERE THE MAGISTRATE INTENDED TO HAND ME OVER TO THE NEXT NAVY GUNBOAT THAT HAPPENED ALONG...
THE THOUGHT OF GOING HOME CLAPPED IN IRONS HELD NO APPEAL. ESPECIALLY WITH BERTIE'S MUMSIE SHARPENING HER FANGS.
FORTUNATELY THE MAGISTRATE WAS ANOTHER HOPELESS SOT. PRETTY FACE, *"GOSH, I'D LOVE ANOTHER GIN AND TONIC, OH, ARE YOU FEELING DROWSY?"*—ETCETERA.
I HOPPED THE FIRST TRAIN I SAW AND STAYED ON 'TIL THE END OF THE LINE, AND WHO DO YOU THINK I FOUND WAITING FOR ME...?
"WHEN I HEARD YOUR NAME, I WONDERED IF YOU COULD POSSIBLY BE WHO I THOUGHT YOU WERE. YOUR UTTER BOORISHNESS SEEMED TO CONFIRM IT.
"TRAVELING BY AEROPLANE WOULD CERTAINLY GIVE ME A SIGNIFICANT HEAD START ON ANY PURSUER—AND I WAS FAIRLY CERTAIN IT WOULDN'T TAKE MUCH TO HAVE YOU EATING OUT OF MY HAND."
THEN YOU—YOUR—HE WAS—
YOU WOULD HAVE KNOWN HIM AS FRANKO. HE WAS THE ONLY MAN I EVER CARED ABOUT, WE WERE COMPLETELY INSEPARABLE.
HE USED TO WRITE TO ME ALL THE TIME. AT THE START OF APRIL, NINETEEN-SEVENTEEN, HE TOLD ME ABOUT THE ***ABSOLUTE HORSE'S ARSE*** WHO'D SUDDENLY JOINED HIS SQUADRON.

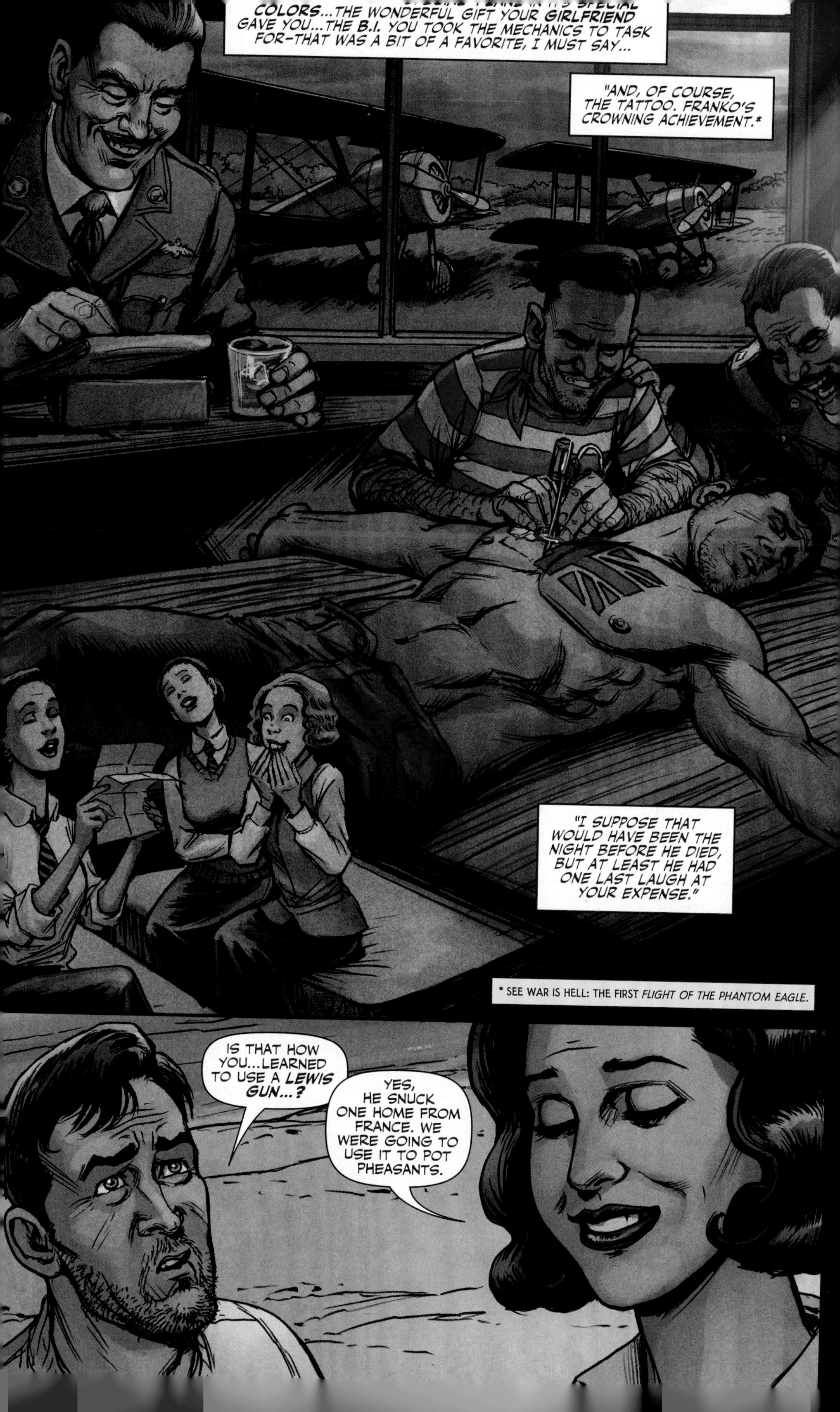
COLORS...THE WONDERFUL GIFT YOUR GIRLFRIEND GAVE YOU...THE B.I. YOU TOOK THE MECHANICS TO TASK FOR—THAT WAS A BIT OF A FAVORITE, I MUST SAY...
"AND, OF COURSE, THE TATTOO. FRANKO'S CROWNING ACHIEVEMENT.*
"I SUPPOSE THAT WOULD HAVE BEEN THE NIGHT BEFORE HE DIED, BUT AT LEAST HE HAD ONE LAST LAUGH AT YOUR EXPENSE."
* SEE WAR IS HELL: THE FIRST FLIGHT OF THE PHANTOM EAGLE.
IS THAT HOW YOU...LEARNED TO USE A LEWIS GUN...?
YES, HE SNUCK ONE HOME FROM FRANCE. WE WERE GOING TO USE IT TO POT PHEASANTS.

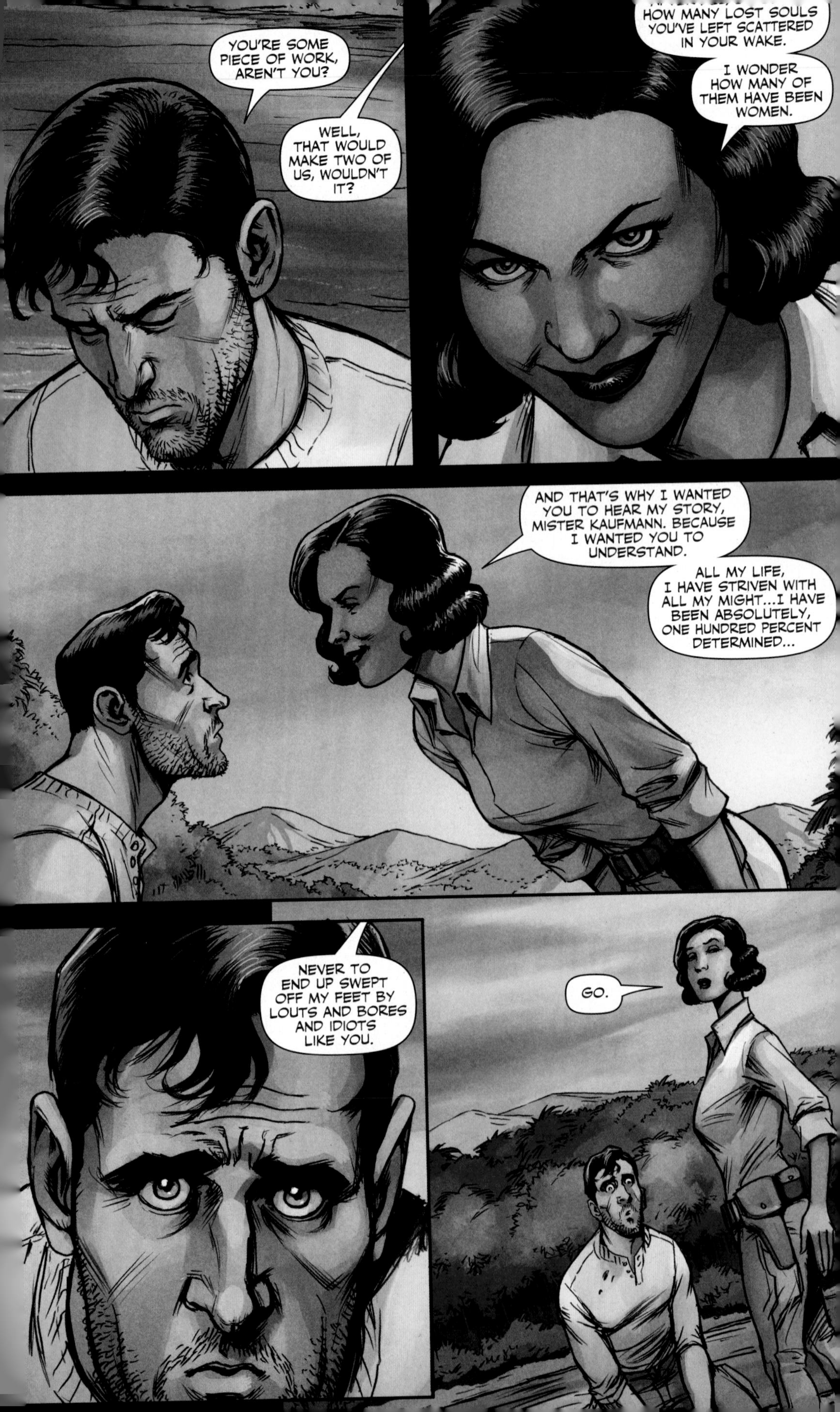
YOU'RE SOME PIECE OF WORK, AREN'T YOU?
WELL, THAT WOULD MAKE TWO OF US, WOULDN'T IT?
HOW MANY LOST SOULS YOU'VE LEFT SCATTERED IN YOUR WAKE.
I WONDER HOW MANY OF THEM HAVE BEEN WOMEN.
AND THAT'S WHY I WANTED YOU TO HEAR MY STORY, MISTER KAUFMANN. BECAUSE I WANTED YOU TO UNDERSTAND.
ALL MY LIFE, I HAVE STRIVEN WITH ALL MY MIGHT...I HAVE BEEN ABSOLUTELY, ONE HUNDRED PERCENT DETERMINED...
NEVER TO END UP SWEPT OFF MY FEET BY LOUTS AND BORES AND IDIOTS LIKE YOU.
GO.

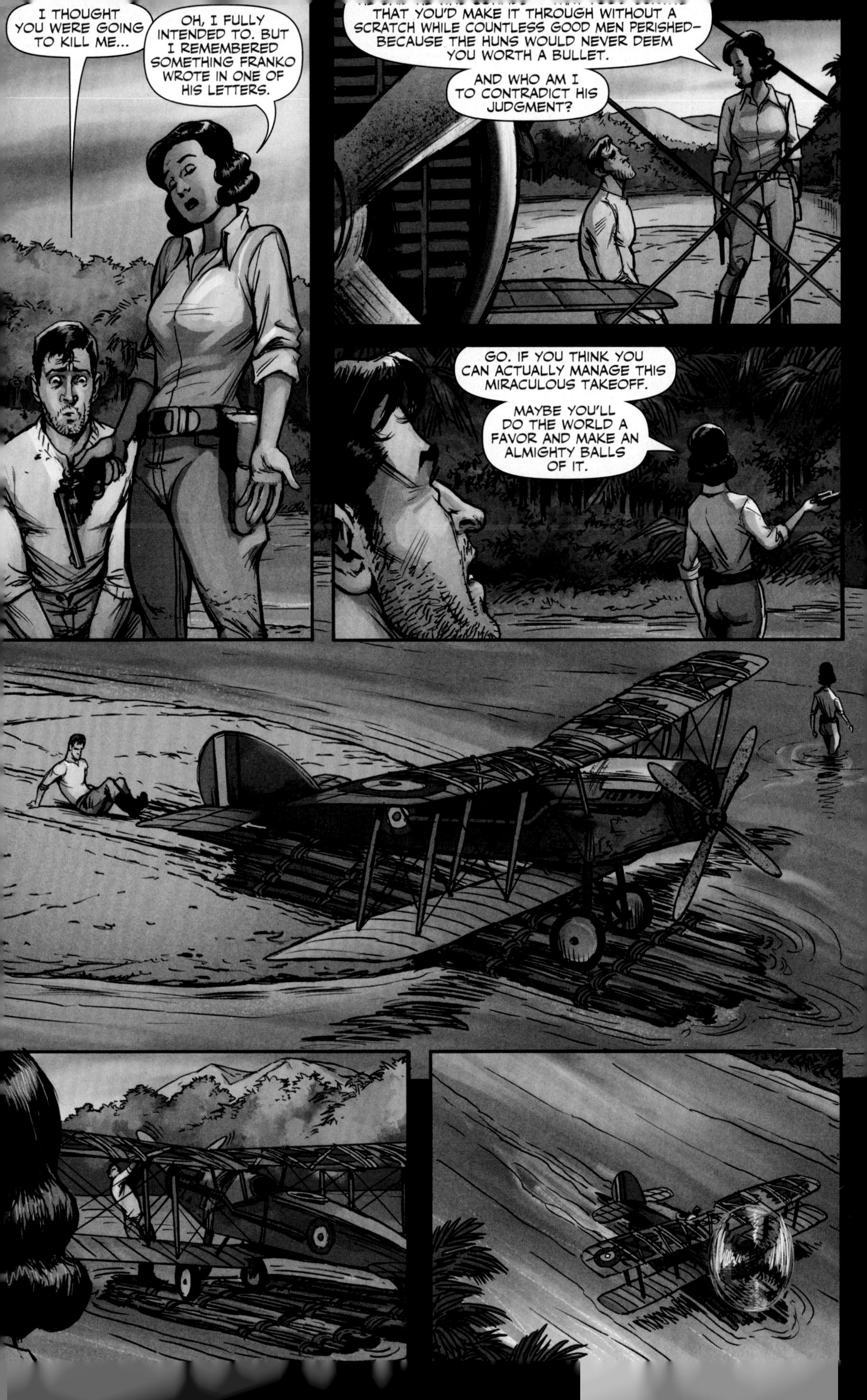
I THOUGHT YOU WERE GOING TO KILL ME...
OH, I FULLY INTENDED TO. BUT I REMEMBERED SOMETHING FRANKO WROTE IN ONE OF HIS LETTERS.
THAT YOU'D MAKE IT THROUGH WITHOUT A SCRATCH WHILE COUNTLESS GOOD MEN PERISHED– BECAUSE THE HUNS WOULD NEVER DEEM YOU WORTH A BULLET.
AND WHO AM I TO CONTRADICT HIS JUDGMENT?
GO. IF YOU THINK YOU CAN ACTUALLY MANAGE THIS MIRACULOUS TAKEOFF.
MAYBE YOU'LL DO THE WORLD A FAVOR AND MAKE AN ALMIGHTY BALLS OF IT.

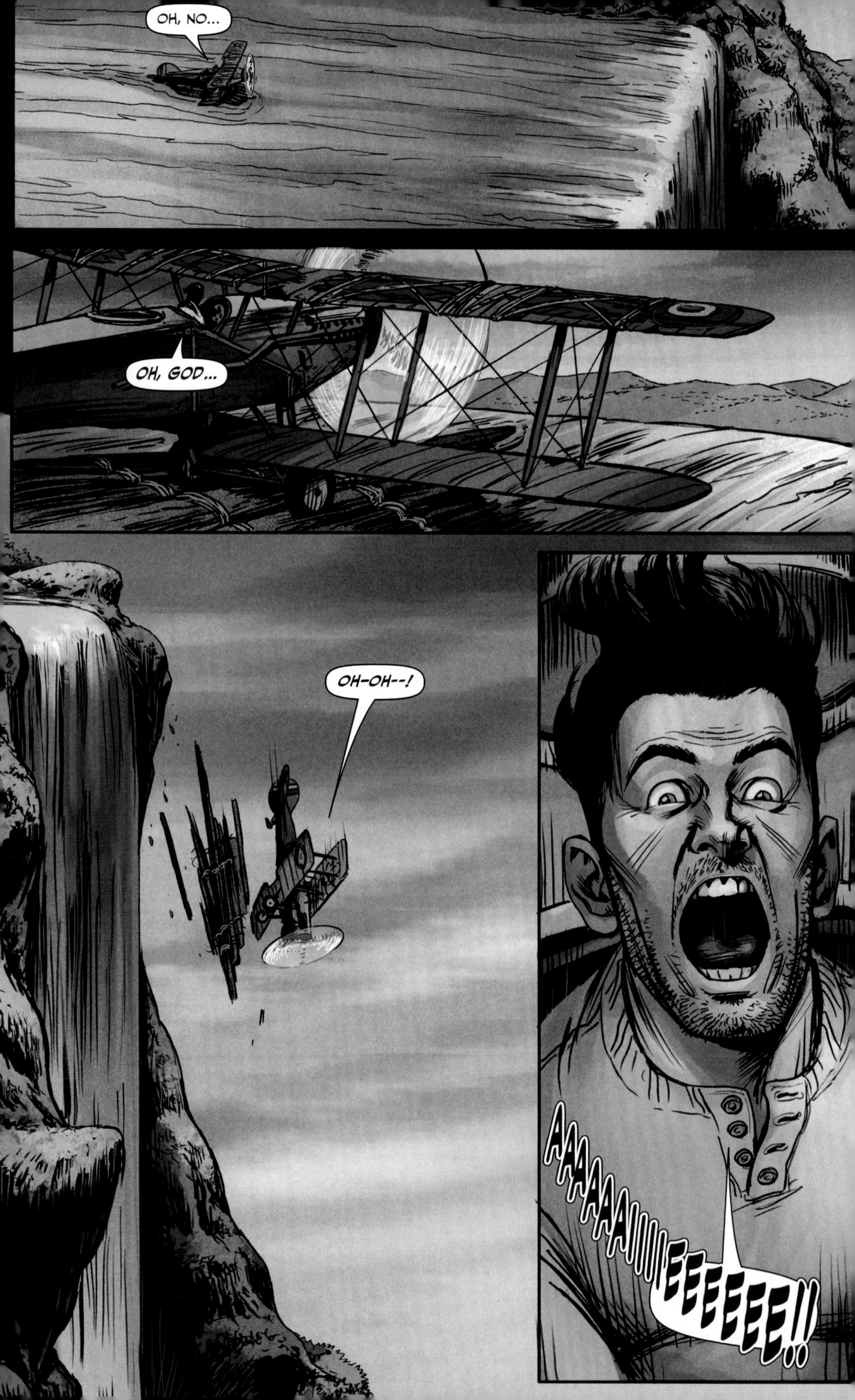
OH, NO...
OH, GOD...
OH-OH--!
AAAAAIIIIIEEEEEEE!!

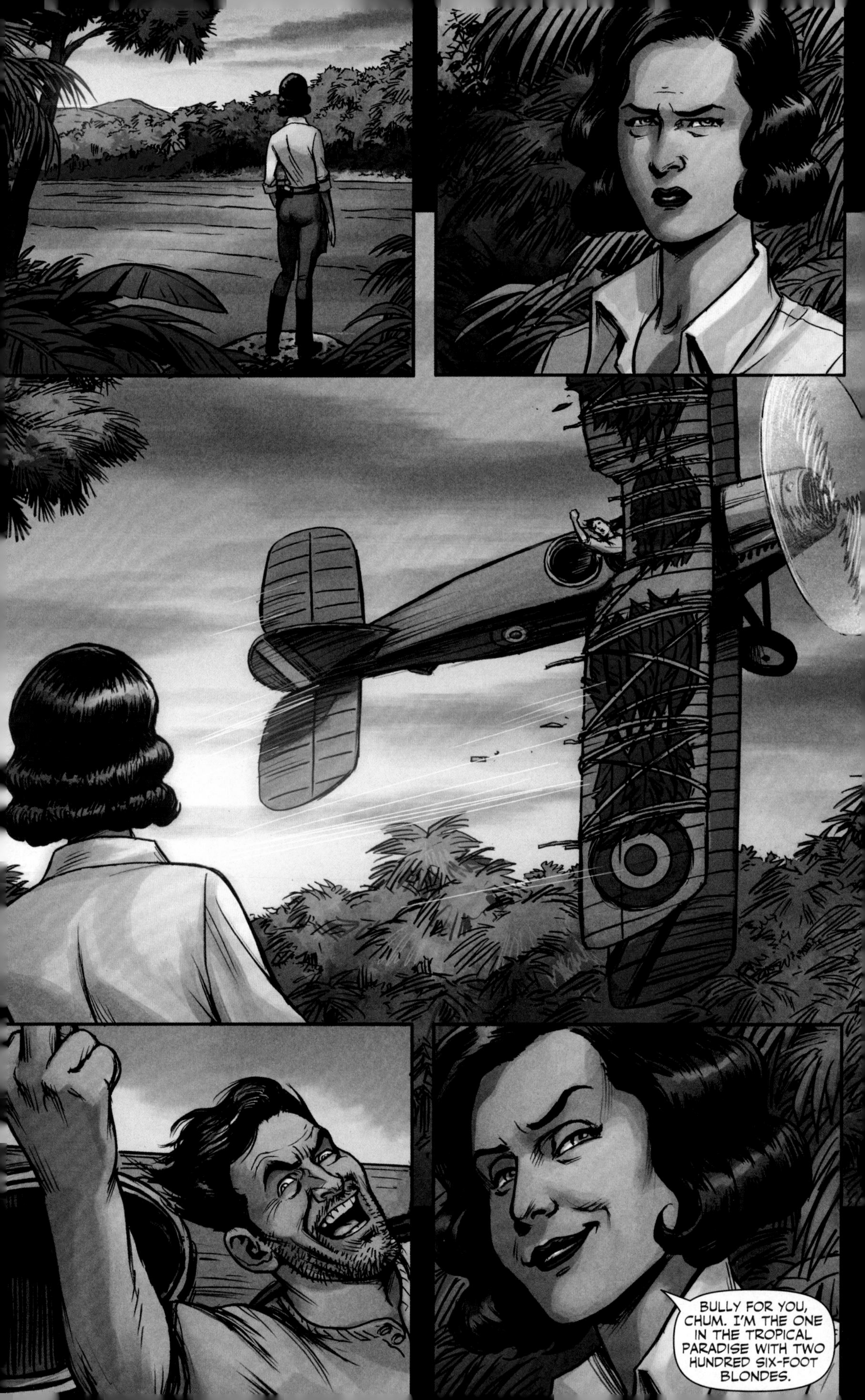
BULLY FOR YOU, CHUM. I'M THE ONE IN THE TROPICAL PARADISE WITH TWO HUNDRED SIX-FOOT BLONDES.

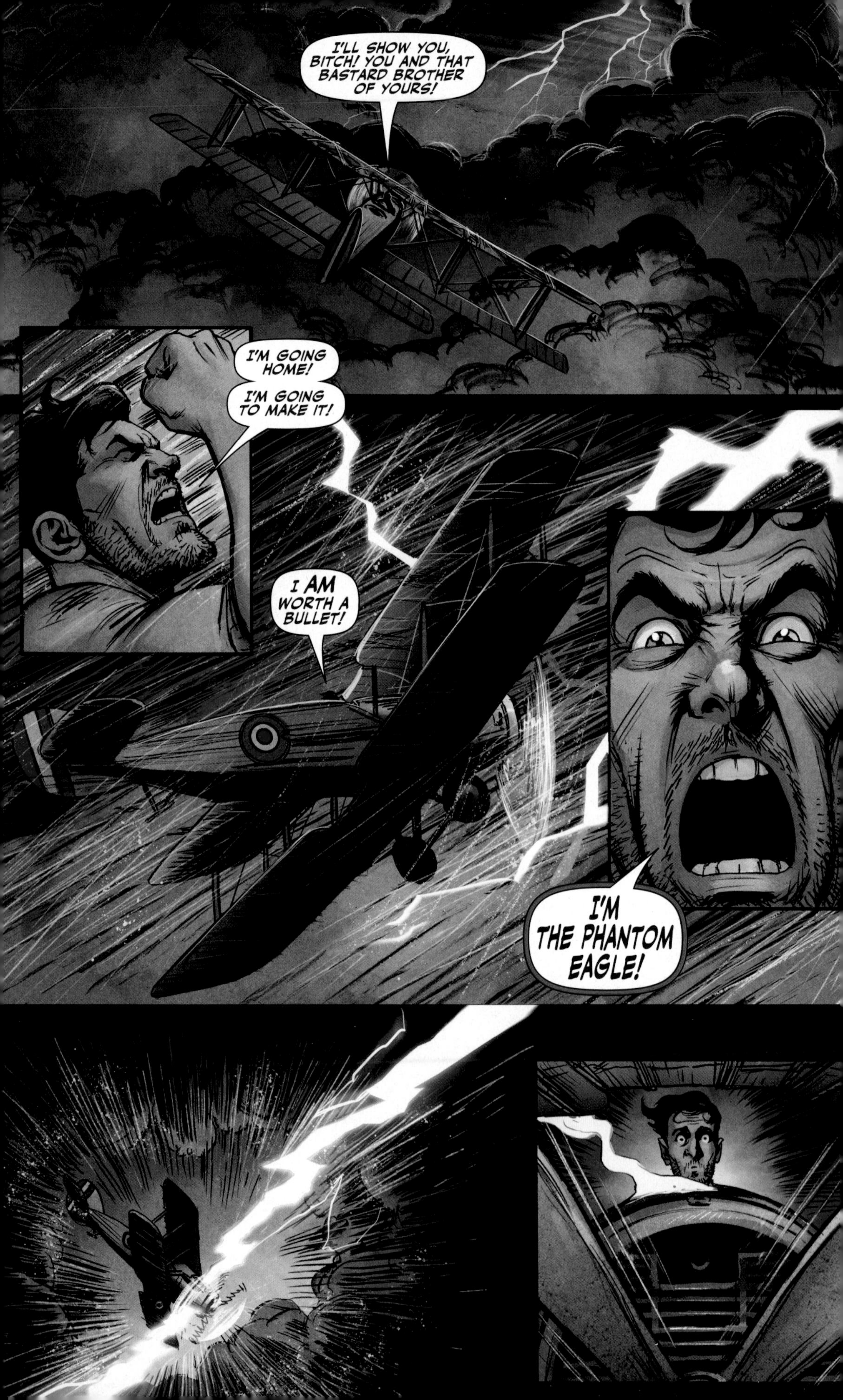

I'LL SHOW YOU, BITCH! YOU AND THAT BASTARD BROTHER OF YOURS!
I'M GOING HOME!
I'M GOING TO MAKE IT!
I AM WORTH A BULLET!
I'M THE PHANTOM EAGLE!

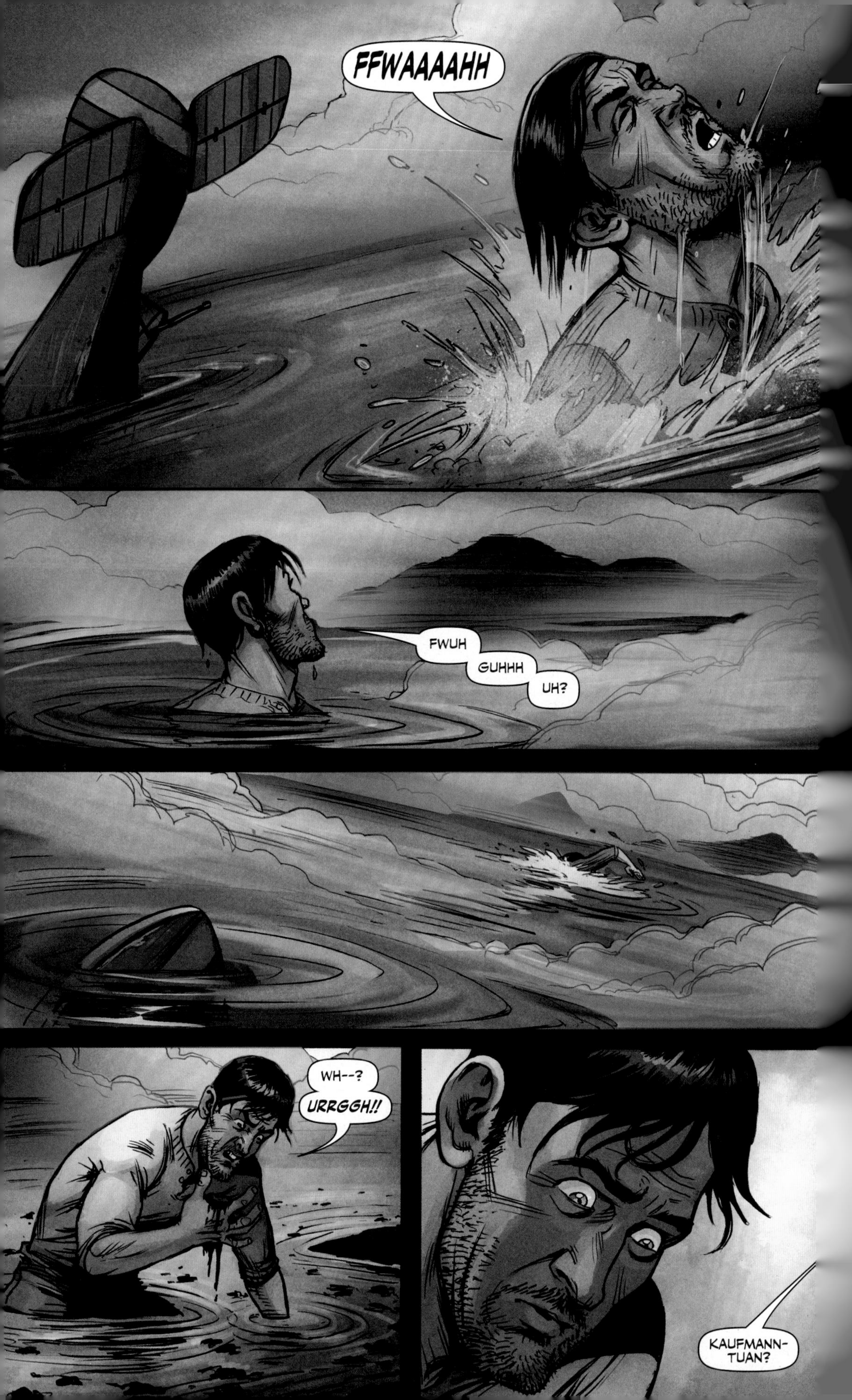
FFWAAAAHH
FWUH
GUHHH
UH?
WH--?
URRGGH!!
KAUFMANN-
TUAN?

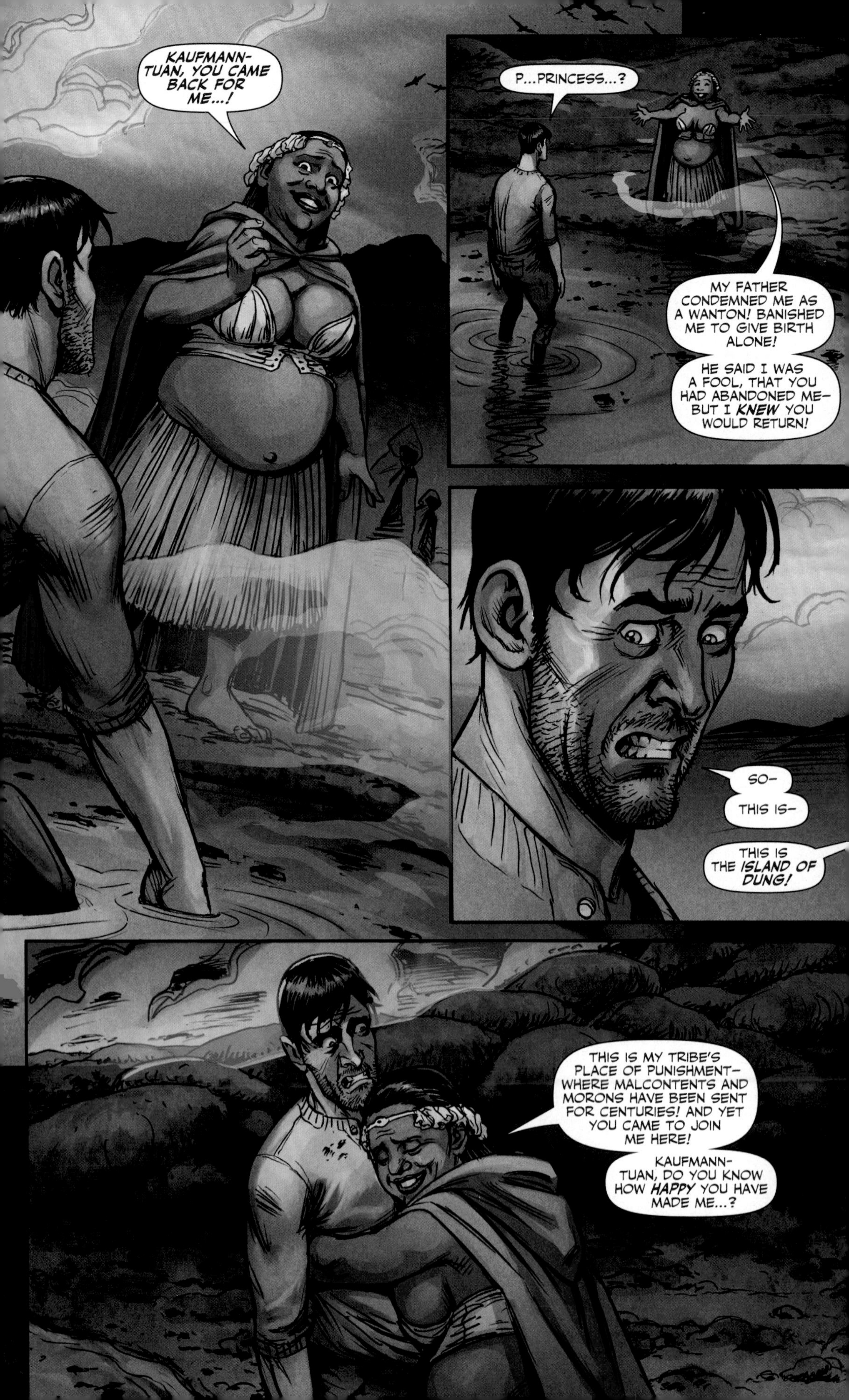
KAUFMANN-TUAN, YOU CAME BACK FOR ME...!
P...PRINCESS...?
MY FATHER CONDEMNED ME AS A WANTON! BANISHED ME TO GIVE BIRTH ALONE!
HE SAID I WAS A FOOL, THAT YOU HAD ABANDONED ME--BUT I *KNEW* YOU WOULD RETURN!
SO-
THIS IS-
THIS IS THE *ISLAND OF DUNG!*
THIS IS MY TRIBE'S PLACE OF PUNISHMENT--WHERE MALCONTENTS AND MORONS HAVE BEEN SENT FOR CENTURIES! AND YET YOU CAME TO JOIN ME HERE!
KAUFMANN-TUAN, DO YOU KNOW HOW *HAPPY* YOU HAVE MADE ME...?

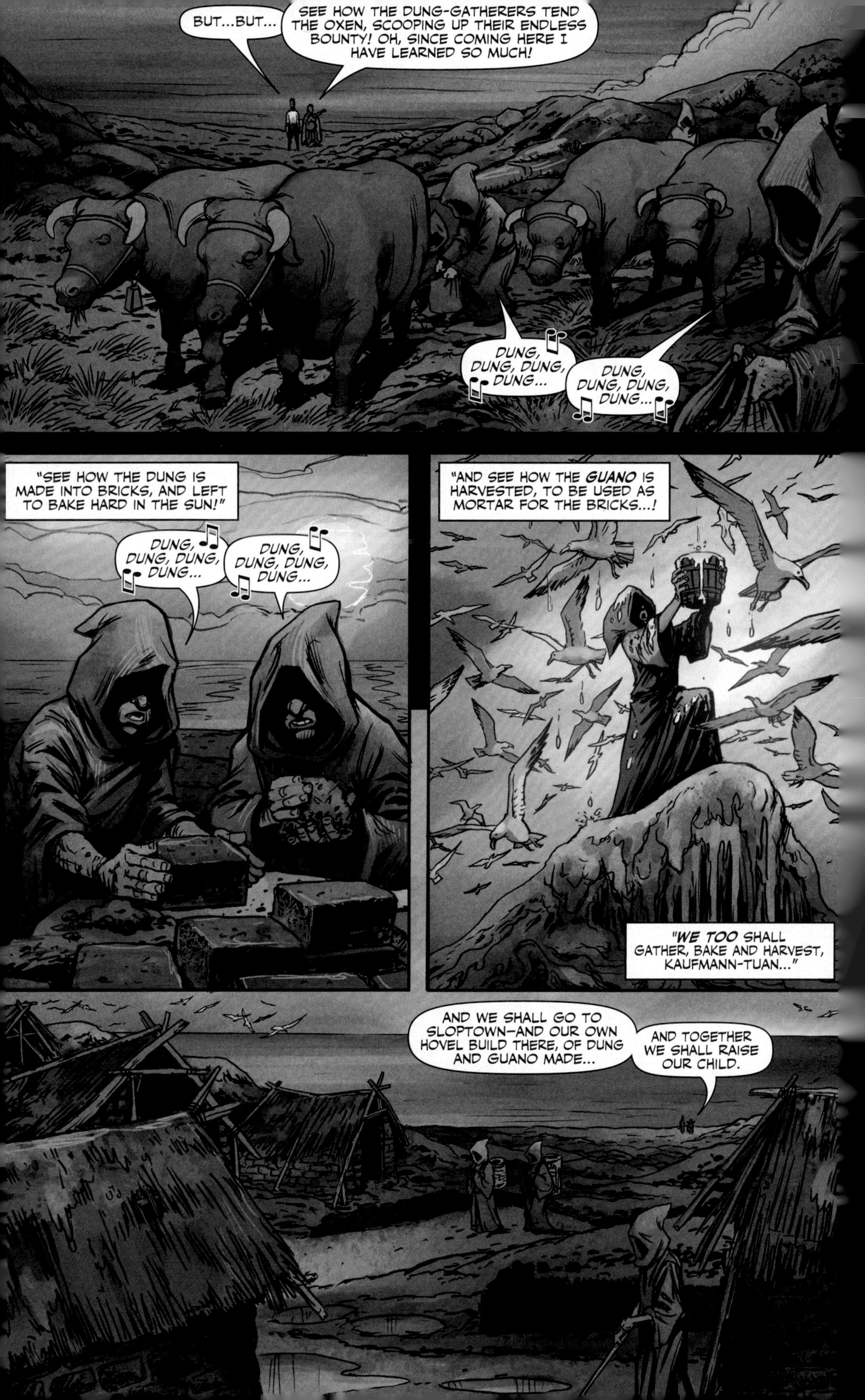
BUT...BUT...
SEE HOW THE DUNG-GATHERERS TEND THE OXEN, SCOOPING UP THEIR ENDLESS BOUNTY! OH, SINCE COMING HERE I HAVE LEARNED SO MUCH!
DUNG, DUNG, DUNG, DUNG...
DUNG, DUNG, DUNG, DUNG...
"SEE HOW THE DUNG IS MADE INTO BRICKS, AND LEFT TO BAKE HARD IN THE SUN!"
DUNG, DUNG, DUNG, DUNG...
DUNG, DUNG, DUNG, DUNG...
"AND SEE HOW THE GUANO IS HARVESTED, TO BE USED AS MORTAR FOR THE BRICKS...!
"WE TOO SHALL GATHER, BAKE AND HARVEST, KAUFMANN-TUAN..."
AND WE SHALL GO TO SLOPTOWN—AND OUR OWN HOVEL BUILD THERE, OF DUNG AND GUANO MADE...
AND TOGETHER WE SHALL RAISE OUR CHILD.

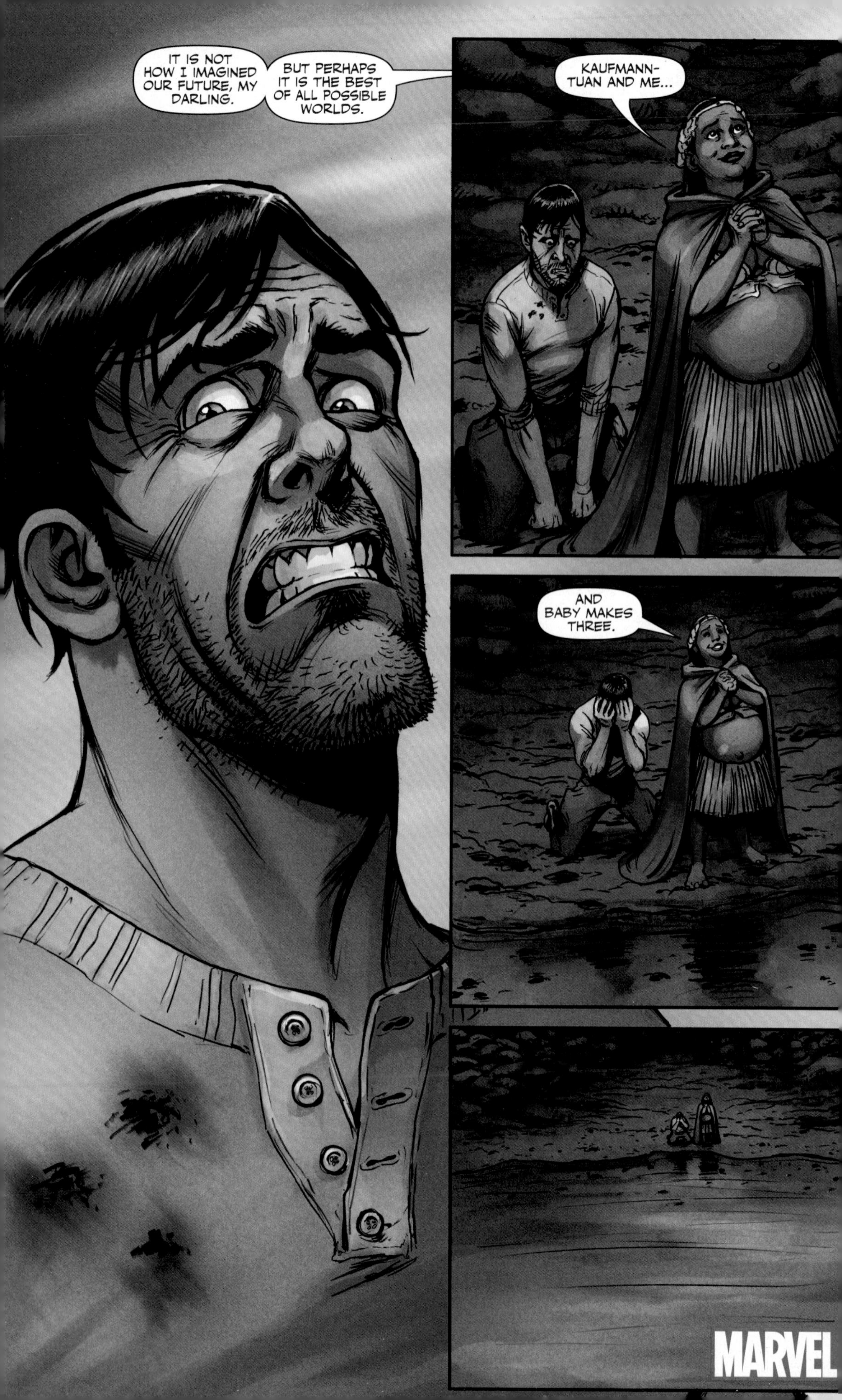
IT IS NOT HOW I IMAGINED OUR FUTURE, MY DARLING.
BUT PERHAPS IT IS THE BEST OF ALL POSSIBLE WORLDS.
KAUFMANN-TUAN AND ME...
AND BABY MAKES THREE.
MARVEL